OXFORD BIBLE SERIES

General Editors
P. R. Ackroyd and G. N. Stanton

OXFORD BIBLE SERIES

General Editors
P. R. Ackroyd and G. N. Stanton

NARRATIVE IN THE HEBREW BIBLE

DAVID M. GUNN
AND
DANNA NOLAN FEWELL

OXFORD UNIVERSITY PRESS

Oxford University Press, Walton Street, Oxford OX2 6DP

Oxford   New York   Toronto
Delhi   Bombay   Calcutta   Madras   Karachi
Kuala Lumpur   Singapore   Hong Kong   Tokyo
Nairobi   Dar es Salaam   Cape Town
Melbourne   Auckland   Madrid
and associated companies in
Berlin   Ibadan

Oxford is a trade mark of Oxford University Press

Published in the United States
by Oxford University Press Inc., New York

British Library Cataloguing in Publication Data
Data available

Library of Congress Cataloging in Publication Data
Narrative in the Hebrew Bible
David M. Gunn & Danna Nolan Fewell.
Includes bibliographical references and indexes.
1. Narration in the Bible.   2. Bible as literature.   3. Bible.
O. T. Genesis—Criticism, interpretation, etc.   (4. Bible. O. T.
Jonah—Criticism, interpretation etc.)   5. Bible. O. T. Daniel—
Criticism, interpretation, etc.   I. Fewell, Danna Nolan.
II. Title.   III. Series.
BS1171.2.G85   1993   221.6'6—dc20
ISBN 0-19-213244-X
0-19-213245-8 (pbk)

3 5 7 9 10 8 6 4 2

Typeset by Graphicraft Typesetters Ltd, Hong Kong
Printed in Great Britain
on acid-free paper by
Biddles Ltd, Guildford and King's Lynn

To

Rebecca Margaret
and Jonathan Farquhar
who waited so long

and to

Aubrey Sinclair
who waited just long enough

GENERAL EDITORS' PREFACE

There are many commentaries on individual books of the Bible, but the reader who wishes to take a broader view has less choice. This series is intended to meet this need. Its structure is thematic, with each volume embracing a number of biblical books. It is designed for use with any of the familiar translations of the Bible; quotations are normally from RSV, but the authors of the individual volumes also use other translations or make their own where this helps to bring out the particular meaning of a passage.

To provide general orientation, there are two volumes of a more introductory character: one considers the Old Testament in its cultural and historical context, the other the New Testament, discussing the origins of Christianity. Four volumes deal with different kinds of material in the Old Testament: narrative, prophecy, poetry/psalmody, wisdom and law. Three volumes handle different aspects of the New Testament: the Gospels, Paul and Pauline Christianity, the varieties of New Testament thought. One volume looks at the nature of biblical interpretation, covering both Testaments.

The authors of the individual volumes write for a general readership. Technical terms and Hebrew or Greek words are explained; the latter are used only when essential to the understanding of the text. The general introductory volumes are designed to stand on their own, providing a framework, but also to serve to raise some of the questions which the remaining volumes examine in closer detail. All the volumes other than the two general ones include discussion of selected biblical passages in greater depth, thus providing examples of the ways in which the interpretation of the text makes possible deeper understanding of the wider issues, both historical and theological, with which the Bible is concerned. Select bibliographies in each volume point the way to further discussion of the many issues which remain open to fuller exploration.

P.R.A.
G.N.S.

PREFACE

No formal aspect of literature has received as much attention
over the past two decades as have the mechanisms of narrative.
As a result of all this attention, we now understand more
precisely what are the various options, and combinations and
permutations of options, for telling a story.

(Alter 1990:171 ¶A)

Robert Alter is here writing about narrative in general, though
through his book on *The Art of Biblical Narrative* (1981 ¶F) he has
done as much as anyone to open up the literary-critical possibilities
for reading the narrative of the Hebrew Bible in particular. (With
other scholars, we use the admittedly problematic term Hebrew Bible
to indicate that this body of text does not have its meaning primarily
in relation to what Christians call the New Testament.) Our present
book is an attempt to steer between discussing mechanisms of biblical narrative and reading particular texts. The former risks becoming
a catalogue of categories and sub-categories, subject to endless exceptions. The latter, while offering inductive possibilities for readers interested in developing for themselves a similar reading method, risks
becoming less a book of introduction to biblical narrative and more a
collection of essays on selected texts. We try to find a balance, therefore, between talking about the method and illustrating the practice.

Our procedure is to alternate between a chapter of methodological discussion and a major reading which is related, though not
slavishly, to that discussion. Some relatively extended interpretations
of particular texts will also be found within the methodological
chapters; by and large, however, illustrations within these chapters
will be of necessity somewhat truncated.

To set our approach to biblical narrative in perspective we indicate in Chapter 1 how literary criticism is related to other dominant
ways of reading the text over the last two thousand years. We
explore similarities and differences among selected readings of the
story of Cain and Abel.

In Chapter 2 we move to a reading of Genesis 38. In his 1981 book (in an essay first published in 1975) Alter took this story of Judah and Tamar as a starting point for his eloquent plea for a 'literary approach' to the narrative of the Hebrew Bible. We also start with this story for our own first extended reading, in part to commemorate Alter's influential book, and in part to celebrate the fact that we no longer have to plead for, but can presume the legitimacy of, a 'literary approach'. (Alter's points often bear repeating and we have incorporated some of them, where appropriate, in our own interpretation.)

Our conviction that characters are of central interest to most ordinary readers of biblical narrative, though perhaps not to some current circles of literary critics, leads us to focus Chapter 3 on characters, with whom we associate also the narrator. Chapter 4 then develops an interpretation of two particular characters, Abraham and Sarah.

Chapter 5 treats some basic notions of plot as well as modifications or alternatives which better accommodate the complexity of actual biblical narratives. An extended reading on the book of Jonah follows in Chapter 6.

In Chapter 7 we explore some other aspects of narrative language which attract us as readers. Repetition, ambiguity, multivalence, and metaphor all contribute to our enlarging of narrative meaning. We suggest some possibilities for interpretation, too, in the way we associate narrative material, tracing allusions and constructing dialogues between texts. The subject of our extended reading in Chapter 8 is Daniel 3, the story of Nebuchadnezzar and the three Jews thrown into the furnace—Shadrach, Meshach, and Abednego.

With Chapter 9 on readers and responsibility we conclude the discussion. As the introductory chapter takes pains to make clear, our method of interpretation and our particular readings imply certain values, stated and unstated. In our final chapter we take up the issue of the ideological dimension of narrative interpretation, with particular attention to Genesis 2–3. As a story of origins this text has generated much discussion about gender and social hierarchy. Does this text define or challenge the status quo (of either the ancient or the modern world)? We lay out some of the debate and open the question, What values are at work when we and others read and champion readings?

Finally, the bibliography lists works cited and influential in our own readings, as well as pointing to a wider range of material available for someone wishing to explore the wealth of this subject beyond the limits of the present book.

Of course, there are other books already written which attempt to do some of what we are also attempting. We have learned from them all and our readers will find them valuable resources.

Robert Alter's *The Art of Biblical Narrative* remains a classic, engagingly written, full of insights, particularly on narrative play with repetition. Adele Berlin's *Poetics and Interpretation of Biblical Narrative* has offered numerous students over the past decade a lucid account of character and point of view, among other subjects. Shimon Bar-Efrat's *Narrative Art in the Bible* is a meticulous analysis of narrator, characters, plot, time and space, and style, replete with copious examples. All three books are accessible to readers who are taking first steps. Meir Sternberg's massive study, *The Poetics of Biblical Narrative: Ideological Literature and the Drama of Reading*, painstakingly explores biblical narrative with elaborate narratology and attentive exegesis. It is a book for more advanced (and patient!) readers.

Our own book bears similarities and differences. It tries to address a wider range of narrative features than either Alter or Berlin. It strikes a different balance between discussing 'mechanics' and presenting 'interpretations' from that found in Bar-Efrat—less of the former, more of the latter. It is more accessible to the introductory reader than Sternberg. Most significant, however, it differs from all these books in its hermeneutical assumptions. Unlike the others, including Sternberg, our book understands interpretation to hinge crucially upon the reader, and not just in terms of a reader's 'competence'. Meaning is not something out there in the text waiting to be discovered. Meaning is always, in the last analysis, the reader's creation, and readers, like texts, come in an infinite variety. No amount of learning to read biblical narrative 'correctly' will lead inexorably through the 'given' poetics of the text to the 'correct' interpretation.

Perhaps, then, because we are unwilling to advocate the possibility of definitive meanings, our book may seem less authoritative than the others. Yet perhaps for that very reason it may open for some readers more possibilities for interpretation. Whatever the case, we would argue that our play with meaning's possibilities is no more or less ideological than the determined discoveries of colleagues. Criticism, by whatever name, is a value-laden enterprise.

This book has been long in the making, longer perhaps than most. It was first commissioned over a decade ago when literary criticism was still struggling to be heard in biblical studies. Today we write about a field of study that has found some maturity. Along the way the project was reconceived as a jointly rather than singly authored one. We like to think that the book is the better for both the wait and our partnership. In any case, both of us owe a special debt of gratitude to Peter Ackroyd, who had confidence in each of us when he could easily have taken a safer route. We are proud to have a book in a series under his general editorship.

We are grateful, too, for his detailed comments and criticisms. And to our other series editor, Graham Stanton, we owe thanks for patience, support, and a gracious and helpful response to our work.

Tim Beal also read the manuscript with characteristic care and acuity, and we are the gainers. We thank him for so generously giving us of his time and critical talents and we deeply appreciate his friendship.

Our students at Columbia and Perkins have met and mulled over much of the material in this book to our advantage. Indeed, the critical explorations they have shared with us are part of the very web and woof of the book. And they have been a crucial stimulus for us. This book is in many ways theirs.

For both of us this book has become something of a milestone (not millstone, though that thought did occasionally occur) in our work as literary critics. Helping to set and maintain us on our way have been some important affirmations from friends and colleagues, among whom we would like to mention Jim Ackerman, Walter Brueggemann, Bob Detweiler, Robert Culley, Carol Newsom, and Vernon Robbins.

Books do not get written in the abstract. They require times to write and places to write in and help from friends and family. We have been very fortunate. Our spouses, David Fewell and Margaret Gunn, have given us unstinting support. Rebecca and Jonathan have shared their father with his writing (and counted the years!); Aubrey has lent her mother to the project, even without exactly knowing it. And specially we want to record our gratitude to Elizabeth Marshall for her generosity in lending her cabin on beautiful Lake Sinclair in the heart of Georgia (nearest phone two miles away!), a tranquil place where the book took its final shape in the spring of 1991.

DAVID M. GUNN
Columbia Theological Seminary

DANNA NOLAN FEWELL
Perkins School of Theology

December 1991

CONTENTS

I

Strategies for Reading

Narrative

Stories are a staple of human life. And stories abound in the Hebrew Bible. For many people in biblically influenced cultures, vague recollections of Abraham and Sarah journeying to the promised land or David felling the giant Goliath are a large part of their small conscious acquaintance with the Bible. For others, however, some of those stories are intimately known. The Jewish community constantly reaffirms its identity by retelling the Passover story from Exodus, just as Christians tell and retell the story of Jesus' last supper from the New Testament. African-Americans, too, have deeply embraced the story of Moses and the children of Israel seeking freedom from slavery. The list could be extended indefinitely.

These biblical stories, like stories everywhere, can powerfully shape people's lives—even when the story may seem innocuous. We can think of stories in alternative ways (following J. Hillis Miller 1990: 68–70 ¶A). Stories order and reorder our experience; that is to say, they *reveal* the way things are in the real world. They reflect a given culture. Alternatively, stories may be thought to *create* the real world. They are 'performative' rather than simply explanatory. They give meaning to life, implicitly making proposals for thought and action which are then embodied in a re-created world. Not only that, they can become 'policemen' of that world. They 'keep us in line and tend to make us more like our neighbors' (Miller: 69). Yet working against that policing function is always another possibility: stories can be subversive, a means of criticizing dominant patterns of thought and institution. Indeed, at times, to narrate an implicitly subversive story is the only safe way for social criticism to be spoken and heard. And, of course, such stories have the potential to create new social worlds.

The terms 'story' and 'narrative' are often used interchangeably, though sometimes 'the story' is a broader term, understood as the events presupposed by 'the narrative' which tells the story in a particular way. But 'narrative' may be a generic term rather like 'storytelling'. We think of narrative in this sense as opposed, say, to lyric poetry, proverbs, or legal codes. What then can we say is typical of narrative?

First, narrative constructs a verbal world that imitates and centres on *human characters* (or personifications), their speech and actions, their relations and desires, their ideas and institutions. Usually there are at least two, but generally three or more characters in a story. As we shall discuss later, the narrator—the voice that tells the story—may usefully be thought of as a character; and a reader or listener is implied, sometimes directly addressed, thus constituting yet another character.

Second, time is crucial for narrative. Unlike the genres just mentioned, which are characterized primarily by non-temporal images (lyrics and proverbs), propositions or admonitions (proverbs and legal codes), narrative is distinguished by *plot*. Put simply, plot is a sequence of actions, often explicitly connected in terms of cause and effect, leading from an initial situation, through complication, to some sense of resolution or 'revelation' (Miller's term). The events of the plot are often explicitly connected by the narrator in terms of cause and effect. Where this is not done, readers tend to supply causality, or at least coherence, for themselves. In short, narrative is generally assumed by hearers and readers to interrelate distinct temporal events, involving several characters, in a coherent whole without extraneous incidents.

Character and plot, then, are distinctive features of narrative. They are also interdependent notions. For a reader, understanding the connection between events often involves deciding what has caused a character to speak or act in a certain way. Understanding a character hangs in part—for there is more to characterization than this—on assessing what he or she says and does, which may be crucial aspects of the plot.

Third, narrative is also a genre which enjoys the *patterning play of words*—'there must be some patterning or repetition of key elements, for example, a trope or system of tropes, or a complex word . . . some form of narrative rhythm modulating that trope or word' (Miller: 75). But again we would observe that this notion is by no means wholly discrete. Patterning language, character, and plot all overlap. Narrators can profoundly shape the terms by which we understand a character through repetition, even by so simple a device as the repeated use of a single epithet (classically 'wily' Odysseus). And a complex figure of speech can lure us to make connections between what otherwise seem extraneous plot elements (as we shall see later, in Chapter 7, when discussing the metaphor of 'house' in the story of King David).

Defining narrative this way—in terms of character, plot, and word-play is but a preliminary step in the exploration of biblical stories. Our own experience in writing this book suggests that no definition is ever satisfactory and that these discriminations between character, plot, and wordplay, like the many other possible analytic categories that we could invoke, are ultimately only heuristic, that is, they serve to open up possibilities of interpretation rather than having some essential reality in themselves. Nevertheless they can help us consider what is happening as we read. We do seem to come to stories with certain expectations. 'That's not much of a story', or 'That's a great story', we may say, without ever having taken a first course in literature. Perhaps our present definition is a matter of expectations rather than of reality. And indeed when we meet a story that defies these expectations we may be inclined to make meaning out of its very deviation from what we expect. Readers seem to have a powerful urge to make sense.

Biblical narrative

The texts

A large part of the Hebrew Bible is narrative. The primary story extends from Genesis to the end of 2 Kings. One way of describing the story is to see the plot as initiated by God, who attempts to establish and sustain a relationship of trust with humankind. A particular family is chosen and promised land and nationhood, gifts which will come to represent God's pledge of commitment and presence in the relationship. For its part, the divinely chosen family seeks to realize its vision of land and nationhood with, and sometimes without, God's assistance. God's desire for relationship and human desire for place and identity prove frequently incompatible and provide the ingredients of conflict in the overall story. Though the gifts are gained, they are lost finally through the people's failure to take seriously their own story and to respond to God's desire.

A second major narrative is the Book of Chronicles, to which Ezra and Nehemiah form a sequel, though these books precede Chronicles in the order of the Hebrew Bible. Prefaced by a genealogical compendium of Israel's story prior to the monarchy, Chronicles is an account of the kingdom of Judah from the death of Saul to the announcement of Judah's restoration from exile. The heart of the story is an elaborate account of how King David established a united state, organized its bureaucracy, founded the temple, provided for its functionaries, and promoted the levitical priesthood. What follows is essentially a falling away from this perceived ideal. The narrative covers the same period as 2 Samuel–2 Kings but presents a distinctive point of view, narrower in its focus and more obvious in its ideology. The books of Ezra and Nehemiah detail the subsequent rebuilding of Jerusalem and the temple, as well as the attempt by both Ezra and Nehemiah to sustain the restored community as a theocratic state in the face of external and internal pressures.

Some of the prophetic books also include narrative, usually retelling in prose the historical circumstances in which the prophet worked and prophesied. In Isaiah and Jeremiah we find material which also appears in segments of 2 Kings. Several psalms of 'historical recital' (Psalms 78, 105, 106, and 136) briefly recount Israel's primary story in poetry, an unusual feature in the Hebrew Bible. Other books contain a type of discourse marginally akin to narrative: visions and divine speeches, for example, often report series of events. Visions, however, often minimize temporality, and divine speeches offer more a catalogue of events than a plot in which tension rises and falls.

Of the remaining narratives, the books of Ruth and Jonah fit into the temporal scheme of the primary story, and further develop the

theme of God's desire for relationship in ways that are both consonant and contrastive with the larger account. Esther and Daniel 1–6
continue Israel's story after the loss of the land. These narratives
capture the crisis of the displaced people faced with foreign rule.
Esther relates the pressures upon national identity in an alien context, and Daniel explores the limits of God's sovereignty and God's
relationship to the rest of humankind. Of all biblical narrative, Job is
the most temporally and geographically elusive. Its distinctiveness
lies not only in its present form—a brief narrative framing an extensive poetic dialogue—but also in its interest in an individual whose
nationality is obscure and whose relationship to Israel is not, on the
surface of the story, of primary importance.

Literary forms and the problem of history

Biblical scholars have for about two centuries focused their attention
on the way the narratives have come to be in their present form.
They have attempted to recover from the Bible its original sources,
written and oral, and to write a history of the development of biblical literature and its conventional literary forms for the purpose of
reconstructing the history of Israel and Israelite religion. Despite
some impressive early hypotheses, the findings of source analysis have
proved mainly inconclusive. Even those critics more interested in the
literary characteristics of the material have attended to questions of
genre or form rather than to the inner workings of the stories themselves. But while definitions of conventional forms can be helpful,
they cannot capture the complexity of meaning produced by biblical
stories.

Form critics have designated a variety of genres in Hebrew narrative. The term 'saga' has been frequently used of the ancestral
narratives in Genesis; 'legend' is sometimes used of the narratives
about Moses in Exodus and Numbers, or about Elijah and Elisha in
1 and 2 Kings; the Joseph story in Genesis has been termed a
'novella' (a story with a compact and pointed plot), as have the books
of Esther, Jonah, and Ruth, and the story of King David's family in
2 Samuel 9–20 and 1 Kings 1–2. Aetiologies or accounts of origins
are found at various places in Genesis–2 Kings. 'Tale' is another
term that has been used to categorize shorter story units.

Often the labels are used to indicate some perceived relation to 'history', though such relations are extremely difficult to determine. In the case of the primary story (Genesis–2 Kings), scholars have been more likely to designate as 'history writing' subject matter closer to the exilic period (sixth century BCE). A major exception has been the story of King David in 2 Samuel 9–20 and 1 Kings 1–2, often thought to be a reliable historical document from close to the time of David. On the other hand, the Chronicler's story, partly because of its (probable) later composition and partly because it has seemed more ideologically 'biased', has long been viewed as historically less reliable than Samuel and Kings generally, despite the fact that it presents itself as 'history writing' no less than those books.

Perhaps some useful distinction might be made in terms of 'imaginative' genres (saga, legend, novella, etc.) and 'recording' genres (anecdote, annalistic extract, memoirs, history writing, etc.). In practice, however, such distinctions are not easily sustained. The difference between fiction and non-fiction, for example, is not always clear, even when dealing with modern genres of 'history' or 'biography'. All history writing involves defining and selecting 'events' and interpreting their relationships, which means constructing a plot and positing the motivation of the participating characters. All authors and editors serve ideological agendas, expressed or unexpressed, and shape their account accordingly. In practice, then, there must always be a distance between the narrative world and the world of 'what actually happened'. Indeed, we could argue that there is no such thing as 'what actually happened'; there are only stories (or histories) of what happened, always relative to the perspective of the story-teller (historian). We shall return to this point later in the chapter. Where ancient 'history-like' writing is concerned, our grasp of sources, literary conventions, and the social location of writer and audience is often minimal. Thus the problem of distinguishing between 'history' and 'fiction' is generally acute. In short, genre definitions narrower than loose terms such as narrative or story, especially where these sub-genres are conceived in terms of historiographical purpose, turn out to be of more limited use in discussing biblical narrative than might be expected.

Nevertheless one distinction—a narratological, not an historical-critical one—that can sometimes prove helpful is between 'dialogic' and 'monologic' narrative (cf. Polzin 1980a: 16–24 ¶C). The dialogic is represented by much of the primary story together with most of the shorter stories such as Ruth, Jonah, Daniel 1–6, and Esther. It is more open to multiple interpretations, entertains within it several ideological points of view or 'voices', often in tension, and is characterized by restraint on the part of the narrator and a premium on 'showing' through characters' actions and dialogue rather than simply 'telling'. The monologic is represented above all by Chronicles, Ezra, and Nehemiah. It has more in common with the rhetoric of public persuasion such as the political speech or the sermon, tends to elicit a narrower range of responses from the reader, minimizes tensions and ideological plurality, and is characterized by a premium on 'telling' through extended monologues from both narrator and characters.

Historical criticism, literary criticism, and the meanings of the text

Until recently a book such as this would have implied, if not claimed outright, that it was concerned with the correct way of interpreting biblical narrative. The objectives would have seemed clear. Despite some differences of approach between practitioners, scholarly analysis of the Bible was aimed at determining *the* meaning of the text. For scholars in the dominant 'historical-critical' school, that meant usually the 'original' meaning, constructed out of hypotheses regarding the compositional history of the text (its sources, editions, etc.), together with identifying and locating its author(s)/editor(s) and 'original' audience/readers. The enterprise suffered, however, from three major and (usually) crippling disadvantages.

First, the paucity of external controls (such as datable literary texts or historical records from ancient Israel) left the process prone to circular argument, a fundamental problem for a method that claimed to be establishing some kind of absolute truth. Assuming existing hypotheses about Israelite literary and political history, the critic would assert that some elements of the relevant text indicated the text's date, place, and purpose. Then the text as a whole would be interpreted to show that it made sense in terms of these parameters. Thus this text would be enlisted in support of the historical-critical hypotheses upon which its interpretation was based and the true meaning of the text would be claimed to have been established. The possibility that there might be (literally) an infinite number of other possibilities was rarely entertained.

Second, the analysis of sources, fundamental to the method, was basically dependent on aesthetic premises which were often arbitrary and rarely acknowledged. Sources were determined by criteria such as vocabulary use and 'contradiction' according to what seemed to the critic to be consistent with the style and thought processes of a single author. Significant expression of ideological tensions or factual contradictions within a single work was deemed unlikely, if not impossible. Invoking the notion of ironic writing to account for some apparent contradictions was usually disallowed. In short, underlying most source criticism has been an aesthetic preference for rationalistic, literal reading of literature.

Third, historical criticism accorded a privilege to the notion of 'original' which is both problematic in itself (why stop at the 'sources', why not the sources of the sources?) and also devastating to the value of the text most people actually read, namely the 'final' canonical text.

One sure effect of this tradition of biblical criticism was to take the possibility of serious initiative in interpretation out of the hands of laypersons and keep it firmly in the hands of scholars. Scholars alone could conduct the arcane arguments about sources and redaction. They then could *tell* others the results of their research. To read the Bible one had to be constantly reading the scholars.

In the same vein, but perhaps even more important, was the assumption that what was being expounded by the historical critic was, if not the correct meaning of the text, at least a step towards the correct meaning. There are two questions here. One is whether critics (readers) think of texts as having ultimately only a single right meaning. The other is whether critics think that there is a single right method of interpretation. For most historical critics the answer to both questions was, yes. The critic was seeking *the* right meaning, and historical criticism was *the* correct method by which to seek it. Historical criticism, indeed, was the summit of the interpretational pyramid. All those layers below were merely relics of bygone mistakes, centuries of wrong interpretations. (The arrogance of this position is, of course, breathtaking, but recognizably Western.)

This present book belongs with a broad movement in recent biblical studies that has broken with the historical-critical tradition in significant ways. Here is not the occasion to develop an argument justifying our position on the question of interpretation. Such arguments are amply indicated in other books (see the bibliography, ¶C), including some in this series (Morgan with Barton 1988; Coggins 1990). Rather here we wish simply to sketch some elements of our position in relation to what has been normative for a century or so.

Where historical criticism sought meaning in the origins or sources of biblical texts, we take the final form (itself a notion not free of problems) as our primary text. Instead of attempting to reconstruct an ancient 'history' we read these narratives as we might read modern novels or short stories, constructing a story world in which questions of human values and belief (and theology) find shape in relation to our own (and our readers') world(s).

Instead of seeking the one legitimate meaning, namely what the text (usually defined as the author) meant in its 'original context', we recognize that texts are multivalent and their meanings radically contextual, inescapably bound up with their interpreters. This reader-oriented approach to textual meaning has its consequences. For example, no matter how persuaded we are of the legitimacy of our own interpretations, we must depend upon some tacit agreement with our larger reading community about reading conventions (method) and broad values if our interpretations are to be taken seriously by anyone but ourselves. (In that sense, hermeneutics or critical theory is logically prior to actual interpretation, though in practice changes usually occur in tandem, as has been the case with the shift from historical to literary criticism.)

In recognizing the subjectivity of reading, therefore, we deny the objectivity that historical criticism claimed was the hallmark of its best scholarship. Such recognition is not, as a recent reviewer proclaimed, an admission of the weakness of our method, but an assertion of its strength, because it is a recognition of what actually happens. Not that we read 'simply' subjectively—as will become apparent, we trust, our method has its own discipline and rigour— but that we see claims of objectivity as too often an unstated defence of the status quo, as shoring up privilege under the guise of neutrality.

Finally, where historical criticism saw texts as fixed expressions of a particular meaning and viewpoint, we understand texts to be inherently unstable, since they contain within themselves the threads of their own unravelling. Language is always slipping. In order to make a point, the narrator must always imply the counterpoint. To construct the narrative world the narrator must suppress something—something that a suspicious reader may choose to dig up. 'Deconstructive' criticism seeks to expound the gaps, the silences, the contradictions, which inhabit all texts, like loose threads in a sweater, waiting to be pulled. We believe that this possibility needs to be faced by any interpreter, including interpreters of a Bible whose meaning has for so long been regarded as a fixture—despite innumerable different interpretations (cf. Miscall 1986: xviii–xxv ¶C).

In short, we find ourselves participants in a major epistemological shift which is, in the larger picture, but a phase in a long-standing Western debate, stretching back to Aristotle and beyond. Stanley Fish (1990 ¶A) has a particularly helpful and accessible discussion of the issues, which he casts in terms of the 'serious' and the 'rhetorical' human. At issue are fundamental views of truth and human nature. The 'serious' human views self and society as objective realities in a world of ostensible, essential truths and values—the 'common-sense' view. Truth is an eternal object which needs to be discovered. Reason and science, re-emphasized by the Enlightenment, are the prescribed tools for revelation. The 'rhetorical' human fashions the world through language, manipulating reality rather than discovering it, since reality is that which is construed as reality rather than some objective essence. On this view 'the givens of any field of activity—including the facts it commands, the procedures it trusts in, and the values it expresses and extends—are socially and politically constructed, are fashioned by [humankind] rather than delivered by God or Nature' (Fish: 209). This world is a carnivalesque one of exuberance and possibility, of enthusiasm and metaphor, of religion, magic, and verbal incantation, where truth is 'an artifact whose fundamental design we often have to alter' (Richard Rorty, cited by Fish: 221). Clearly our own inclination is to align with the 'rhetorical' human, despite the problems that view raises for much traditional Western understanding of God, truth, and the Bible.

For more than a century, historical criticism was the dominant method of biblical interpretation in the universities of Europe and America (as well as other European outposts). Both of us were taught that it was the only 'responsible' method for biblical scholars. Instead it has become for us a distinctly secondary line of inquiry. We do not think that historical-critical analysis, interesting as it might be, is a necessary major precondition of our reading. Sometimes, as in the case of the book of Jonah, we may make reference to historical events and draw for 'culture code' upon Assyrian imperial annals or palace reliefs depicting aggressive militarism, or even the place of the text in a hypothetical history of biblical literature. Usually, however, we find ourselves appealing less to 'history' behind the text than to information that is part of the world of the biblical text itself. Thus most of what we need to know about Jonah's world, including Nineveh and the temple, comes from within the (larger) biblical story, especially Genesis–2 Kings.

We often read across source boundaries as historical critics have conventionally defined them. When we do, we are reading the final, canonical form of the text. Sometimes source analysis can be helpful to us by drawing attention to disjunctions in a narrative, disjunctions which have been treated as signs of disparate sources but which for us can have a major impact on how we construct the meaning of the narrative taken as a whole. At other times historical-critical studies seem irrelevant to the way we are reading. More often, like many different kinds of analysis, critical and pre-critical, such studies may provide us with useful observations and insights—here and there.

In practice, therefore, we refer little in this present book to standard historical-critical work on the Bible. That is not to denigrate historical criticism. It has been a powerful movement in biblical studies, instrumental (following the spirit of the Renaissance) in opening the Bible to scrutiny as a document of human literature, and in that sense a profoundly 'literary' study. Its future seems to us to lie in a major reconstruction of its programme in terms of social world studies, with its positivistic ('objective') notion of 'history' radically reconceived. As already indicated, history may be better thought of as an ideological and social construct, inevitably subjective, and existing on a continuum with notions such as 'myth' and 'fiction'.

None of this means that we think the Bible to have nothing to do with history. It simply means that, by and large, we are not addressing historical questions directly. We have other fish to fry. Some scholars have tried to argue recently that for interpretation to be truly liberating, it must be anchored in an historical analysis (Wimbush 1989 ¶D). Without dismissing the power in that argument, we doubt that it is necessarily true—from both theoretical and practical points of view. As far as practice is concerned, we might witness the power of the readings produced in the central American 'base communities', hardly dependent upon historical analysis of the production of the text, though crucially related to an understanding of the current social situation of the readers. And we have found something similar take place in a very different context in North America, among seminary students in our own institutions or largely middle-class participants in church Bible studies.

Varieties of interpretation: Genesis 4 through 2000 years

Our discussion of literary criticism in relation to historical criticism perhaps needs to be put into a larger context. It is not as though historical criticism has always reigned supreme. In fact, its time has been relatively short, about two centuries at most. The history of the interpretation of biblical narrative is a play of continuity and discontinuity over two millennia. So far we have been speaking of interpretation in the abstract. To glimpse something concrete of the rich variety of biblical interpretation over those two millennia let us consider some readings of a particular biblical narrative—Genesis 4, the story of Cain and Abel. This survey is intended to serve two ends: to put in historical perspective historical-critical claims to truth, and to provide a backdrop against which our own approach to biblical narrative may be more clearly defined.

What we shall observe with the Cain and Abel story is typical of the interpretation of biblical stories. We shall see major differences between interpreters, but also some significant continuities. This survey, then, will both illustrate some of the lines of difference which we have just been discussing and contest the sharpness of those lines. Like our method, and indeed all strategies for reading texts, our history of interpretation is itself fraught with risk as its categories struggle to sustain themselves against an infinitude of other possibilities.

Philo

The story of Cain and Abel in Genesis 4 is our text (for bibliography, see ¶H.2). One of the earliest extensive interpretations is that of Philo, a learned Jew of Alexandria in Egypt from *c*.20 BCE to 50 CE. In one treatise he deals with Genesis 4: 2–4. Addressing an audience brought up in a Hellenistic cultural tradition, he reads his text with close attention to verbal details, typical of a Jewish exegete, but also in terms of Greek philosophical and ethical categories. Why, for example, is Abel, the younger, mentioned before his elder brother in verse 2? The answer is that while vice (Cain) is older in terms of time, virtue (Abel) is prior in value—a point backed by experience (where youth's passion gives way, he claims, to the philosophical calm of older age) and scripture (the law of the rights of the first-born son of a man with two wives, Deuteronomy 21: 15–17). While on the subject of virtue and vice, he elaborates an allegory of the two women mentioned in Deuteronomy 21: 15–17, viewing one as a courtesan, the other as a chaste woman, each pressing her claims upon 'the mind'. We may be reminded of the 'strange woman' and 'woman wisdom' competing for the attention of the young man in Proverbs 1–9. And like that part of scripture Philo's text is starkly androcentric. The mind, the subject, is always male. With virtue's victory, the mind becomes, like Abel, a shepherd, controlling the unreasoning 'lower' faculties (the sheep).

Why, asks Philo, is Cain's offering rejected? The answer is found in verbal detail. Cain brings his offering not immediately but only 'after some days'. Furthermore, he offers some of the fruits, but it is not said that he offers the first-fruits. Abel, by contrast, is said to offer the firstlings of his flock. (A scholar recently published an argument resting on exactly the same point.) A meditation follows, first on the subject of prompt and willing service and then on the true nature of first-fruits—whatever are first in value, namely the virtues. To 'offer' these is to meditate upon them. And with this thought, Leviticus 2: 14 comes into play. The offering is to be 'new, roasted, sliced, pounded'. These, then, must be of fresh inspired thoughts, hardened by the fire of close reasoning, divided by careful analysis, and pounded in by the discipline of repeated meditation. Some of us, present day interpreters, may recognize an exegetical tradition that still lives in many a pulpit.

In a second treatise Philo deals with other parts of the story. The summons to Abel to go out into the field or 'plain' is viewed as a summons to disputation. Philo has little interest in the literal level of the text. The characters are opposing principles, Virtue and Vice, love of self and love of God. The story concerns the contest of values. 'Plain', he argues, is elsewhere in Genesis a figure for such a contest. Jacob calls Leah and Rachel to the plain because there he 'tends his flocks', which means, as we have seen, that he disciplines his lower impulses. That is what Joseph's brothers are learning to do, so that naturally his father sends him there to be taught by them. (That he needs teaching is obvious, given that he wears a multi-coloured patchwork of inconsistent tenets.)

Untrained in dialectic, Abel is foolish to accept Cain's challenge. Thought and speech should always be married. (Moses, deferring to Aaron, was wiser than Abel.) Glib fools may be despised, but silent wise men are ineffective. Nevertheless, the seeming victory is a defeat. Abel speaks to God through his blood. His life (that is, blood) is no longer speechless but has a voice which God hears. Cain's curse comes to him 'from the earth', that is, from the senses (the 'lower' part of a person) which are his chosen field. So virtuous, God-centred thought triumphs over vicious, self-centred senses.

Targum Pseudo-Jonathan

Another early Jewish interpretation appears in the Targum Pseudo-Jonathan, an Aramaic paraphrase of the biblical text (see ¶H.2). Though given its present shape after the seventh century CE it probably embodies much earlier material. Here Cain is viewed as bringing first-fruits which are indeed the seeds of flax, a detail probably deduced from Leviticus 19: 19 and Deuteronomy 22: 4. The detail adds specificity lacking in the text, probably on the assumption that the interpreter is doing nothing more than making explicit the implicit. Understood, too, is the harmony or consistency of scripture.

The interpreter can safely turn to Leviticus and Deuteronomy for information. That we saw to be Philo's principle also.

The detail of the flax has perhaps a further purpose. It blocks the interpretation that sees Cain's offering rejected because it did not precisely fulfil the rules. On the contrary, the Targum goes on to elaborate God's speech to Cain (vv. 6–7) and to add a debate between the brothers (v. 8) that suggests another cause. How the gift was received is not the issue, God seems to be saying. Rather the real question is whether Cain is satisfied that he has worked well. Compared with that issue any guilt incurred for infraction of rules is inconsequential. On the other hand serious failure will be judged, not now, but later, on the 'day of the great judgement'. The point is how in the mean time he will handle his frustration, the temptation to evil, over which he does have power. In the field it becomes clear, as he argues with his brother, that Cain does not accept God's point. He asserts that though the world was created in love 'it is not ordered by the issue of good works, because there is partiality in judgement'. Abel retorts (self-righteously, perhaps) that there *is* justice—his offering was accepted because his work was better. Cain responds with a flat denial of judgement, judge, world hereafter (the day of judgement?), reward for the righteous or reckoning for the wicked. Abel flatly affirms these things. Cain picks up a stone (indicating perhaps that this was not premeditated murder) and drives it into Abel's forehead, so slaying him.

Here we have a powerful reading that highlights the issue of theodicy (God's justice), an issue that has loomed large for many a reader of Genesis 4, and an issue that haunts the whole Hebrew Bible. The interpretation is sensitive to details present in the text. It is sensitive, also, to what is not said, the 'gaps' in the text. Perhaps it is the text's silence about any prior antagonism between the brothers, as well as its failure to indict *clearly* Cain's sacrifice as the reason for its rejection, that has led the interpreter to build a reading around Cain's frustration and anger. The anger, properly addressed to God, Cain redirects instead to his self-righteous brother and lets it boil over into a murderous impulse. Later in the Bible an equally frustrated Job will be challenged by even more drastic circumstances to question God's justice and will refuse to submit to the judgement of several self-righteous 'brothers', but with a very different outcome.

The comparison, together with the Targumist's exposition of verse 7 in terms of God's gift to Cain of 'the power of the inclination of evil', may suggest that here in Genesis 4, too, God is no innocently detached third party but is deeply implicated in what looks like a test of the human's ability to command the power of evil.

Indeed, the question of evil is embedded in the Targumist's reading from the start. Verse 1 begins, 'And Adam was aware that Eve his wife had conceived from Sammael the angel, and she became pregnant and bore Cain, and he was like those on high, not like those below; and she said, "I have acquired a man, the angel of the Lord"'. Why is Adam removed from being Cain's father, and where does Sammael come from?

To the first question we might answer that, whereas in Gen. 5: 3 it is said that 'Adam begat a son in his own likeness, after his image, and called his name Seth', the parallel construction in Gen. 4: 1 has only 'Adam knew Eve his wife, and she conceived and bore Cain . . .' For a patriarchal tradition of interpretation which has already pinned the blame for the expulsion from the garden (the 'Fall') on Eve, these contrasting statements offer a splendid opportunity again to remove the patriarch from direct responsibility. Thus here the verb 'to know', is simply read literally as a verb of cognition rather than as a sexual metaphor: 'Adam knew that Eve his wife conceived . . .' Language is wonderfully flexible.

Who then was the father? The answer is bound up with the age-old question of evil's entry into a world created by a good God. Judaism (in cabalistic mysticism, for example) has always entertained the possibility that evil is part of God from the beginning. Here, however, the Targumist is perhaps pushing in the other direction, the direction that Christianity has conventionally taken. Evil infiltrates the world from powers outside God. Hence this particular solution: a complicit woman and an evil angel bring homicide into the human realm. In a stroke, God and the primal man are rendered blameless and the woman, again, is made the scapegoat. Thus, despite the surface differences between their interpretations, Philo and the Targumist have some important ideological ground in common.

Finally, before we leave the Targum, we might note a more practical concern of the reader emerging in the paraphrase. If this book of Genesis is an account, complete in itself, of how the world began and grew, it must imply the answer to a practical question. Who did Cain and Abel marry? The question is a perennial one for those who regard the book as a (largely) literal and comprehensive account of sacred history with its own complete internal logic. The same question is still asked today. The Targum offers an answer, which cautiously adds no new birth notice, but simply expands what is already there: 'And [Eve] went on to bear from Adam, her husband, his twin sister and Abel.'

Luther

Let us now jump some centuries, to the European 'Renaissance' and enter the formative phase of Protestant Christian interpretation. Martin Luther in Germany and John Calvin in French-speaking Switzerland were both professors of Old Testament. For Luther, in his commentary on Genesis (1535 ¶H.2), reaching chapter 4 was something of a relief and a chance to make clear yet again what he was doing.

At last we have passed over that expanse of text on which all expositors have toiled exceedingly—to some degree also we ourselves, although its entire content was rather clear to us because we did not concern ourselves with allegories but adhered to the historical and strict meaning. Since the majority of the interpreters did not concern themselves with this but attached greater importance to Origen, Dionysius, and others than to Moses himself, it is no wonder that they went astray. The chapters which now follow are less subject to debate and are clearer. Moreover, they support our conviction; for nobody can fail to see that Moses does not intend to present allegories but simply to write the history of the primitive world.

Commenting on verse 1, he targets the phrase that intrigued the Targumist, 'And Adam knew Eve his wife'. Lest anyone should be offended at Scripture's mentioning of such an act, Luther notes that though Adam had fallen he was still subject to the promise that from him would be born a shoot of life. Hence he understood that he had to produce offspring, especially since the command to increase and multiply (Gen. 1: 28) 'had been reaffirmed in the promise of the Seed who would crush the serpent's head' (Gen. 3: 15). Accordingly, in

Luther's judgement, 'Adam did not know his Eve simply as a result of the passion of his flesh; but the need of achieving salvation through the blessed Seed impelled him too.' So we learn from this exercise in the 'plain sense of Scripture' that Moses' history of the primitive world was infused with christological intentions.

Addressing himself further to the question of whether sexual intercourse ('the work of procreation') is good or shameful, he urges that it is essentially good, since it is part of God's creation, and would have been 'a very pure and very honourable work' had 'man' not fallen: 'Just as no one [i.e. no man] has misgivings about conversing, eating, or drinking with his wife—for all these are honourable actions—so also the act of begetting would have been something most highly regarded.' But 'sin and the curse' interposed, so that 'procreation remained in nature when it had become depraved; but there was added to it that poison of the devil, namely, the prurience of the flesh and the execrable lust which is also the cause of sundry adversities and sins, all of which nature in its unimpaired state would have been spared.' To cement his point he appeals to experience, though which part of it is his own is unclear. 'We know from experience the excessive desire of the flesh, and for many not even marriage is an adequate remedy.'

Now comes the major thrust (if we may put it that way) of his exposition. For having shown that for Moses to speak of Adam's sexual intercourse is 'no disgrace' he wants to add that 'it was also necessary for him to impart this teaching and to write it down because of future heresies . . . [he refers to sects advocating celibacy], but especially because of the papacy.' He proceeds to attack the church's rule of celibacy for priests, monks, and nuns—a rule, he says, which disregards the divine command to multiply—'as if the life of married people, of which Moses is speaking here, were detestable and reprehensible. But the Holy Spirit has a purer mouth and purer eyes than the pope.' He throws in for good measure several anecdotes purporting to demonstrate the hideous results of enforced celibacy—a papal pond in Rome with the heads of 6,000 infants, and a cellar in an Austrian nunnery with infant corpses in jars.

Whether Luther's readers respond with chilled spines or incredulity, few will fail to remark the commentator's passionate conviction. Luther's reading of Moses' ancient history is inextricably a product of Luther's own religious crusade.

At this point the tone of the commentary changes abruptly. The scholar observes that the word 'to know' has no equivalent in Latin or Greek. It means, he says, not only abstract knowledge, but feeling and experience. Thus Adam knew Eve, his wife, 'not objectively or speculatively, but he actually experienced his Eve as a woman'. Attention to details of the language takes him further. When it says simply that Adam knew Eve and that Eve conceived and bore Cain, here is evidence that physical conditions were generally better then than in Luther's own time: 'For at that time there were not so many ineffective cohabitations as there are in this declining world; but when Eve was known only once by Adam, she immediately became pregnant.' The comment, in its literal construction of the text, is worthy of the Targumist.

So, too, is the next, bringing the commentary on the verse to an end, though it constructs a meaning that the Targumist would have been unable to recognize. The question arises, why does Moses say 'She bore Cain' and not, as later, 'She bore *her son* Seth'? Why are blessed Abel and cursed Cain not called sons? 'The answer is that this happens on account of their descendants . . . it was Seth from whose descendants Christ, the promised Seed, would be born. And so Seth was the first who received the name of son.' Luther ends where he began, with christology.

Calvin

Calvin, too, in his commentary on Genesis (1554 ¶H.2), notes on verse 1 that the injunction to increase and multiply was not abolished by sin. Indeed, 'the heart of Adam was divinely confirmed, so that he did not shrink with horror from the production of offspring.' But if he recognized, in having children, 'the truly paternal moderation of God's anger', he also was forced to taste, when Cain slew Abel, 'the bitter fruits of his own sin'. Unlike the Targumist, therefore, Calvin places the blame for Cain's sin ultimately at Adam's door. Here a strong (Augustinian) doctrine of original sin is driving the reading.

But Calvin does not wish to dwell too long on such broad themes. Rather, 'let us follow the narration of Moses', he urges:

Although Moses does not state that Cain and Abel were twins, it yet seems to me probable that they were so; for after he has said that Eve, by her first conception, brought forth her first-born, he soon after subjoins that she also bore another; and thus, while commemorating a double birth, he speaks only of one conception. Let those who think differently enjoy their own opinion; to me, however, it appears accordant with reason, when the world had to be replenished with inhabitants, that not only Cain and Abel should have been brought forth at one birth, but many also afterwards, both males and females.

So the subject, and perhaps the tradition, of the Targumist appears again.

He continues with attention to the awkward grammar of the phrase 'I have gotten a man *'et YHWH*'. He offers several possibilities. Some translate '*with* the LORD', or '*from* the LORD', suggesting that 'Eve is giving thanks to God for having begun to raise up a posterity through her, though she was deserving of perpetual barrenness, as well as of utter destruction'. Others, 'with greater subtlety', translate, 'I have gotten the man *of* the LORD'. The implication of this reading is that 'Eve understood that she already possessed that conqueror of the serpent, who had been divinely promised to her'. Hence Eve's faith is celebrated, except that she mistook Cain for Christ. Calvin is sceptical. Rather the genuine sense seems to be 'that while Eve congratulates herself on the birth of a son, she offers him to God, as the first-fruits of his race'. The best translation is, therefore, 'I have obtained a man from the LORD'. Moreover, he adds, with an eye for a peculiarity of the word choice, 'she calls a new-born infant a man, because she saw the human race renewed, which both she and her husband had ruined by their own fault'.

When eventually he reaches verse 8, he addresses the problem of what Cain said to Abel. The Hebrew text lacks the phrase included in the Greek Septuagint and most versions, 'Let us go into the field'. It just has an ellipsis: 'And Cain said to Abel his brother . . .' Calvin, following the Hebrew, recognizes the ellipsis and debates what is to be understood. The Latin Vulgate, similar to the Greek, has 'Let us go outside'. On that interpretation, Cain is hypocritically concealing his anger, pretending fraternal concord, and looking for an opportunity to do his dastardly deed. Calvin sees some homiletical possibilities therein. But he wonders whether the speech is more directly a response to what has just gone before, God's rebuke. 'I certainly rather incline to the opinion that he did not keep his malignant feelings within his own breast, but that he broke forth in accusation against his brother, and angrily declared to him the cause of his dejection.' That the narrative continues with the brothers going out into the field ('When they were in the field . . .') is important. That means, Calvin observes, that although Cain may have already complained to Abel at home, 'he had yet so covered the diabolical fury with which he burned, that Abel suspected nothing worse'. Unlike (perhaps) the Targumist, however, Calvin sees the deed in the field as premeditated—vengeance deferred. 'This single deed of guilt clearly shows whither Satan will hurry men, when they harden their mind in wickedness, so that in the end their obstinacy is worthy of the utmost extremes of punishment.' He concludes, then, by relating this story of murder to a theology of judgement.

The Anchor Bible: Speiser

Coming now to the latter part of the twentieth century, we take up the Jewish American scholar E. A. Speiser's commentary on Genesis (1964 ¶H.2), the first in the Anchor Bible series, possibly the most widely sold 'critical' commentary series of the century. Its scholarly tradition is mainstream 'historical critical'. Speiser characterizes the meaning of the text in his very first sentences. 'The story of early man is now carried a step further, embracing the conflict between the pastoral and the agricultural ways of life. The conflict is depicted in terms of the impact on the given individuals.' So much for that. Next he turns to some matters of more burning interest. On the translation of verse 1, he argues that 'know' is inadequate and 'had experience of' is better. The stem of the Hebrew word in question *yd'*, is applied 'not only to normal marital situations . . . but also to clandestine conduct . . . and even homosexuality'. Use of the term is 'thus not a matter of delicate usage, as is sometimes alleged'. And to make his point stick he delivers his *coup de grâce*, the datum drawn from comparative philology. Akkadian 'extends [the term] to dogs'. Paragraphs of philological elaboration follow.

More complex, he avers, is the problem of how to understand verse 7. What does it mean, for example, that 'sin is couching at the door'? The solution, centring on the term 'to couch', is to be found via an alleged Akkadian 'loan word' signifying demon. All now falls into place, he believes, and a correct translation can be offered: 'Surely, if you act right, it should mean exaltation. But if you do not, sin is the demon at the door, whose urge is toward you; yet you can be its master.' With this matter solved he concludes his comment on the story.

Readers who have found the comment a little thin may turn to the notes and find, for example, that the phrase *'et YHWH* used of Eve's bearing Cain, translated 'with the help of Yahweh,' has been the subject of considerable suspicion and speculation. Speiser feels that we should note, therefore, that Akkadian personal names 'often employ the corresponding element *itti*, e.g., *Itti-Bel-balatu* "With Bel there is life"'. Or, for those of us, like Calvin and the Targumist, interested in what Cain said (v. 8), Speiser simply states categorically that the Hebrew text was accidentally shortened and that the ancient versions supply the missing clause, 'Let us go outside'.

Speiser's, then, is an interpretation perhaps more interesting for what it fails to say than what it says. Comparative philology offers a useful strategy for constructing a reading that says nothing about possible theological issues or themes (e.g. theodicy, sin, and judgement), nothing about the individual characters and their intentions or emotions, nothing even about Speiser's own claim that the story really depicts a social rather than individual conflict. Still, we do learn that in Akkadian dogs 'have experience of' other dogs.

Westermann

Though Speiser's commentary in many respects epitomizes a major and still prevalent vein of twentieth-century scholarship, historical criticism can offer richer theological interpretation. The protestant German scholar Claus Westermann's extensive commentary (1974/1984 ¶H.2), is instructive. Westermann begins with a short history of interpretation since the rise of historical criticism, observing two main lines of interpretation: the 'individual-primeval' and the 'collective'. The former takes the individuals, like Adam and Eve in the Garden, as paradigm figures of humanity in basic relationships. The latter, predominant in historical criticism for most of the twentieth century (Speiser is typical), finds the story to have originated in a tribal history of desert Kenites and to be really about an opposition between arable land and the desert. (In a sense, then, the story would be an allegory of societal conflict.) Westermann, however, sees no convincing clues to an earlier narrative of tribal history. Nor does he see collective interpretations actually paying much attention to the sequence of events narrated in the existing text. More satisfactory for him is the 'individual' understanding of the Jewish commentator Umberto Cassuto (1961): 'Cain, who killed his brother, is the prototype of the murderer. All human beings are brothers and whoever sheds human blood sheds the blood of his brother.'

Westermann takes the story as an integral part of the 'Yahwist' or 'J' narrative (one of the main sources thought to comprise the Pentateuch/Torah). Like Genesis 3, the Cain and Abel story deals with a crime and its punishment, but while Genesis 2–3 'deals with people before God in the community of husband and wife', chapter 4 'deals with the individual before God in brotherly relationship'. Both relationships are basic to human community, just as the different occupations of the brothers belong together as the staple of social life. 'Man' is not just Adam and Eve, but also Cain and Abel. If the relationship of man and woman to each other is one of mutual help, another possibility, of enmity and opposition, exists in Genesis 4. Here we find a crucial value judgement informing Westermann's reading: 'Brothers are naturally rivals, as the patriarchal history shows; rivalry, competition, quarrels, enmity are rooted in being brothers. This does not normally grow out of the partnership of man and woman, nor out of the relationship between parent and child, though it is a possibility. But it does normally grow out of the mutual coexistence of equals because the possibility of conflict is there.'

The story is not, therefore, simply about the intensification of sin, as is often urged, for the subjects and sins of Genesis 2–3 and 4 are different. Genesis 4 deals with basic elements of society—the positive, namely the division of labour, and the negative, namely the conflicts springing from rivalry.

Relating his interpretation now to Christian explanations of the 'Fall', Westermann urges that traditionally, by isolating Genesis 2–3, such interpretations have placed emphasis on 'sin in the area of sex', whereas 'sin in the area of social conduct retreated frighteningly into the background'. The New Testament's 'individual' interpretation (Matt. 23: 35; 1 John 3: 12; Heb. 11: 4 and 12: 24), he argues, takes up the Rabbinic interpretation of the story which sets it in a theological scheme contrasting the righteous one and the malefactor. So Cain is the evil one, Abel the just one whose sacrifice—martyrdom —is offered 'out of faith'. Westermann, on the other hand, views Cain, whose crime lies not in his sacrifice but in his killing of his brother, as a victim of typical human 'brotherly' rivalry. Yet he sees this alternative interpretation as not opposed to the message of the New Testament as a whole. When Christians 'have recognized once more the proper meaning of the text', the meaning intended in the context of Genesis 1–11, they will 'see it in the context of the social accusations of the prophets and, following this same path, in the context of the social aspect of the proclamation of Jesus, thus opening it anew'.

Finally, we might note the way Westermann deals with some perennial questions. Eve uses 'man' to describe her child because she sees in him the future man; rather than 'acquiring' him she has 'created' him, so that her boast is 'that she has brought forth a man in a way that corresponds to the creation of the man by the creator'. The problematic *'et YHWH* remains problematic, after a long discussion, though the critic prefers the sense, 'together with', 'equally with', 'like'. Likewise the difficulty of verses 6–7 can find no satisfactory resolution, though that does not necessarily affect an understanding of the narrative as a whole. In any case, the sentences may not be 'original'.

And what, finally, is to be said of God's involvement in the story? Why does God have no regard for Cain's sacrifice? Firmly rejecting any explanation in terms of a faulty attitude or offering, Westermann locates in the rejection a sign of the immutable: 'It is fated by God to be so.' The regard and disregard of sacrifices 'must remain without explanation.' On the other hand, it is clear that the narrator sees the matter of divine 'regard' as decisive in provoking conflict between brothers. Westermann takes the issue no further.

Reading for liberation: Boesak and Mosala

We began our journey with Philo in Africa. Now we return to Africa, to recent readings of the Cain and Abel story by Alan Boesak (1984) and Itumeleng Mosala (1987 and cf. 1991). (See bibliography, ¶H.2; and Gerald West 1989.) Both men, Christians and Black South Africans, are consciously relating their interpretations to their context of struggle against apartheid in South Africa.

Noting the narrative's reiteration of the term 'brother', Boesak elaborates his own evaluation of 'brotherhood'. 'It means to seek together for true humanity; to attempt together to make something of God's objectives visibly operative in the world; to let something of God's own heart become visible in fraternal relationships; and, in corporate relationship to history, to humanize the world and keep it humanized.' Cain's murder is not just a murder, it is fratricide. Discussing the expulsion of Cain from the land, Boesak observes how this curse strikes at Cain's very way of life, bound up with the land, so that his fear is understandable. Instead he is forced away from the land where God had given birth to humanity, where men were to live in community, 'as men, brothers, real people'. Even the earth refuses to be fruitful for him, choking on the blood of his brother, unable to respond to Cain, its relationship with him ruptured. And, condemned to be a wanderer, he will never belong to a land, be 'at home', again.

Boesak speaks to his own contemporary situation. The story affirms that oppressors shall have no place on God's earth. 'Oppressors have no home. Oppressors do not belong to, are not at home in God's objectives for this world. They have gone out of bounds.' The rupture of the fraternal bond is also a rupture of the bond with God. Cain 'brotherless' is also Cain 'Godless'. Cain is removed from God's presence. Thus the fate of the violent oppressor is to live in anxiety and fear. So the Whites of South Africa live, anxious and fearful. And, ironically, the most fearful think that they can resolve their fear, secure peace, by intimidating and destroying others. Why does Cain survive? He lives in order to warn of what happens when God is not sought. He also lives in order to seek forgiveness—as the murderer on the cross found forgiveness from Jesus. Can anything change? Boesak invokes Jesus' reversal of

Lamech's words. Jesus' message is not vengeance seventy-seven times, but forgiveness seventy times seven. Can Blacks in South Africa transcend their situation, asks Boesak, and forgive like this? People who have seen their children shot in the streets? No one should speak too hastily about forgiveness, he feels. Nevertheless, 'With God all things are possible, including forgiveness welling up out of the hearts of suffering and oppressed Black South Africans. That too. Precisely that.'

Finally comes the birth of Seth, of whom Eve says, 'God has given me another son in the place of Abel whom Cain killed'. Eve, observes the interpreter realistically, recognizes the awful past. But she also sees God wishing to begin all over again with this new child. 'The story ends not in tragedy but in words of hope: "At that time men began to call upon the name of the LORD" (Gen. 5: 26).' Boesak concludes: 'After murder, terror, inhumanity, apartheid, and the gobbling up of the profits of apartheid, and finally death—after all this, God still wishes to begin all over again with us.'

Mosala, unlike Boesak, understands his own reading to relate to an historical-critical analysis. What ideological or spiritual agendas motivate the text in its original historical context? What social, cultural, class, gender, and racial issues of the time inform the text? Mosala locates the story in the so-called 'J' or 'Yahwist' document (one of the original sources of Genesis, according to historical-critical hypothesis), which he views as the work of royal scribes of the Solomonic monarchy. Thus the narrative's dominant ideological concerns are those of the state, which needs to justify the creation of large privately owned estates together with the dispossession of most peasant farmers from their inherited plots. The story legitimizes this process of dispossession by a new class of estate holders under the protection of the monarchy. 'Clearly, Cain the tiller of the soil must be seen to represent the freeholding peasantry who become locked in a life-and-death struggle with the emergent royal [and landed] classes, represented in this story by Abel. Obviously, the text favors Abel and enlists divine pleasure on his side.' Abel is depicted as a pastoralist for reasons to do with the new division of labour, although Mosala is less than clear on this point.

On his major point, however, he is insistent. The story is an ideological production of the monarchic state. By making Cain, the historical victim, into the story's oppressor and the historical victor, the pastoralist Abel, into the story's victim, the narrative lends legitimacy to the dispossession of the tenth- and ninth-century Cains, the small peasant freeholders.

For Mosala the question of the acceptability of Cain's sacrifice to God becomes focused on the question of how the monarchy exacted tribute from village peasants. And finally, he observes that though, historically speaking, the death of Abel may indicate some resistance by the peasant class, the account has been reshaped to deplore the fact—in the interests of the ruling class that produced the text.

Similarity and difference

There are many observations that could be made about this survey of interpretations. We make a few in the cause of stimulating some re-evaluation of what is accepted as legitimate interpretation as well as how this particular story may be understood.

For our own part, we are struck first by threads that reappear over the centuries, no matter what the dominant interpretive mode. The grammatical peculiarity *'et YHWH* demands attention, as does the difficulty in construing a literal sense of verses 6–7. Why speak of a child as a 'man'? And what is the significance of the apparent ellipsis in the Hebrew text in verse 8 ('And Cain said to Abel . . .')? These are matters of *detailed grammatical and literal construction*. Even the most obvious allegorist, Philo, attends to them.

The question of twins will not go away, though the modern critics have done their best to dismiss it. This, too, is a matter of literal detail. The question arises when interpreters understand the text as a window into a story world that is the same as the 'real' world. It is a world complete in all its details, whether or not these are expressed explicitly by the text. Thus 'missing' detail can always be supplied from clues in the text and inferences drawn from contemporary life and logic. Often, as in the twins suggestion, a premium is placed upon the most economical explanation, the one that appears to add least to the text.

Details of linguistic difference are also favourite starting points for building themes of consequence. Why, for instance, is the formula for the birth of Cain different from that of Seth? For the Targumist that difference opens a way into the question of evil's presence in the world. For Luther it anchors perhaps his most important point, the christological intention of this primeval story. Some thematic issues too, such as theodicy, surface constantly, even if some of our particular interpreters manage to sideline them. Why does God regard the one sacrifice and disregard the other? Is God's treatment of Cain just? Attempts to single out some failure in the offering itself have an unstable history.

On the other hand, we are also struck by some gaps. One is of particular importance to us. None of the commentators is willing to explore *the character of God* too far. Loyalty to established dogma concerning the divinity seems to be determinative. What God does is generally assumed to be unchallengeable, despite the fact that the question of justice in God's initial treatment of Cain is raised as early as the Targum. But we could ask whether, even if the rejection of Cain's offering were just (which we cannot know), was it wise? Does God bear no responsibility for the murder? Why does God, in answer to Cain's anger (v. 5) make the enigmatic and provocative speech about 'doing well' (vv. 6–7)—a speech which we could reasonably judge to be calculated to intensify Cain's frustration. Far from being inconsequential to the meaning of the narrative as Westermann would have it, we might argue that it is the crux, where angry frustration turns into homicidal frustration.

Blocking awkward questions about God's intentions, desires, and accountability is a widespread practice—though not universal (witness, for example, Voltaire ¶H.2)—in the interpretation of biblical narrative. The same tendency can be seen in Genesis 2–3 where God's intention in placing the tree of the knowledge of good and evil in the garden is rarely considered. That what God does·may be mistaken, let alone culpable, is normally out of bounds to interpreters of biblical narrative. But God is a character in the story, not to be confused too quickly with the God who transcends the story, the God of religious faith. Our own reading takes the anthropomorphic qualities (including gender) of the biblical character, God, seriously. The character seems to be constructed on a divine–human continuum. The YHWH (the LORD) of these narratives is not the philosopher's omni-God, all knowing, all powerful, and all present. This God is amazingly powerful but also vulnerable. This God discerns with uncanny accuracy but also feels his way. Hence our reading of Cain and Abel could not so easily stop the question of God's motivation with the assertion that this is not a proper question or that Cain is simply confronted with the immutable.

An important feature of the readings that clearly affects interpretation is *the literary context* in which the text is read. Philo has no hesitation in citing evidence from elsewhere in the Torah. Luther reaches back to Genesis 1 and leaps beyond the Hebrew Bible into the New Testament. Calvin is more cautious, and tends to stay with his given text, but he treats the story as part of a much larger story, 'the narration of Moses'. Westermann appeals to Genesis 2–3 (and also Genesis 11) but, unlike Luther or Calvin, for example, will not invoke Genesis 1, since to do so would cross source-critical boundaries. Genesis 1 is thought to be a priestly composition (P), while Genesis 2–3 and 11, like Genesis 4, are considered to come from the Yahwist source (J). On the other hand Westermann is also interested in relating his own interpretation of Genesis 4 to New Testament interpretations of the text. But unlike Luther he does not assume that the two interpretations need to be entirely consonant. In various ways, therefore, despite their differences, all the commentators adopt some kind of 'canonical' approach.

We find our own reading method connected variously with the commentators here. We would assume Genesis–2 Kings to be our primary narrative, irrespective of putative sources, and the Hebrew Bible to be its larger literary context. Hence we would have no hesitation about invoking Genesis 1 if it seemed relevant. Indeed, we would make much more of the relation of Genesis 4 to the larger narrative (Genesis–2 Kings) than any of the commentators. Division between brothers marks the story powerfully, whether between individuals—for example, Jacob and Esau, Joseph and his brothers, Abimelech and his brothers, Absalom and Amnon, Solomon and Adonijah—or corporate entities—Gilead against Ephraim (Judges 12), Israel against Benjamin and Jabesh-Gilead (Judges 20–1), Israel against Judah (1 Kings 12, etc.). Extending the reading this way lends support to Boesak's focus on the theme of brotherhood.

Finally we would note that like Westermann, when reading in a Christian context, we have an interest in relating our reading to the New Testament but are not willing to let the New Testament determine our interpretation.

A further point that strikes us from the survey is *the constant and complex interplay of literal and allegorical/metaphorical interpretation.* While commentators may express their disquiet about other interpreters' methods (as opposed to their specific results) the distinctions they draw are often less clear-cut than may at first appear. Luther disparages earlier (Christian) allegorical exegesis as having little to do with what Moses intended. Yet his own interpretation of Seth's 'sonship' as pointing to Christ, the Son, may seem to many readers hardly an obvious historical-literal reading. On the face of it, Philo's allegorical account of the main characters as figures of virtue (noble God-centred reason) and vice (base self-centred feelings) has more literal connection with the text. We noted that the distance between Philo's allegory and the modern 'collective' interpretation of the text is not so far. Each picks up an aspect of the text—Cain's anger, the characters' occupations—and from it determines an underlying thematic structure. Westermann's critique of the collective interpretation—that it has too little connection with the surface sequence of events (plot?)—would seem to apply to Philo, too, though no more perhaps than to Mosala's historical-sociological analysis. On this point our own preference, methodologically speaking, lies with Westermann. We incline to a reading method that takes seriously the 'surface' of the narrative, treating its characters (at least initially) as discrete persons and the sequential unfolding of the story as significant. We do not limit narrative meaning to the literal 'surface' of the text. We are not 'formalists'. But we believe that interpretation becomes increasingly tenuous as it loses touch with the surface of the narrative. (Perhaps here we still share a Reformation legacy.)

Even more important from our own point of view is the obvious part played by *the ideologies or value systems of the interpreters.* Even Speiser, who seems on the face of things to believe in little except the value of Akkadian, perhaps tells us by his detachment that he is avoiding theological engagement. Having embraced the liberal critical position, he was distinctly out of step with the mainstream of Jewish scholars of his time. By contrast, Luther's christological orientation and anti-papal polemic is patent. We might guess at a deep-seated belief in stern discipline from Calvin's relish of the theme of judgement. The androcentric/patriarchal values shared by Philo and the Targumist would doubtless extend to other commentators were we to make a closer analysis.

Westermann's conviction that equality (brotherhood) breeds conflict is interesting, especially given that he finds marriage and parent–child relationships to be much less conducive to disruption. We find that a strange statement. His world seems radically different from ours. A feminist critique might suggest, on the other hand, that it is simpler than that. Here is a classic statement of patriarchy —which is, of course, committed to hierarchy as the natural order, including both marriage and parenthood. Moreover, the understanding of brotherhood as intrinsically competitive is itself a product of patriarchy, especially in its capitalist version. We might well wonder about those twin sisters. Is it of no consequence that this story is told of brothers and not sisters? Could a patriarchal narrator have sustained a story of two sisters arguing over God and a sacrifice to the point of one killing the other? For that matter, do brothers indeed symbolize for all readers endemic conflict? Boesak speaks against that view. Or perhaps Westermann's value judgement is one of political ideology, favouring authoritarian versus egalitarian institutions. Or perhaps it is both patriarchal and politically authoritarian.

For their part, Boesak and Mosala make no bones about their interest. They are reading passionately for liberation and that in a particular context, the struggle in South Africa. Their candour is refreshing.

The *religious traditions of commentators* obviously shape interpretations. In this respect we can do no other than join the crowd. Both of us are Christians, currently teaching in protestant seminaries, though our specific traditions within protestantism diverge. Of course, the relationship of religious tradition to interpretation is complex. At some points it is clear that the universalities of human experience and the communion of scholarship (the 'intertextuality' of biblical commentary) have a way of subverting sharp lines of division. To read within traditional boundaries, yet seek constantly to cross (and occasionally subvert) them, seems to us a worthwhile enterprise.

Several of the commentators are explicit about their seeking and promoting the *'correct' reading*. We hope that the account just given may help relativize such claims, including those that will continue to be made. Mosala, for example, insists that a reading for liberation requires a historical-critical analysis as well as 'a basis in critical theoretical perspectives which can expose the deep structure of a text'—by which he means that only an historical and sociological analysis from a materialist (e.g. Marxist) perspective will do. Our own experience of reading Boesak and Mosala with African Americans who sense a kinship with the struggle in South Africa suggests, at a practical level, that Mosala's interpretational strategy has a limited power to engage a wide audience. (This is also West's critique, 1989 ¶H.2.) It is essentially an academic endeavour, technically out of the reach of most readers, and we would say academically vulnerable at its base, namely its historical claims regarding the provenance of the text (in the present case, the claim that the Cain and Abel story is a product of the Solomonic monarchy). With most biblical literature, such claims are tenuous at best. They may or may not be 'correct'. Resting on such shifting sands, the claim that this method is 'required' is problematic to say the least (and Mosala would probably now modify his argument). By contrast, Boesak's reading is of a kind that is accessible to, and can be practised by, many who are familiar with the text.

To say this is not to dismiss Mosala's point that the production of texts is an ideological act. On the contrary. But there are more ways of countering ideological coercion by texts than historical-materialist analysis. Our own strategy, given the acute problems involved in analysing the production of biblical texts, is to sharpen our awareness of the ideological dimensions of *reading* them. Something of this position will therefore emerge as the book proceeds, and we shall return explicitly to the issue again in the final chapter.

This account of some previous readings of a particular story should lend some further perspective to our own interests and method of interpretation. In terms of the last century or so of historical-critical scholarship, we claim to be supporting a significantly new way of reading narrative in the Hebrew Bible. In the larger picture, however, it becomes apparent that while dominant assumptions, goals, and strategies regarding interpretation come and go, there remains a web of connection. Our own book is simply part of this ebb and flow of interests and approaches. Much of what we do with narrative has been done in one form or another already, many times, over many centuries.

We are not offering the correct way of reading the Bible. Rather we are suggesting lines of interpretation and a reading method for people of our own times who share something of our own culture. Our hope is to provoke enlivening engagement with biblical stories.

2

Tamar and Judah: Genesis 38

Our book moves, we have said, between readings of texts and discussions of method. This first extended reading illustrates broadly from one particular story, in Genesis 38, the kinds of questions we shall be asking and the kinds of observations we shall be making about Hebrew narrative in general.

It happened at that time that Judah went down from his brothers, and turned aside to a man, an Adullamite, whose name was Hirah. And Judah saw there the daughter of a Canaanite man, whose name was Shua; he took her and went into her, and she conceived and bore a son, and he called his name Er. Again she conceived and bore a son, and she called his name Onan. And again she bore yet another son, and she called his name Shelah. He [Judah] happened to be in Chezib when she bore him. (Gen. 38: 1–5)

'It happened at that time' raises the first question: what time? We have introduced the narrative as a discrete story, but the beginning invites us to reconsider the story's boundaries. Alter (1981: 3–12 ¶F) makes a compelling case based on theme, motif, and language for the connection of this episode with its literary frame, the story of Joseph (deaths of sons; contrast of mourning/consolation; recognition as a recurrent motif (Genesis 37, 38, 42, 45); deceptive garments; symbol of the kid goat; opening formulas: 'Judah went down' and 'Joseph was taken down' (38: 1 and 39: 1); sexual incontinence contrasted with sexual continence (Genesis 38 and 39).

The temporal formula, a less subtle connective, indicates sequence and simultaneity. The episode involving Judah obviously follows upon his conspiracy with his brothers, but occurs at the same time as

Joseph's experiences in Potiphar's house and in prison. The phrase suggests something like 'meanwhile' or 'in the meantime'.

Once the context is established, the preceding episode provides temporal depth to Judah's character. It suggests, for example, the possible motivation for his departure. His father's inconsolable grief is, perhaps, a too-constant reminder of his part in the conspiracy against his brother Joseph. A little distance provides relief from his guilt.

His inspiration to dispose of his brother as a piece of merchandise offers a clue as to how he conducts his personal relationships. The abrupt way the narrator has him 'see,' 'take' (NRSV and others have 'marry', but Hebrew normally says 'take for a woman (wife)' to indicate 'marry') and 'enter' (NRSV, more coyly, has 'go in to') the daughter of Shua reinforces the notion that Judah has little regard for the civilities of relationship. He takes and disposes in much the same vein; which is to say, Judah relates to people in terms of what benefits him. The woman is given no name, which further underscores her lack of value in his sight, except for sex and pro-creation. It is telling that almost the same set of verbs—see, take, and lie with—are the terms used only a few chapters earlier to preface Shechem's rape of Dinah (Genesis 34).

This part of the exposition indicates subtly the nature of Judah's values. He names the first-born, but his wife names the other two sons. Judah's interest in his sons ceases once he has an heir, someone to carry on his line and his name.

Similar information is found in the allusion to Chezib. The Masoretic Text says that *he* (not she, as the ancient Greek and some English versions would have it) was in Chezib when the third son is born. Chezib, a place-name found nowhere else in the Hebrew Bible, means something like 'falsehood' or 'lie'. That Judah is in a place of 'deception' while his wife is busy having a baby prompts us to suspect him of being both irresponsible and unfaithful, characteristics of his later treatment of his daughter-in-law.

And Judah took a wife for Er his first-born, and her name was Tamar. But it happened that Er, Judah's first-born, was evil in the sight of YHWH, and YHWH slew him. So Judah said to Onan, 'Go into your brother's wife, and do a brother-in-law's duty to her, and raise up

seed (offspring) for your brother.' But Onan knew that the seed would
not be his; so it would happen that whenever he went into his brother's
wife he would spill (his semen) on the ground, so as not to give seed to
his brother. But what he did was evil in the sight of YHWH, and he slew
him also. So Judah said to Tamar his daughter-in-law, 'Remain a
widow in your father's house, till Shelah my son grows up', for he
thought—lest he die, like his brothers. So Tamar went and dwelled
in her father's house.   (Gen. 38: 6–11)

This portion of the exposition shows Judah the controller. He
may have chosen his own wife, but he does not allow his son the
same privilege. He will determine his own line. But his control slips
when God enters the picture.

Judah does not count on his son Er's 'evil'. If he knows about it,
he has taken no account of it. He certainly is not expecting divine
punishment—after all, he and his brothers suffered no consequences
for their dealings with Joseph. If he does not know, then his sense of
control is all the more ironic, an irony which recurs with his second
son Onan.

The first son is dead, but we do not see Judah mourn. Unlike his
father Jacob, Judah gets on with life—still, as he imagines, in
control. He demands that Onan perform as surrogate husband in
order to father yet another generation of the first-born line. Like his
brother before him, Onan is given no choice concerning this woman
Tamar. But again there is a limit to Judah's power. His control
cannot really extend into the bedroom and certainly not into the
realm of the divine. Because what Judah does not know, he cannot
control—and Judah does not seem to know of God's part in all this.

When his second son dies, he is suddenly less anxious to build his
family through the woman Tamar. To Tamar he claims that his
third (and last) son Shelah is not old enough to act as surrogate, but
the narrator gives us a glimpse of Judah's real reason for hesitation:
he thinks that the woman Tamar has had something to do with the
deaths of his sons. Hence the dramatic irony: we know what Judah
does not, namely, that Er and Onan have died as a result of their
own evil. God, not Tamar, has killed them.

Once we recognize the discrepancy between the public and the
private Judah, we can rest assured that he never intends to summon

Tamar for the third son. This is a 'don't call us, we'll call you' speech if ever there was one! Tamar can remain a childless widow in her father's house.

The days went by, and the wife of Judah, Shua's daughter, died, and Judah was comforted, and he went up to Timnah to his sheep-shearers, he and his friend Hirah the Adullamite. And Tamar was told, 'Your father-in-law is going up to Timnah to shear his sheep.' So she took off her widow's clothes, and put on a veil, wrapping herself up, and sat at the entrance to Enaim, which is on the road to Timnah; for she saw that Shelah was grown up, and she had not been given to him as a wife. And Judah saw her and thought her to be a whore, for she had covered her face. He turned aside to her on the road and said, 'Come, let me come into you', for he did not know that she was his daughter-in-law. So she said, 'What will you give me, that you may come into me?' He said, 'I will send you a kid from the flock.' But she said, 'Only if you give me a pledge, till you send it.' He said, 'What pledge shall I give you?' She said, 'Your signet and your cord, and your staff that is in your hand.' So he gave them to her, and went into her, and she conceived by him. Then she arose and went away, took off her veil, and dressed in her widow's clothes. (Gen. 38: 12–19)

The narrator begins a new phase of the story. The simple phrase indicating the passage of time, literally 'the days multiplied', prepares us for Tamar's perception, reported in verse 14, that Judah did not intend to keep his promise (Alter 1981: 7). The third death in Judah's family is recounted in laconic fashion, with no explanation. Rather the focus immediately moves to Judah's response, with the cryptic observation, '*and* [he] was comforted' ('*when* [he] was comforted,' as in RSV, is interpretive), immediately followed by the announcement of his trip to Timnah to the sheep-shearing. Close attention to the language used here is rewarding. While it is customary to understand the mention of comfort (or consolation) as indicating the passing of a period of mourning (so, for example, NRSV), there is no compelling reason to read the term only this way. The ambiguity of the phrase 'and he was comforted'—consoled in his mourning for her, or relieved because she has died?—is as striking in Hebrew as in English. The narrator could easily have made it clear that Judah mourned for her by using language specifically of mourning ('*bl, spd*). Instead, in contrast to Jacob who 'mourned for his son many days' and 'refused to be comforted' (Gen. 37: 34–5), Judah is simply 'comforted' and off to the sheep-shearing—a time of eating, drinking, and general festivities. So we are hardly surprised to see him making straight for the prostitute, the moment he sees her. (While seeing 'comfort' as mourning, Alter none the less observes the contrast with Jacob's refusal to be consoled.)

Apparently Tamar knows her father-in-law well enough, too, so that when the word gets to her that he is going to the sheep-shearing she knows what sort of things he has in mind. As so often in biblical stories, vital pieces of information are passed from character to character by anonymous informants. Knowledge is power, and the story world, like our own, is full of busybodies, brokering rumour, breaking secrets, and subverting the independence of individuals. We may imagine the scandalized, or at least disapproving, gossip that works its way quickly from Judah's house to Tamar's on the news of Judah's unseemly trip to Timnah.

Gossip or not, Judah, as a man, can do as he pleases. The woman Tamar, as her widow's garments remind us, is in a different position. Comforted or not, she is expected to remain where Judah has put her, a widow in her father's house. To get out of her widow's clothes permanently she must put them aside temporarily. Thus her changing of clothes, which neatly frames her dangerous deception, is symbolic of her larger goal.

With this deception of Judah Tamar counters Judah's deception of her. And she does so, appropriately, by manipulating his sexuality. (As Alter observes, it is also appropriate inasmuch as it recapitulates Judah's own deception of his father with the blood-stained garment purported to belong to Joseph.) For he has kept her celibate while her childbearing years have gone by. The exercise of her sexuality could give her status, a status which he has effectively denied her. The exercise of his sexuality is for him simply a source of pleasure. In other words, she is using his desire for pleasure to gain her own security (for sons are a woman's security in a patriarchal society). What is casual for him is critical for her; and the imbalance is symptomatic of the relation between men and women in the social world of the story.

Tamar loiters by the side of the road at the 'entrance to Enaim'. Here again is language at play. The phrase could equally be translated the 'opening of eyes'. The place is nowhere else mentioned in the Hebrew Bible and could well be fictional, perhaps a conceptual word-play on Gen. 3: 7—'Then their eyes were opened (*pqh*) and they knew they were naked'. In any case it makes a fine irony. For where Judah sees a prostitute we know that he is in fact seeing someone else. It is as though his eyes are closed. But in due course his sight of this woman will lead to his eyes being opened to his unjust treatment of Tamar. (While noticing word-play in a place name we could speculate about Timnah, from 'counting,' 'reckoning'—so was Judah on the way to a reckoning!)

Judah's perception of Tamar is just what she has expected it to be: he thinks she is a prostitute and jumps to take advantage of this obviously available woman. Alter comments:

Wasting no time with preliminaries, Judah immediately tells her, '[Look here,] let me lie with you' (literally, 'let me come to you', or even, 'let me enter you'), to which Tamar responds like a hard-headed businesswoman, finally exacting the rather serious pledge of Judah's seal and cord and staff, which as the legal surrogate of the bearer would have been a kind of ancient Near Eastern equivalent of all a person's major credit cards.   (Alter 1981: 89)

Tamar is not to be flustered by his abruptness. She matches his directness with her own: 'Look here, I want to have sex with you', he says. 'What's it worth to you to have sex with me?' she says. Tamar clearly knows the man with whom she is dealing. She knows the promise of payment from Judah means nothing. After all, had he not promised to give her to his son Shelah? Of course, his lack of payment is to her good fortune, because to make her scheme work, she must have something that can be identified as his. Perhaps her original plan was to steal such an object in the course of their 'business'. But his lack of collateral and the urgency of his desire plays right into her hand. Judah, the self-interested deceiver, lays himself open with a remarkable want of circumspection. For what Tamar asks as pledge and what Judah is prepared to give are, as Alter observes, extraordinary tokens of value and identity.

That Tamar does not hesitate to name her pledge demonstrates that she has carefully thought this through. The objects she insists upon also have another level of significance. Through the names of the objects, she mocks him and declares her purpose, though Judah is unaware of anything but his 'need'. She asks for 'your seal (*hotamka*) and your cord (*petileka*), and your staff (*mattka*) which is in your hand'. The word *hotam* may remind us of *hotan*, 'father-in-law'; *petileka* conceals *peti*, 'simpleton' (and so *peti leka*, 'you have a simpleton [on your hands]!'); and *matteh* is surely a sexual euphemism as in so many other languages. But more than that, this last term is supremely appropriate. For it is also a homonym of 'tribe'. Give me the staff which is in your hand. Give me the sexual intercourse which is in your power to give. Give me the tribe which is within your grasp. And indeed he does, unknowingly. Though we might be inclined to put it the other way around: it is she who grants him a line.

Judah sent the kid by the hand of his friend the Adullamite, to take back the pledge from the hand of the woman, but he could not find her. So he asked the men of her place, 'Where is the sanctuary woman who was at Enaim on the road?' But they said, 'There has been no sanctuary woman here.' So he returned to Judah, and said, 'I have not found her; and also the men of the place said, "There has been no sanctuary woman here".' And Judah said, 'Let her take the things for herself, lest we become a laughing-stock; look, I sent this kid, and you could not find her.'   (Gen. 38: 20–3)

The previous scene ended with Tamar as subject, from conception back to her resuming the garments of widowhood. Now the narrator resumes the story from Judah's point of view: Judah sends the kid 'to get the pledge' (not make good his payment) from 'the woman' (not Tamar, since he does not know that she is Tamar). He sends a proxy, his friend Hirah. Why? Is he keeping a low profile because he is now very anxious about the how the whole affair might look if people were to learn just what he had done? Left his credit cards with a prostitute? Unbelievable! What a fool!

But Hirah cannot find the woman. Of course he cannot. Yet he has a double difficulty, since he asks not for a *zonah*, prostitute, but for a *qedeshah*, a sanctuary woman, a 'holy woman' (from the word *qadosh*, 'holy'). By mistranslating *qedeshah* as 'harlot', the RSV and other versions miss the point of the narrator's careful word choice (which Alter has nicely observed). The *qedeshah* is not an ordinary prostitute, but a woman who engages in sexual activity with worshippers as an expression of fertility or as a symbol of the worshipper's union with the divine. Judah's double standard is wonderfully encapsulated in this choice of words. He is more than ready, privately, to have sex with a prostitute. And the narrator has made it crystal clear that this is precisely what he thought he was doing: 'and Judah saw her and took her for a whore' (v. 15). But now that the business has a public dimension, Judah is constructing a public face. To leave his valuables with a sanctuary woman rather than a prostitute was to put his behaviour a notch up the social scale of acceptability. So Hirah, apparently under the impression that he is looking for a *qedeshah*, goes asking the wrong question.

Perhaps Judah had thought Hirah would take the point and discreetly broaden the scope of his search. But he does not, and naïvely reports back that the men of the place (and who better to know than the men) claimed that no *qedeshah* had been there. Rather than clarify the issue with his simple-minded friend, Judah decides that things have gone far enough. He expresses what he most fears, that he be mocked publicly for his folly. But even in admitting his vulnerability he manages to implicate his friend (and spread the blame): 'Let her keep the things as her own, lest *we* be laughed at.' And his speech ends with lame self-justification. After all, he wants everyone to know, Judah is an honourable man. He pays his debts: 'See, I sent this kid, but you could not find her.'

It happened about three months later that Judah was told, 'Tamar your daughter-in-law has been acting like a whore; and moreover she is pregnant by whoring around.' So Judah said, 'Bring her out, and let her be burned.' As she was being brought out, she, on her part, sent word to her father-in-law, 'By the man to whom these belong, I am pregnant.' And she said, 'Recognize, if you will, whose these are, the signet and the cord and the staff.' And Judah recognized them. So he said, 'She is more righteous than I, inasmuch as I did not give her to my son Shelah.' And he never again slept with her. (Gen. 38: 24–6)

Once again the scandalmongers are at work. Tamar's pregnancy is showing and since she is not married her condition is ascribed to her prostituting herself. Now the community's double standard is showing also. A widower's intercourse with a prostitute, even if it is not deemed respectable, is plainly common and tolerated. But a widow's intercourse is deemed prostitution, 'whoring around', and the subject of outrage. Judah immediately seizes on that outrage and his voice becomes its prime expression: 'Bring her out and let her be burned!' His own double standard merges with his interest in another matter: now he has the problem of Tamar and Shelah permanently solved. With his daughter-in-law out of the way he is free to marry Shelah off to whomever he pleases.

The sexual double standard is not the only focus of an ironic reading here. There is also the matter of responsibility. Judah has been only too ready to blame Tamar and unwilling to take any responsibility for her once he was rid of her from his house. Now, when it suits his moral posture and his plans for his son, he is only too ready to assume responsibility over her as family head (as the community prompts—'Tamar *your daughter-in-law* has been acting the whore' (cf. Deut. 22: 20–1)) and make judgement against her. (Actually the law prescribes stoning, not burning; cf. Deut. 22: 20–1.)

The narrator returns us momentarily to Tamar's point of view— 'she sent word to her *father-in-law*'—with the term 'father-in-law' expressing *her* sense of the relation of responsibility Judah bears towards her. Her insistence that he 'recognize, please, to whom these [objects] belong' is in fact her insistence that he 'recognize' his responsibility toward her. He must see and acknowledge for himself the objects he left in her care. (Note too how this recognition scene connects this story with the previous one (chapter 37), which ends with Jacob recognizing Joseph's bloody robe and drawing a wrong conclusion—see Alter 1981: 10–11.)

We may also notice the separation between the two people. He gives to someone else the orders for her execution. She sends by someone else her message of incrimination. And in his final speech Judah does not address Tamar but rather talks about her to bystanders. 'She is [not *you are*] more righteous than I.' We are not even sure she is present. We do not know that she ever hears from Judah's lips her justification. He did not see her during his intercourse with her. He passed judgement on her from a safe distance. Now he does not want to make a confession of guilt to her face. He never asks her pardon. Rather he is only concerned with his public face, with making the best of his embarrassment, with impressing the community by the immediacy of his concession (hardly confession).

He diverts attention away from the question of his own promiscuity on to the matter of levirate marriage: 'she is more righteous than I, *inasmuch as I did not give her to my son Shelah.*' And lurking in that qualifying clause is already an attempt at justification, since (as we know from Onan's attitude, from the law which allows for refusal, and from the book of Ruth) he may expect that at least some of the men in his audience will deem this custom to be an unduly onerous one and will sympathize with his attempt to evade it. Along with this rhetorical move comes a gross overstatement, 'she is more righteous than I'—as if Judah has also been righteous. He refers, of course, to his duty to carry out justice, to rid his house of harlotry. We may decide, however, that burning the woman would never cleanse his house, since the harlotry is his.

Separation extends beyond this climactic moment. The narrator adds one final word about the relationship: 'And he did not lie with her again.' Commentators, eager to rehabilitate their hero, have usually seen this note as functioning to clear Judah of the charge of incest. Yet the laws prohibiting sexual intercourse between in-laws clearly presuppose a living spouse—male control of sexual property is at issue, as in many of the sexual prohibitions in the Hebrew Bible—and in the case of levirate marriage male relatives are required to do what otherwise would be prohibited. Rather than seeing this ultimate separation as Judah's response to a problem of incest we see it rather as the embodiment of his underlying resentment against her, his final attempt to control the woman who had refused to be controlled by him, his inability to consummate an intimate relationship with anyone who insists on holding him accountable for the way he treats people. Better for. Judah to own a woman who will make no demands, like the daughter of Shua, or to buy the temporary services of a nameless, faceless woman whom he will never have to see again. A woman with rights and the initiative to secure them is certainly not Judah's kind of woman. 'And he never again slept with her.' The Hebrew euphemism for sexual intercourse here is the verb 'to know' (Alter translates 'and he had no carnal knowledge of her again'). The word choice is apt. Judah did not know her when he sent her away to her father's house, and he did not know her when he lay with her. When he does come to know her it is more than he cares to know, and he has no wish to know her further, for she forced him to know himself.

It happened, when it was time for her to deliver, that, behold, there were twins in her womb. And it happened, when she was delivering, one put out a hand; and the midwife took and bound on his hand a scarlet thread, saying, 'This came out first'. But it happened that as he pulled his hand back, behold, his brother came out; and she said, 'What a breach you have made for yourself!' Therefore his name was called Perez. Afterward his brother came out with the scarlet thread upon his hand; and his name was called Zerah.   (Gen. 38: 27–30)

The story ends much the way it began, with the births of Judah's sons. From Judah's point of view, this final scene corrects an imbalance. He has lost two sons; now the two sons are replaced—much as in the story of Job. The family he seeks to establish for himself at the beginning gradually dissolves in the course of the story, but the family established at the end is established in spite of himself so to speak. These sons eventually go with him down to Egypt (we assume that Tamar does too, though she is never mentioned), and it is this firstborn, Perez, through whom Judah's line gains prominence.

If one reads this episode as part of the patriarchal story, one can hardly miss the common motif of brothers struggling for status. Beginning with the competition between Cain and Abel, we have watched parental favouritism and the custom of primogeniture create strife between siblings as they struggle for birthright, blessing, inheritance, power. Indeed, this is the conflict which led Judah to leave his family of origin to begin with. Consequently, the symbolism of Perez's breach suggests 'like father, like son'.

But Perez is not merely like Judah. He is like his mother who, breaking all the rules of social respectability, breached the walls of the prison to which Judah had consigned her and punctured the patriarch's veneer of righteousness. Yet in a crucial respect he is unlike his mother, inasmuch as he, already privileged as a male, pushes past his brother to gain the greater privilege of the first-born male, whereas she merely reaches past Judah to grasp her due.

Unlike the beginning of the story the ending focuses upon the mother. The birthing experience of Shua's daughter is reported merely by 'she bore'. Her significance seems to lie in the fact that she is a channel for the family Judah is building. With a nice touch of poetic justice Tamar treats Judah the same way. He merely provides the seed she needs so badly. Here at the end we see Tamar building her own family and consequently her own future.

Of course, significance is an elusive notion. Shift perspective just a little, step back from the immediate experience of a woman trying to survive, and we may find ourselves back in the patriarchal story, the story of the line of Abraham, a male line. Then Tamar becomes, like the daughter of Shua, just another channel for the male seed. How two-edged her story ends. She is triumphal in her own story in the birth of sons, yet eclipsed in the ongoing story by those sons and their unrighteous father.

3

Characters and Narrators

'Literature is written by, for, and about people', writes literary critic Mieke Bal. 'That remains a truism, so banal that we often tend to forget it, and so problematic that we as often repress it with the same ease' (1985: 80 ¶A). If literature in general is written by, for, and about people, certainly no less can be said of biblical literature specifically.

Readers and people

What is it about Genesis 38 that sparks the interest of modern readers? It might in fact be difficult for some to relate to parts of the plot or to the social world of the story. After all, readers in the western world, for example, do not have a system of levirate marriage and are unlikely to want to promote one. Most of us now deem the arranged marriage a quaint and old-fashioned custom, though it is a common enough practice in many other parts of the world. Foreign, too, is a death sentence for adultery and the practice of cult prostitution. Yet most of us, having read this story, would probably claim some understanding of its characters. We can recognize the protective (and ambitious) parent. We recognize people who say one thing when they think another. We may recognize women who struggle against a double standard. We may even recognize the predicament of those who have to prostitute themselves for survival. We recognize people driven by concern for public approval. We know controllers, subverters, deceivers, and gossips. We know people who are maternal, desperate, daring, shrewd. We know some who are perceptive about themselves and others, and some who are blind to themselves and who misjudge others. And we know many who exemplify various mixtures of these traits.

The power of narrative lies in its ability to imitate life, to evoke a world that is like ours, to reproduce life-like events and situations, to recreate people that we understand and to whom we relate. And we become acquainted with these people in much the same way we get to know people in real life.

Nothing is simpler than to create for oneself the idea of a human being, a figure and a character, from a series of glimpses and anecdotes. Creation of this kind we practise every day; we are continually piecing together our fragmentary evidence about the people around us and moulding their images in thought. It is the way in which we make our world; partially, imperfectly, very much at haphazard, but still perpetually, everybody deals with this experience like an artist.

(Percy Lubbock, quoted in Chatman 1978: 128 ¶A)

We may not be dealing with real people when we encounter biblical characters, but we are using our experiences of real people to help us understand these linguistic constructions. We come to understand both in much the same way. We listen to what they say and how they say it. We watch what they do. We note how other people respond to them and what others say about them. We put together pieces of a personality, whether real or fictive, as we might put together a puzzle. And even when we deal with literary characters, we come to understand these artistic constructions by using psychological insight acquired through our dealings with the real world (Chatman: 126).

'Psychologizing' has long been taboo in the field of biblical interpretation. Reflections on the human mind and behaviour, so the argument goes, was either beyond, or not of interest to, the ancient writer. So modern readers are to be dissuaded from imposing their own psychological insight on to the biblical text.

Historical critics have discouraged us from 'psychologizing' by positing a major gap between the interests of the biblical writers and those of modern Western readers. While today we may be interested in real people and actual events, the Hebrew Bible, many critics have argued, is not history in the modern sense of the term, but theological literature with a long and complex composition history. Its characters are not historical personages about whom we can ask, What did they really do? And what did they really think? Rather, the characters are constrained by literary convention and primitive imagination—and fragmented by multiple literary sources. If biblical writers had wanted us to understand more about the internal workings of these characters, they would have been more explicit. The power of the text lies not in its characterization, but in its classification as *Heilsgeschichte*, God's salvation history of the chosen people. Put in literary terms, the power lies in the plot: the pattern of God's mighty acts in history.

At root, this prohibition against attempting to understand the mental and emotional processes of characters presupposes that biblical literature is unsophisticated and thus unconcerned with the intricacies of human thought and behaviour. It also expresses the fear that interpreters will fall victim to uncontrollable flights of fancy or, at the very least, will inappropriately impose modern psychological categories on texts entirely too ancient and different from contemporary experience.

Even some literary critics in recent decades have resisted delving into the intricacies of character. As a result of work with cultural myths and folk-tales, structuralists and formalists have sometimes relegated characters to being mere functions of the plot (cf. the influential work of Vladimir Propp 1928/1968 ¶A). The idea is that we constantly tell the same stories—stories, the structuralists would argue, that address deep-seated cultural tensions and dichotomies (cf. Leach 1969 ¶F)—with the same plots and the same kinds of characters. Characters, according to structuralist and formalist theory, have no psychological core, no individual identity. They are 'actants'—senders, objects, receivers, helpers, opponents, and subjects—who do what the folk-tale or mythic (or other) genres dictate that they do. They are cardboard characters, 'types', who fill the slots and act out the plots that are already provided. The emphasis is on what they do, not who they are. In other words, plot takes the primary seat again. (David Jobling's structuralist study of Jonathan introduces this approach well, 1978 ¶F.)

A common presumption is that folk genres are primitive kinds of literature employing rudimentary characterization. Legends or fairy tales, for example, are usually read in terms of character 'types'—the brave young hero, the beautiful princess, the good fairy, or the wicked witch—perhaps in response to the reader's sense of sameness in the telling of these tales. This understanding of genre has also influenced biblical interpreters since much historical-critical, especially form-critical, work has designated the basic narrative genre in the Hebrew Bible as saga (German *Sage*, 'folk-tale').

Genre expectations of other kinds (particularly notions of the Bible as hallowed and authoritative) have also limited readers' willingness to engage in extensive character construction. Human characters, for example, have been expected to be either good or bad, models to emulate or abhor, 'types', in fact. Likewise with the character of God—many readers within orthodox faith communities are taught from childhood that the divinity will exhibit traits such as being always completely good, just, and in the right, as well as all-powerful, totally in control of all that happens, and knowing all (past, present, and future). Thoughts, feelings, and actions that appear to conflict with such expectations (jealousy, anger, violence, favouritism, change of mind, lack of knowledge, or failure to anticipate developments) are then either ignored or rationalized as good, just, etc., or these values are redefined to fit the behaviour of the divinity.

We wish here to subvert the notion of 'type' when it comes to biblical characters. Confidence in the identification of biblical narrative as saga or folk-tale has waned. In any case, the notion that folk genres are primitive and somehow limited in their potential for complex characterization is problematic and, in the end, a matter of the reader's perspective. Reticence does not necessarily mean emptiness. Simplicity may indicate openness to inference rather than closure. Furthermore, even though stories appear to be similar, they are never identical. Genres are constantly being stretched and broken, and every different text is potentially subversive of the genre. We can choose to read for sameness or for difference. We can search for the complexity of characters or settle for types. We can allow the Bible the kind of complexity that we find in other kinds of literature or we can deplete its richness by confining it to convention.

So we ask, why *not* psychologize? 'Narrative evokes a world', writes Seymour Chatman, 'and since it is no more than an evocation, we are left free to enrich it with whatever real or fictive experience we acquire' (1978: 120 ¶A). That holds doubly true for story characters. Why should we not speculate about the behaviour of biblical characters? We speculate about real people all the time. As long as our inference and speculation is recognized for what it is and does not attempt to masquerade as a final and definitive interpretation, why should we not use our understanding of human nature to envision and enliven the characters we encounter in biblical literature?

As readers, we are not mere recipients of a given meaning. The text only comes alive when we engage it. Certainly, if we wish to read in such a way that we can share our reading with others, we are limited in the extent of our engagement—limited, for example, to what others may be willing to recognize as interpretation 'connected with' or 'based on' or 'arising from' the text. But since meaning is a product of the interaction between reader and text, what counts as 'in' the text is always significantly determined by reading conventions and readerly values, as we saw in our brief account of the ways the Cain and Abel story has been read over the centuries. (Thus the metaphor that locates meaning spatially 'in' or 'arising from' the text, like the distinction between 'exegesis' and 'eisegesis,' reading 'out of' and 'into' the text, can be seriously misleading because it tells only part of the story.) As critics, we can settle for current conventions or seek to change them. For our own part, we have found that extending questions about characters beyond the norms of traditional biblical criticism can truly enliven the encounter of reader and narrative text. And if such questions facilitate an intimate relationship between reader and text, if they serve as midwife to meaning born from the manifold possibilities latent 'in' both reader and text, then why should we not ask them?

Why should we not question what motivates characters to do what they do? Why should we not ponder why the woman in the garden picked the fruit and why the man stood passively by while she did it? Why should we not wonder what was going through Abraham's mind when he sold Sarah to the Pharaoh, or when he allowed Hagar and Ishmael to be sent into the wilderness, or when he went to sacrifice Isaac his son on Mount Moriah? And why should we not speculate, as did the ancient rabbis, about Sarah's response when she heard of Abraham's trip to Moriah?

Because literary characters come to us through an artistic medium, we realize, of course, that we are not dealing with real people. The biblical narrator's customary reticence about characters may remind us further that these people are literary constructs. The economy with which biblical characters are presented has long been frustrating to readers used to narratives with elaborate and explicit description. Biblical characters are seldom described in any detail. Their thoughts are rarely revealed. The reasons for their actions are only occasionally reported. Yet, centuries of readers and listeners have related to their stories. Why? Because the open construction of biblical characters has allowed, even compelled, readers to imagine, to speculate, to *psychologize*, if you will, about what makes these people tick. Readers are quick to fill gaps, to give voice to the silences about character, even when they are unaware of doing so.

The challenge, then, is to be conscious of our speculation and, as a check, to relate it constantly to what other readers are likely to regard as explicit features of the text. How do we go about reconstructing biblical character? Let us begin our study by considering the sources of information available.

Character can be revealed through the report of actions; through appearance, gestures, posture, costume; through one character's comments on another; through direct speech by the character; through inward speech, either summarized or quoted as interior monologue; or through statements by the narrator about the attitudes and intentions of the personages, which may come either as flat assertions or motivated explanations.

(Alter 1981: 116–17 ¶F)

If understanding characters in biblical narrative is rather like getting to know people in real life, we might start with assumptions about appearance, profession or position. A particular action or conversation may also prompt initial approval or disapproval. In effect, what we start with is a hypothesis which we then test and elaborate as we draw on information as it becomes available. For the purpose of discussion it seems helpful to think of two major sources of information, namely the narrator and the characters themselves. We shall begin by treating these separately. As our exploration proceeds, however, we shall find that we are not simply gathering information from these sources but observing the interplay between them and evaluating discrepant data.

The narrator

One obvious difference between art and life is the narrator. Some of us wish we had an omniscient narrator in our own lives—someone to consult for the scoop on the people we meet (and on ourselves, for that matter). A forlorn wish. Narrative does provide us something of that luxury. We experience biblical characters as mediated through a narrator who selects and shapes what we experience.

While in some biblical literature the narrator may not be easily distinguished from the author (as in the book of Nehemiah, narrated in the first person by Nehemiah himself), this is not usually or obviously the case. Historical criticism, for example, has taught us that the authorship of Genesis–2 Kings is a complex matter, involving probably various authors and editors from various time periods. This narrative corpus, however, posits a narrator who has first-hand knowledge of events from creation to exile and signals no change of narrator (except where Moses takes on an extended first-person narration) from beginning to end. It is clear, moreover, from the vast amount of pseudepigraphal literature (writings under assumed names, as The Testament of Abraham or The Book of Enoch) that the distinction between author and narrator was well recognized in the ancient world. Even in the more discursive literature like Proverbs or Ecclesiastes, the speaking voice (Solomon, son of David, speaking as a father in Proverbs; or Qoheleth, son of David, speaking as one disillusioned with wisdom in Ecclesiastes) takes on a personality that appears to be separate from the author. Again, if we look at the narrator of the book of Esther we may observe that, though the author is undoubtedly Jewish, the narrator speaks of 'the Jews' and 'Mordecai the Jew' as though she or he shares no identity with them. A similar strategy is used by the Jewish historian Josephus, who presents his story of the Jews through a narrator who sounds like a Roman. We would urge the reader of biblical narrative, therefore, to observe that the narrator is not the author but a fictional construct.

To define the narrator as fictional construct is to put the narrator into a category similar to the characters. Indeed, it might be helpful sometimes to think of the narrator as a character, distinct from the other characters. The narrator is a character who tells the story while other characters enact it. Because the narrator controls the story's presentation, it is the narrator's point of view that could be said to predominate over all others. And it is, in fact, the narrator who determines how other points of view emerge. (Nevertheless, how we evaluate those points of view and, indeed, the narrator's own point of view is ultimately not the narrator's but the reader's to determine.)

Reliability

'The Bible', claims Meir Sternberg, 'always tells the truth in that its narrator is absolutely and straightforwardly reliable' (1985: 51 ¶F). Reliability in this literary sense is defined in terms of the story world; it is not a claim about absolute truth (though many readers of the Bible make no such distinction). A reliable narrator always gives us accurate information; or put another way, does not make mistakes, give false or unintentionally misleading information, or deliberately deceive us. Other characters may do so, but not the reliable narrator.

Where character is concerned, Alter spells out a scale of certainty: character revealed through actions or appearance 'leaves us substantially in the realm of inference'; direct speech by or about a character 'lead[s] us from inference to the weighing of claims'; the report of inward speech offers us 'relative certainty', at least about the character's conscious intentions; finally, with 'the reliable narrator's explicit statement of what the characters feel, intend, desire . . . we are accorded certainty' (1981: 116–17 ¶F).

Out of this list, there are two types of information for which the narrator is solely responsible. First, the narrator relates characters' actions. We usually accept such reports at face value although, as Alter observes, we may not know what motivates the people concerned. As in real life, we often learn as much about people from what they do as from what they say. In the direct narration of action, *what* the narrator reports is crucial for our basic knowledge of the person. *How* the narrator reports may also guide our inferences.

Consider what can be learned of Judah in the exposition to Genesis 38. The peremptory account of Judah's 'seeing, taking, and having intercourse with' the nameless daughter of Shua, along with equally featureless reports of her childbearing, may give the impression that Judah is mainly interested in filling physical needs and familial goals. And indeed, this hypothesis gains support as we see Judah so determined to protect his final son, so readily 'comforted' after his wife's death, and so eager to engage the services of a prostitute immediately following the woman's demise.

The second type of information is the narrator's revelation of internal speech or feeling. When the narrator claims this kind of knowledge, we can usually trust what we are being told. Often this information reveals a character's perception (or lack of perception) of a situation. Tamar changes her clothes and sits by the road to Timnah, 'for she saw that Shelah was grown up, and she had not been given to him in marriage'. The narrator never tells us explicitly that she intends to intercept Judah. But by sharing with us her perspective, the narrator leaves us in no doubt that she is indeed planning an encounter with Judah and that the reason has to do with her social rights. The woman beside the road catches Judah's interest because, the narrator tells us, 'he thought her to be a harlot'. Judah proceeds to proposition her 'for he did not know she was his daughter-in-law'. By communicating Judah's misperceptions, the narrator explains why Judah behaves the way he does with this woman. He would not, of course, have gone through with a negotiation if he had realized who she actually was.

In short, information conveyed directly by the narrator always carries more weight than that mediated through some other source (usually another character). Some of this material we can accept without question, as in the revelation of internal thought or emotion, and use in our reconstruction of character. Other information comes to us uninterpreted, as in the reporting of action. It is then up to us to infer the reasons underlying a character's behaviour in light of other data.

In practice, some such scale of reliability is a helpful rule of thumb in reading biblical narrative. The claim, however, that the biblical narrator is always 'absolutely and straightforwardly reliable' cannot be sustained without significant modification. First, we would need to divide up a story like Genesis–2 Kings into separate units or layers, much like the 'sources' of the historical critics, and then contain our readings within those boundaries. Otherwise we run into major disjunctions in the text—temporal, spatial, and simply factual regarding the actions of characters—which are highly problematic for the notion of a straightforwardly reliable narrator. Second, we would need to ignore the possibility that a narrator attuned to deploying irony against characters might deploy it against readers, for example by intruding ironic as well as 'straightforward' evaluative comment. Sternberg effectively follows both strategies to avoid raising difficulties with his poetics (Gunn 1987; 1990 ¶F).

As far as irony is concerned, the treatment of David and Solomon in 1 Kings may suffice to make the point. We are told in Kings of David's and Solomon's rectitude in such positive terms that we may be led to see in these monarchs some absolute standards of behaviour. Except that the little word 'except' (*raq*) creeps into the evaluation.

David 'did what was right in YHWH's eyes and did not turn aside from anything that he commanded him all the days of his life, except in the matter of Uriah the Hittite' (1 Kgs. 15: 5). 'Except' can have a powerful effect on the way we read the sentence if we recognize the matter of Uriah the Hittite to be the pivotal episode in David's life, representing a peak of grasping for whatever was good in his own eyes. 'Solomon', we are told in 1 Kgs. 3: 3, 'loved YHWH, walking in the statutes of David his father; except he sacrificed and burnt incense at the high places.' But then we come to the closing phase of his story. We contemplate the multiplication of his foreign brides and calculate some seven hundred (and more) altars set up to foreign gods, replete with sundry mentions of his 'going after' them and an angry condemnation by God (1 Kgs. 11: 3, 7, 8). Then we may choose to read that apparently innocuous 'except' as packing quite a punch. An ironic reading of the 'except' clause can turn the narrator's evaluation from laudatory to condemnatory in a stroke.

The possibility of irony is therefore inherently destabilizing where the relationship between narrator and reader is concerned. It precludes any possibility of simple 'straightforward' or literal reading being an infallible reading strategy. Sternberg claims, 'The reader cannot go far wrong even if he [*sic*] does little more than follow the

statements made and the incidents enacted on the narrative surface.'
Such a claim seriously underestimates the problems of literal,
'surface' reading.

Where facticity ('what actually happened' in the story world) is
concerned, the case of David and Goliath is enough to make the
point. Who did kill Goliath (cf. 1 Samuel 17 and 2 Sam. 21: 19)? Or,
to take another much argued case, just when did what tribes take
possession of the land (cf. Joshua 10–12 and Judges 1)? Historical
critics have not been entirely off the mark in determining 'inconsistency' or 'contradiction' in these biblical texts. The mention of
Elhanan as the slayer of Goliath (2 Sam. 21: 19) really does disturb
convictions of reliability whether we are talking in historical or literary categories. Perhaps it is no accident that Sternberg condemns 2
Samuel 21–24 as a 'sorry stretch of discourse', a 'hodgepodge' which
'has the least pretensions to literariness and . . . hardly coheres as
more than an appendix' (1985: 40, 42 ¶F). (For another view, see
Brueggemann 1988 ¶N.3, or Gunn 1988 ¶N.3, 1989 ¶N.)

In practice, therefore, most biblical literary critics who take the
narrator's reliability as assured avoid such major disjunctions of
information, often by confining their reading to stretches of text
which exclude the conflicting statements. For historical critics, most
of whom assume a wholly reliable narrator (without ever articulat-
ing the assumption), 'contradictions' are a prime sign of disparate
narrators. Irony is strongly discounted as a possible solution. The
way out is to postulate disparate 'sources' which have been put
together by an unreliable editor.

Plainly this is a complex matter. If we are to read, say, Genesis–2
Kings as related by a single narrator, we shall need to entertain the
possibility that this narrator is less than straightforwardly reliable,
perhaps sometimes unsure of the 'facts', and perhaps, too, prone to
use conflicting facts and evaluations ironically against the reader, as a
device to shake the reader's assurance. Or we could conceive of the
story as a story told by various narrators, now the one, now another,
intruding without warning—none wholly reliable because always
subject to subversion by another.

Description

The narrator will sometimes establish for us something of the appearance, profession, or social situation of the character under scrutiny. How significant such description will turn out to be as the story progresses may vary considerably, but as a rule such items of information do engage a reader's social awareness and elicit interesting *a priori* evaluations. Such initial judgements may indeed help the reader to understand a character or, alternatively, may lead the reader astray to the point where the pertinent social code (ancient or modern) is called into question.

Physical description is sparse in biblical narrative, but occasionally a very general description of a character's appearance or a particular physical characteristic is mentioned. Perhaps the most common description is that a character is beautiful (either 'beautiful', 'beautiful of form', '[very] beautiful [or 'good'] of appearance', or 'good-looking'). For example, Rebekah (Gen. 24: 16), Rachel (Gen. 29: 17), Joseph (Gen. 39: 6), David (1 Sam. 16: 12), Abigail (1 Sam. 25: 3), Bathsheba (2 Sam. 11: 2), Tamar (David's daughter; 2 Sam. 13: 1), Absalom (2 Sam. 14: 25), and Tamar (Absalom's daughter; 2 Sam. 14: 27) are all said to be beautiful. As far as Rebekah, Rachel, Joseph, Bathsheba, and David's daughter Tamar are concerned, the information usually communicates their sexual desirability in stories of courtship, seduction, or rape. David's and Absalom's appearance perhaps relates directly to their ability to charm. Abigail's beauty enhances both her desirability and her capacity to charm. Absalom's daughter Tamar has no story, but the comment that she was a beautiful woman (like her desolate namesake aunt) sets an ominous tone in a family where women are 'taken' for their beauty (cf. 2 Samuel 11 and 13).

In Judges 3 the narrator remarks that Ehud the Benjaminite is left-handed and Eglon the Moabite king is fat. At first we may think these descriptions are incidental to the story, but we soon learn that Ehud's left-handedness, because unexpected by his adversaries, makes possible his treachery, while Eglon's size makes him an easy target. As Alter has observed, Eglon's name suggests the Hebrew *'egel*, 'calf.' 'The ruler of the occupying Moabite power turns out to be a fatted calf readied for slaughter . . .' (1981: 39 ¶F). Furthermore, the yoking of the adjective *bari'*, 'fat', and Eglon, 'calf', reminds us of the fat cows in Pharaoh's dream (Genesis 41), whose fate was to be devoured by the thin cows. (The word *bari'* occurs infrequently; its only earlier occurrence in Genesis–2 Kings is in Genesis 41.)

By naming a character the narrator may indicate a person's work or social role or status. Naming Ruth as 'the Moabite' defines her in terms of foreignness, reflecting perhaps the way the Bethlehemite community perceives her. Naming Dinah as 'the daughter of Leah' (Gen. 34: 1) establishes at the very beginning of her story that she belongs to the less favoured of Jacob's families, that she is daughter to the unloved wife. Later this familial epithet will also help us understand why of all her brothers it is Simeon and Levi who personally kill Shechem her rapist, for they alone are her full brothers. Michal, greeting a dancing David bringing the ark into Jerusalem, is named 'daughter of Saul' (2 Sam. 6: 16, 20, 23). The narrator may be suggesting that as daughter of a king she has her view of what is appropriate behaviour for a king (and David's behaviour is off the mark). But the name also loads the interchange between king and queen/princess because it encapsulates the ambiguity of David's relationship with her—she is alien to him, as daughter of his enemy, the man he has supplanted, yet she has been necessary to him as representing political alliance with the house of Saul and thus legitimation. (Indeed, the naming throughout this passage repays subtle attention: notice, for example, how Michal sees '*King* David' leaping and dancing, and despises him; then comes out to meet simply 'David' though addressing him, scornfully, as 'the king of Israel'.)

Sometimes a brief description will open up meaning in similar ways. Thus Esau is a 'skilful hunter, a man of the field', a phrase that immediately sets up a contrast between him and his younger brother, Jacob (Gen. 25: 27). It is, of course, Esau's vocation that allows him to be an easy dupe for the scheming of Rebekah and her favourite son. Esau's unsuccessful hunting expedition (Genesis 25) gives Jacob the opportunity to acquire the birthright for a bowl of beans. And because Esau's hunting takes him far afield (Genesis 27) Jacob is able to steal his older brother's blessing from their unknowing father, Isaac.

Deborah is a prophetess who 'was judging Israel at that time' (Judg. 4: 4). Describing her as a prophetess marks her out as a distinctive leader, one like Abraham (Gen. 20: 7), Moses (Deut. 18: 15–22; 34: 10), and Miriam (Exod. 15: 20). Thus she is invested with an authority that helps us understand Barak's relation to her—his deference to her summons, for example. It also leads us to adopt her (prophetic) point of view, namely that the bizarre set of events culminating in the killing of Sisera and deliverance of Israel is indeed a manifestation of the hand of YHWH. Deborah is also described as 'woman of *lappidot*', which we may initially be tempted (by the patriarchal context of the story, if not our own) to consider a label of status, namely 'wife of Lappidot'. As the story continues, however, it looks more and more like an epithet of character, namely 'a fiery woman' (literally, 'a woman of fiery flashes').

Abigail's husband, Nabal, is introduced as 'a man in Maon whose business was in Carmel. The man was very rich; he had three thousand sheep and a thousand goats' (1 Sam. 25: 2). The place-names provide significant information. Maon is a town in Judah, just south of Hebron, the major political centre in the south at the time of the story. That probably means that Nabal was a person with important political status, which David might well hope to usurp. Carmel is further south in a region where David's band of outlaws would have freer rein. The man's wealth not only helps explain his own proud sense of self-sufficiency; it also gives us a clue to David's interest in receiving 'gifts' from him and, doubly, in the prospect of inheriting his wealth through his widow.

Evaluation

The narrator may also qualify our perception of a character by comment that is explicitly evaluative rather than descriptive (though as we have seen description often harbours evaluation).

Sometimes it may be merely a matter of a straightforward word or two. 'Noah was a righteous (*tsadiq*) man; blameless (*tamim*) he was in his generation; Noah walked with God' (Gen. 6: 9). 'There was a man in the land of Uz and his name was Job; and that man was blameless (*tam*) and upright (*yashar*); and he feared God and turned away from evil' (Job 1: 1). '[Samuel's] sons did not walk in his ways but turned aside after gain; they took bribes and caused justice to be turned aside' (1 Sam. 8: 3). Rehoboam (or Abijah—the text is ambiguous) 'showed discretion in detailing his sons to take charge of all the fortified cities throughout the whole territory of Judah and Benjamin' (2 Chron. 11: 23; NEB). Rehoboam 'did what was wrong [evil], for he did not set his heart on seeking guidance from YHWH' (2 Chron. 12: 14). Jehoshaphat, king of Judah, 'did wrong in joining with [Ahaziah king of Israel] to build ships for trade with Tarshish . . .' (2 Chron. 20: 35; NEB). 'I gave my brother Hanani, and Hananiah, the citadel governor, command over Jerusalem, for he was a more trustworthy and God-fearing man than most' (Neh. 7: 2).

Perhaps what is most interesting here is that clear examples of direct and unambiguous evaluation by the narrator are hard to find. This is so, even in a text like Chronicles where the narrator appears to see people and events in a much more simplistic way than the narrator of Genesis–2 Kings, who is given to cultivating ambiguity. (None of the sentences quoted above from Chronicles occurs in the equivalent places in Kings.) Evaluative judgements in both works more often take an indirect form, expressed through the viewpoint of YHWH.

One of the most striking explanatory statements from the narrator of Genesis–2 Kings is found in 2 Kings 17 which recounts how the Assyrians destroyed the northern kingdom of Israel. Here the narrator uncharacteristically comments at length on the event as the culmination of a whole series of events. The view is urged that the disaster was in fact the work of YHWH, who was provoked to anger by the people's worship of other gods and by their departure from YHWH's laws. In effect, the narrator is making a judgement on the corporate character of Israel, the nation conceived as a whole.

In 2 Kings 17, therefore, as well as in other places, the narrator's evaluation of a character is indirect, tied to and mediated through YHWH's point of view. Typical is the comment made about both Er and Onan, that they 'did evil in the sight of YHWH' (Gen. 38: 7, 10). In cases like these the narrator's viewpoint is not made explicit but we usually assume that the narrator is aligning with YHWH's point of view and so echoing the view that the deed was 'evil'.

Likewise, in the judgement against King Manasseh:

Manasseh also shed a great deal of innocent blood, until he had filled Jerusalem from end to end, quite apart from the sin which he made

Judah to sin, to do evil in the sight of YHWH. But the rest of Manasseh's affairs and everything he did, and what sins he committed, are they not written in the book of the chronicles of the kings of Judah? (2 Kgs. 21: 16–17)

Here the narrator observes not only that Manasseh did evil in the sight of YHWH but that he 'committed sin' and made Judah 'to sin, to do evil in the sight of YHWH'. Sin is defined from YHWH's point of view, but again it seems reasonable to assume that the narrator identifies with that assessment, unless something else in the context should suggest otherwise. Finally, we may notice the narrator's somewhat surreptitious (Bar-Efrat uses the term 'covert'; 1989: 32–4 ¶F) evaluation by use of the phrase 'Manasseh shed very much innocent blood'. With the term 'innocent' the narrator condemns Manasseh directly, without recourse to YHWH's point of view. Taken together, the narrator's and YHWH's viewpoints may be seen to converge in a strong judgement on the king.

At other times, however, the narrator's evaluative words may be quite subtle, allowing several possible interpretations or allowing the reader's basic understanding to slide or shift in the course of the story. These are the kinds of evaluation that require more critical assessment on the reader's part.

In the story of David's family concerning Amnon's rape of his sister Tamar (2 Samuel 13), Amnon's friend and adviser, Jonadab, is introduced as a 'very wise [*hakam*] man'. We may think that the narrator is commending to us this man. Yet as the story progresses from the narrator's simple announcement that Amnon loved his sister Tamar to the culmination of Jonadab's plan in the devastating rape and eviction of Tamar, we learn that the narrator has used the adjective 'wise', as also the verb 'to love', with tongue in cheek. No doubt Amnon believed he loved Tamar, and no doubt he and others in David's court (and doubtless Jonadab himself) considered Jonadab a very wise man. But we come to recognize in this tale what we know from our own lives, that there is love and lust, wisdom and machination, and that the one too often masquerades as the other. (By translating *hakam* as 'crafty,' RSV and NRSV crassly undermine the narrator's seduction of the reader; likewise, in verses 5–6, the translation 'pretend to be ill', instead of 'be ill', unnecessarily dissipates the narrator's irony, as also 'lust' instead of 'love' in verse 15, NRSV.)

The narrator's identification of Jonadab as Amnon's 'friend' is yet another seduction of the reader. Later in the story, after Absalom has murdered Amnon, and David has been led to believe that Absalom has killed all his sons, we hear Jonadab comforting David, 'Let not my lord suppose that they have killed all the young men the king's sons, for Amnon alone is dead, for by the command of Absalom this has been determined from the day he raped his sister Tamar' (13: 32). As we learn what Jonadab knows and how long he has known it, we realize that, rather than being Amnon's friend and adviser, Jonadab is a traitor to Amnon and most likely a secret helper of Absalom. (See Mieke Bal on 'truth value' in 1985: 34–6 ¶A.)

Boaz is introduced in Ruth 2 as an *'ish gibbor hayil*. In a military context that would mean something like 'a mighty man of strength'. In a civil context strength may be taken as 'wealth' or 'worth', and so 'a man of substance' (NEB: 'a well-to-do man') or 'a great man of importance' or a 'a very worthy man'. The label, therefore, might indicate his financial well-being (wealth), his social status (importance), his moral character (worth), or perhaps all of these. If the term is taken as one of moral evaluation, however, we cannot initially be certain that this is the narrator's evaluation, for, as would be the case with the term 'a man of great wealth', it might simply reflect how Boaz is viewed by the Bethlehem community at large. As readers, we would do well to leave open a decision on the matter until more evidence of the narrator's view of Boaz is forthcoming. In the meantime, the introduction of Boaz with this label may prompt us, as we read on, not only to be making our own evaluation of Boaz's 'worth' but also to be reflecting on what constitutes the measure of 'worth' in this story.

Jacob is a 'quiet man' (NRSV, translating the Hebrew *'ish tam*; Gen. 25: 27). More often the adjective means, as we have seen in the cases of Noah and Job, 'blameless' or 'innocent', and it can even be translated 'perfect' (KJV on Job 1: 1). But how can Jacob the archetypical deceiver be described as blameless or perfect? (Obviously the NRSV sees a problem with this description and chooses a non-evaluative adjective. In no other case, however, does the word mean 'quiet'.) The narrator's statement is at odds with what we know of the character. In short, the narrator teases us and forces us to consider several interpretive possibilities.

If 'blameless' is being elevated as the primary meaning here, might the narrator be suggesting that Jacob is never completely responsible for his trickeries? If 'perfect' is our guide, we might consider the possibility of physical perfection (cf. Song of Songs 5: 2; 6: 9). In other words, in contrast to the red, hairy Esau, Jacob looked perfect. If cultural values are the criteria for perfection, perhaps the observation is being made that Jacob values the right things—the vocation of herder, the birthright, and the blessing (the first two of which are taken lightly by Esau). We might wonder, is 'perfect' directly related to Jacob's 'dwelling in tents'? Is he perfect because he stays at home, unlike Esau who wanders the steppes? Moreover, we might want finally to ask 'perfect in whose point of view'? Who thought Jacob was perfect? Of all the participants in the story, narrator and characters alike, Rebekah alone emerges as the likely candidate. While 'Isaac loved Esau because [he put] game in his mouth, Rebekah loved Jacob' perhaps because he was perfect as far as she was concerned; that is, he remained at home close to her.

The characters

Speech, context, and contrast

We have looked at some of the direct ways the narrator may prompt us to conceive of the characters. Alternatively, the narrator will step aside and allow the characters to speak for themselves. For, of course, what characters say and how they say it may tell us much about the kind of people they are. Furthermore, close attention to the context of a character's speech, the circumstances in which the speech takes place, can help us to decide what to make of it. Since biblical characters seldom appear alone, we can compare and contrast characters, take note of how they speak to each other, and, in the end, see how one person can help to define another.

A delightful episode in which characters are humorously constructed in contrast to each other is found at the beginning of the story of Samson in Judges 13. An angel's intrusion into the mundane world of Manoah and his wife ('his woman' is the Hebrew expression) produces some interesting effects. The angel (the Hebrew word also means simply 'messenger') appears to the child-less woman and announces that, though she is barren and has no children, she shall in fact bear a son. Moreover, she is to observe certain rules, both she and her child, rules that remind us of those enjoined upon a 'Nazirite' (Num. 6: 1–21). This, then, is to be no ordinary child, but one born out of barrenness to be dedicated, separated to God.

The wife or woman—as we shall call her, following the text, since she is given no name of her own—senses from the outset that she is in the presence of the divine (13: 6). 'A man of God came to me', the woman tells her man, 'and his appearance was like the appearance of a divine messenger, very awesome [or 'fearful']' (13: 6). For her that appears to be sufficient. She recognizes the divine message. She does not need more. 'I did not ask him where he came from, and he did not tell me his name, but he said to me . . .'

Manoah, by contrast, is far from content. His wife tells him that she has had a man visit her and, in the same breath, that she is going to have a baby! Who exactly was this 'man of God'? Was he really a messenger from God? What business had he going directly to Manoah's wife with this 'communication' instead of introducing himself first to the man of the house as only right and proper? And what if, *if*, the visitor were a messenger of YHWH? Was he, Manoah, sure that he knew precisely what being a Nazirite entailed? Should they not have plans for the boy, a pedagogical programme, a clear definition of those rather ambiguous rules? (Did they all apply to the boy or were some only for the mother?) All very problematic! So why not try a little test? Why not ask God to send the man back? And just in case the visitor should indeed be God's messenger he, Manoah, could avoid appearing to doubt God. He could use the excuse that he and his wife needed further details of what to do with the boy.

As it happens, none of the foregoing account of Manoah's interior response is explicit in the text, but it is one likely reading, given what follows.

So Manoah entreated YHWH and said, 'YHWH, please, let the man of God whom you sent come again to us, and teach us what we are to do with the boy who is to be born.' And God listened to [or 'obeyed'] the voice of Manoah—and the messenger of God came again to the woman as she sat in the field, and Manoah her man was not with her. (Judg. 13: 8–9)

Irony is piled on gentle irony. Despite Manoah's subtle inclusion of himself into the audience ('come again to *us*, and teach *us* what *we* are to do'), God 'listens to' Manoah but deliberately sends his messenger back to the woman when Manoah is not with her, just as before. This time the wife fetches Manoah:

And the woman hurried and ran and told her man and said to him, 'Look, he has appeared to me, the man who came that day to me.' And Manoah got up and went after his woman, and came to the man and said to him, 'Are you the man who spoke to this woman?'

(Judg. 13: 10–11)

The wife's words are interestingly divided between her trust in the epiphany ('he has appeared to me', not 'he has come to me') and her sense of her husband's doubt ('the man,' not 'the messenger' or even 'the man of God'). Manoah's words may be read as bluntly sceptical. Eliminating all talk of divine possibilities, he rather insinuates impropriety by setting 'the man' in relation to 'this woman'. Compounding the insinuation, moreover, is his objectification of her as 'this woman' as though that were the visitor's point of view. At the same time, by not using 'my woman' as we might have expected, he distances himself from her. His suspicion is showing.

The visitor's frankness (and perhaps his refusal to be rankled), however, pushes Manoah into playing his next card:

So Manoah said, 'When [or 'If'!] your words come to pass, what guidelines exist for the boy, and what is he to do?' (Judg. 13: 12)

Notice that he does not, to the man, include himself in this attempt to clarify responsibility—no 'us' or 'we'! And perhaps in the same spirit, he gets in reply even less than the original message to his wife on the previous occasion! Pointedly *nothing* is said of Samson or

Manoah. And though the instructions to the woman about herself are repeated, they are now framed, for Manoah's benefit, by an audacious claim to authority over her: 'All that I have told the woman, let her observe . . . All that I have commanded her, she shall observe' (13: 13–14). Or, as the REB puts it, 'She must do whatever I say'! The visitor even impishly adopts Manoah's language, referring not to 'your wife' but to 'the woman.' We can almost hear divine laughter.

Manoah, however, is not through (13: 15) and he is not yet willing to let the visitor go: 'May we urge you to stay? Let us prepare a young goat for you' (REB). Perhaps he is testing the visitor. Is he indeed a divine messenger, that is, an angel, or merely a human who will eat meat? Or perhaps this is a test of hospitality. A man who has had sex with his wife would be unwilling to accept his hospitality, because to do so would massively compound the injury.

Without completely giving away the guessing game, the messenger of YHWH tries valiantly to make it easy for Manoah. 'Though you urge me to stay, I shall not eat your food; but prepare a whole-offering if you will, and offer that to the LORD' (REB).

But the visitor's refusal to eat and his suggestion that his portion instead be offered to God are still not enough for Manoah who *still* 'did not know that he was the messenger of YHWH'. (By this stage a reader may be strongly reminded of Gideon's interminable tests in Judges 6–7—Gideon who also had difficulty in recognizing a divine visitor and also tried the food test [6: 11–24].) Manoah presses to know the man's name, wrapping the request, as he had done earlier, in an ambiguous expression of expectation. 'What is your name? So when (if!) your words come to pass we may honour you' (13: 17).

The visitor tries one last verbal clue. 'How come you ask my name, when it is Wonderful?' But Manoah is too stubbornly in search of the tangible.

The messenger resorts to a final strategy. It takes a mystery of great wonder, as the divine visitor ascends in the sacrificial flame into the heavens and appears no more, before Manoah, his scepticism satisfied at last, recognizes his identity. Manoah's wife knows the divine when it appears. Manoah only knows it when it disappears.

But now that he knows, he knows even more—'We shall surely die, for we have seen God!' (13: 22). For Manoah knows the rules of holiness. He panics, as indeed those 'rules' suggest he should. Again we are reminded of Gideon, who cries, when recognition finally dawns, 'Alas, O YHWH God! For now I have seen the messenger of YHWH face to face.' On that occasion YHWH reassures Gideon: 'Peace to you; do not fear, you shall not die' (Judg. 6: 22–3). On this occasion Manoah's wife plays God's role. Her attitude is clear: What matter the rules? Manoah has seen God but learned little. If killing were intended, why accept the offering, quite apart from taking so much trouble to announce these things?

And the woman bore a son, and called his name Samson; and the boy grew, and YHWH blessed him. (Judg. 13: 24)

In the contrast of characters a thematic statement about religious experience is developed. There is the man, Manoah, who must have a name, must be sure, must map out the future, must fit his experience to the norms and expectations of ordinary social life and the standard rules of religion. There is the man's wife, 'the woman', who is deprived of a name, yet who is blessed in her barrenness, knows a divine word when she hears it, trusts God, and is satisfied to ask (or presume) no more. There are two ways of relating to the divine. They seem to be related not just to the particular man, Manoah, and the particular woman, his wife, but perhaps also stereotypically to 'man' and 'woman'. The narrator's deployment of those terms takes them beyond the point of simple redundancy. Their repetition shapes one of the frames through which we see the story. The culturally constructed stereotype of women's intuitive and men's rationalistic ways of knowing is one that has currency still today. These characters, as man and woman, are still recognizable. Perhaps what is most curious, however, is that in this particular man's world, this patriarchy where the man is named and the woman is '*his* woman', it is the man's way that is mocked.

The stereotyped contrast, however, is not the whole story of characterization here. The woman's relationship with the man is more subtly developed than we have suggested so far.

As Alter has noticed, when reporting to her husband the first time what the angel has said to her, she withholds something. 'For the boy shall be a Nazirite to God from the womb', the messenger announces, 'and he shall begin to deliver Israel from the hand of the

Philistines' (13: 5). 'For the boy shall be a Nazirite to God from the womb', reports the woman, 'to the day of his death' (13: 7). Intuitively she substitutes death for deliverance, a proleptic substitution. For in the event, Samson's suicide will effect the beginning of deliverance, as he brings low Dagon, the oppressing god of the Philistines, and implicitly manifests the power of YHWH, the delivering god of Israel (16: 28–30). Thus when she substitutes the one phrase for the other, she does so in a way that is intuitively consonant with the way the story will move. So far the stereotype holds.

On the other hand, in the immediate context, her withholding of talk about deliverance from the hand of the Philistines looks like something else. She keeps the point of the pronouncement, with all its intimations of violent danger and death, to herself. Like Mary in Luke's Gospel, she keeps this thing, pondering it in her heart (Luke 2: 19). She has a life independent of her husband and she has the power to keep powerful knowledge from him. Does she fear to put the idea of a child destined for warfare in her husband's head? Does she hope to thwart the divine purpose? Or does she wish to see divine purpose work out its own way, unencumbered by her husband's control? Of course, more simply, she may be simply blocking her fear, as she trembles for the future of her unborn child. But we are reminded of her later rebuke of her fearful husband. That would suggest that here at the beginning also she takes charge. In other words, Manoah's wife takes on a special life of her own, with its own special relationship to the man who ostensibly defines her. She is not simply a stereotype.

Finally, an aspect of characterization that we may easily overlook. The messenger, as we watch him in contrast to Manoah, has a wonderful sense of humour. But is he acting independently on YHWH's behalf, or is he a direct reflex of God, a manifestation of the divine? Is it then YHWH who has the sense of humour?

Responses and reliability

Characters often speak about themselves and other characters and can be an important source of information in the reconstruction of personality. Readers must keep in mind, however, that what characters say about themselves and about one another cannot always be relied upon since characters in biblical narrative, mimicking real life, speak to specific occasions and convey only limited human viewpoints, frequently prejudiced and self-serving. The point is worth stressing, for a reading of biblical narrative that probes beneath the surface of speech enables a reader to build a much richer story world.

Public and private speeches, for example, may differ in terms of reliability. Judah's conceding Tamar's righteousness is a case in point (Gen. 38: 26). The implicating objects and the public nature of the confrontation tell us that Judah is working hard to save face.

Likewise, David's public speeches expressing concern for the welfare of the house of Saul are also suspicious. While his past friendship with Jonathan might make him sentimental about his friend's family, David's ambition should warn the reader against taking his public rhetoric of concern simply at face value. When he laments the deaths of Saul and Jonathan (2 Sam. 1: 17–27) is he truly expressing his personal grief or is his lament for the benefit of the people who had followed Saul but who he now hopes will turn their political allegiance to him? When he asks 'Is there still anyone left in the house of Saul, that I may deal loyally (kindly) with him for Jonathan's sake?' (2 Sam. 9: 1) we might wonder if he is truly interested in dealing loyally or if he wants to unearth any potential contenders to the throne. Told of Jonathan's lame son, Mephibosheth, David summons the man and tells him, 'you shall eat at my table always'. Is this a gesture of honour and caretaking or a move designed to enable David to keep a close eye on this potential political threat? Public situations do not necessarily reveal the private person. (See further Gunn 1978 ¶N.3, Perdue 1984 ¶N.3, and Alter 1981: 116–19 ¶F, who notes the predominance of public speech by David until the death of Uriah.)

We know that threatening situations can also colour a character's speech. In 1 Samuel 25 we read a remarkable speech by a woman, Abigail. She addresses David, whose story is in its 'wilderness' phase—in exile from Saul's court, he roams the country with a band of armed men. His men have gone to Nabal, Abigail's husband, asking for hospitality in return for protecting, as they claim, Nabal's sheep. Nabal refuses, in contemptuous terms. 'Who is David? Who is the son of Jesse? There are many servants these days breaking away from their masters. Am I to take my bread and my water and my meat—that I have slaughtered for my shearers—and give it to men who come from I don't know where?' (vv. 10–11). David's men take this response back to their leader.

Abigail, goaded into action by the servants' anxious report that 'evil is aimed against our master and against all his house', quickly gathers a substantial gift of food and wine (not water!), and rides post-haste to intercept a furious David who is indeed on his way to wipe out Nabal and his household. When she meets David she claims that the lack of hospitality was really an oversight on her own part: 'On me alone, my lord, be the guilt . . . I, your handmaid, did not see my lord's young men whom you sent . . . Pray forgive your handmaid's trespass.' At the same time she keeps blame directed at her husband by heaping opprobrium upon him—'fool [*Nabal*] is his name and folly [*nebalah*] is with him'. Tactfully ignoring all the armed men, she speaks as though David has already done the religiously correct thing. He has been restrained by God from taking vengeance. Only then does she offer the food and drink. Her timing thus avoids having the gift appear openly to be a bribe. She proceeds to paint David's future in the brightest of terms: 'YHWH will certainly make my lord a secure house . . . my lord's life will be bound in the bundle of the living in the care of YHWH your God.' She pictures David as the chosen of God, able only to do good.

The context of her speech prevents us from accepting at face value Abigail's picture of David, as also her unqualified condemnation of her husband. Is David truly without blemish? Had Nabal no justification for his behaviour? What is the true nature of David's unsolicited 'protection' of Nabal's flocks?

The servants speak to Abigail of David's men being a 'wall to us both by night and by day, all the time we were with them guarding the sheep', but never define the nature of the threat beyond the 'wall'. Moreover, the servants have every reason to put the best possible complexion on the behaviour of David's men. Either they persuade Abigail to intercede and to placate the armed band or they are all dead men. The fact is, we have no reliable information to make us sure that David's 'protection' is legitimate. Nabal, therefore, may be foolish to oppose David, but not necessarily unprincipled.

He may have a certain right on his side. His folly would then be that he is a proud and unbending man, convinced that he is master in his own house, master of his own land.

Apart from the dubious nature of David's protection business, the haste and vehemence with which David orders reprisals against the whole of Nabal's household does him little credit. Abigail's speech may proclaim a God-fearing man, content to let YHWH take care of vengeance, but we know that what has been decisive in that regard has been Abigail's intervention. Her speech makes clear that she is a very shrewd woman. She is also, we are told, a physically attractive one (v. 3). It is unlikely that David's decision against bloodshed is purely a matter of being persuaded on theological grounds. We may guess that, like us, David hears Abigail at the end of her speech discreetly offering to join him: 'And when YHWH has dealt well with my lord, then remember your handmaid' (v. 31). For sure enough, when the time is ripe and Nabal dead, David does exactly that—he sends and takes her for his wife. 'And Abigail hurried and rose and mounted on an ass, and her five maidens attended her; she went after the messengers of David, and became his wife' (v. 42).

Contradiction, point of view, and irony

We may also seek to fathom characters by measuring what they say against what they do. We listen to their speech, observe their actions, and look for congruence or discrepancy. In effect, we are comparing and contrasting the voices of character and narrator. A character speaks, the narrator recounts action. When there is incongruity, we often find that the narrator's report of action is a more reliable indicator of character than the character's speech. In much the same way, we may find the narrator's voice offering a significant and authoritative alternative when characters say one thing and the narrator tells us that actually they are thinking another.

For readers to think in this way, in terms of two voices, is useful because it involves recognizing two discrete points of view which may or may not converge. Indeed failure to make this distinction between points of view is one of the most common sources of confusion in the interpretation of biblical texts. In other words, readers often assume that the thoughts and values of a character are also the thoughts and values of the narrator, and are, consequently, the opinions and values that the narrator is urging the reader to adopt. When, however, the perspectives of character and narrator are separated, the story gains depth and dimension because it is being seen from different angles. By recognizing the plurality of perspectives the reader can also resist the simplistic idea that a narrative pushes only one kind of rhetoric, that it offers only one basic message, one model of living, one meaning.

Often a character's thought, speech, and action are congruent. When they are not, we see different points of view, and irony, at work. A simple and crucial case of contradiction may be seen in the exposition of the story of Judah and Tamar in Genesis 38. Judah's sons die, the narrator tells us, because they do 'evil in YHWH's sight'. Judah has a different view which becomes clear when he sends Tamar back to her father's house, 'lest', as he says to himself, '[Shelah], too, die like his brothers'. In other words, he views Tamar to be a jinx, whereas the narrator has made it clear that the deaths are God's responsibility. The reader who keeps clear the different points of view is in a position to consider Judah's readiness to blame the woman rather than see any fault in his sons, to recognize unequivocally Tamar's innocence, and to sense her bitter frustration at being denied marriage after two inexplicable (she is not aware that they are YHWH's doing) deaths which she knows are not her fault.

Genesis 33 offers us another case where the narrator's voice inclines us against accepting the character's speech as representing what the character truly intends. The story concerns the last meeting between Jacob and Esau. After Esau has accepted Jacob's conciliatory gift, Esau insists that they journey on together. Jacob demurs, 'Let my lord pass on before his servant, and I, I will lead on at the slower pace of the cattle before me and at the pace of the children, until I come to my lord in Seir' (33: 14). Both Esau and the reader are led by Jacob's speech to believe that he will follow Esau to his home. The narrator, however, remarks 'So Esau returned that day on his way to Seir. But Jacob journeyed to Succoth, and built himself a house, and made shelters for his cattle . . .' (33: 16–17). What we discover from this discrepancy between speech and action is that Jacob, for all his desire to placate Esau, is still the deceiver, concerned for his security, but hardly his integrity.

In Judges 19, it is because the narrator has already given us a version of an event that we find ourselves viewing with some scepticism a character's public account, howbeit passionately related, of the same event. The Levite, having handed over his concubine to a mob intent on raping him, equivocates on the details when he seeks to incite the congregation of Israel to take revenge on Gibeah. He avoids describing himself as the intended object of rape; instead, he claims that the men wanted to kill him. He avoids implicating himself in the woman's death; instead, he simply states that she was raped and is dead. His speech reduces a situation of complex culpability to a simple scenario of himself as victim with the entire male population of Gibeah at fault. If his view of the woman as a disposable possession was not already apparent to the reader in the preceding scene, it should be by the end of his speech. Attention to the narrator's account will find him out.

One of the more troubling kinds of contradiction for the religious reader is when the narrator stands in disagreement with God. After Jehu's blood-bath in Samaria and Jezreel, God says to him, 'Because you have been good in doing what is right in my eyes—according to all that was in my heart you have done to the house of Ahab—your sons to the fourth generation shall sit on the throne of Israel' (2 Kgs. 10: 30). But the narrator is much less enamoured with the hero and frames God's speech with bitter indictment: 'Only [or 'except'], the sins of Jeroboam the son of Nebat, which he made Israel to sin—Jehu did not turn aside from them, namely the golden calves that were in Bethel, and in Dan . . . And Jehu did not take care to walk in the law of YHWH the God of Israel with all his heart; he did not turn aside from the sins of Jeroboam, which he made Israel to sin' (10: 29, 31). Furthermore, for all God's promises of prosperity, the narrator reveals that 'in those days YHWH began to cut off parts of Israel. Hazael defeated them throughout Israel's territory: from the Jordan eastward, all the land of Gilead, the Gadites, and the Reubenites, and the Manassites, from Aroer, which is by the Wadi Arnon, that is, Gilead and Bashan' (10: 32–3; cf. God's attitude in Hos. 1: 4–5).

Contradiction, of course, can work on several levels. When more meanings are present than the characters involved can recognize, irony is present. Irony as an ingredient or mode of narration varies

within the Hebrew Bible. Genesis–2 Kings is particularly rich in
irony, Chronicles much less so. That difference is typical of the
difference between dialogic and monologic narrative.

Irony is incongruity of knowledge, value, or point of view.
Characters think they know what they are doing when in fact they
may be doing something rather different, just as Judah thought he
was engaging the services of a prostitute, when in fact he was having
sex with his daughter-in-law. Characters may see the world one way
when in fact it is different. Judah thought the woman caused the
deaths of his sons, when their deaths were their own fault or, at
least, God's doing. Characters may enact values different from those
they propound. Judah was anxious to burn his daughter-in-law for
committing the same sin of which he was guilty.

Sometimes the discrepancy of knowledge is contained within the
story world, so that some characters know more than others, just as
Tamar knew more than her father-in-law. In 2 Samuel 11, both Joab
and David are in a position to savour the irony of Uriah carrying the
letter which is also his warrant of execution. In such cases the reader
is also aware of the irony. At other times the reader alone is in a
position to appreciate it. To Joab, at the news of Uriah's death,
David sends the message, 'Do not let this thing be evil in your sight,
for the sword devours at random.' But to the reader the narrator
observes a few verses later, 'But the thing that David had done was
evil in sight of YHWH.'

Verbal irony, language that can be interpreted as understating
or counterstating what, on the surface, it seems to mean, also often
bypasses the characters en route from narrator to reader. 'In those
days there was no king in Israel; all the people did what was right in
their own eyes', observes the narrator repeatedly amidst the accounts
of chaotic self-interest at the end of Judges. Are we to read this as a
recommendation of kingship as a cure of ills? If we do, we must
ignore both the story of Abimelech (Judges 9) and most of the
resulting history of the monarchy in Samuel and Kings. There
kingship seems no major barrier to the further exercise of corrosive
self-interest. Furthermore, the narrator has slipped in a decisively
different evaluative standard from that of the earlier stories of
Judges. In the earlier episodes, 'the eyes of YHWH' are the standard
of judgement for Israel's behaviour (Judg. 2: 11; 3: 7, 12; 4: 1; 6: 1;

10: 6; 13: 1); now the people rely upon their own 'eyes' for guidance. A similar shift is reflected, a little later in the larger story, in YHWH's lament at the people's insistence on a monarchy: 'they have rejected me from being king over them' (1 Sam. 8: 7). Political 'progress' might very well be religious and moral regress.

Reconstructing characters

When reconstructing a character, that is, putting together all the text's clues about a character, readers (often subconsciously) formulate some idea of the *kind* of person playing out the story. In this respect, even after many years, modern literary critics still find useful E. M. Forster's (1927 ¶A) distinction between round and flat characters (cf. Chatman 1978: 131–4 ¶A; Alter 1990: 54–6 ¶A).

A flat character possesses few qualities or personality traits (perhaps only one) and, hence, is often rather predictable. Such a character may or may not be a conventional type. She or he may be as superficial as an agent, a person who is necessary merely to keep the plot going, a messenger, for example. On the other hand, some flat characters can be a vital presence in the story. God, for example, is a flat character in many biblical stories. Defined often by a single or few traits (for example, steadfast, merciful, and concerned for justice), God may none the less participate decisively in the story.

Unlike flat characters, round characters exhibit a conglomeration of traits, many of which are even contradictory. Such diversity and inconsistency may convey realism. We are well aware that, in the real world, neither we nor people we know exhibit consistent behaviour. We differ within ourselves. Consequently, we relate more readily to round characters in literature. They have the capacity to grow, to develop, to change their minds, to surprise the reader as well as the other characters in the story. We remember these characters because we cannot pin-point them. They, like the real people in our lives, are elusive, always evading complete definition or explanation.

In biblical literature, round and flat characterizations often shift. A flat character in one episode may become a round character in the next and vice versa. Sarah, for example, is not much more than her husband's shadow as he wanders through most of the pages of Genesis. In Genesis 16 and 21, however, she exposes more of her complexity and draws the reader's attention, if only temporarily, away from Abraham.

This propensity for characters to shift in and out of focus should warn readers against too quickly or rigidly identifying a story's central character(s). We tend to sort out major and minor characters by the amount of explicit attention—literally how much 'page space'—the narrator gives them, and that is certainly one way of thinking of centrality. Identifying who is 'major' and who is 'minor', however, is often a matter of the reader's perspective (including ideology/values). Tradition, inasmuch as it has named the book after her, declares Esther to be the central character in the book of Esther. Some commentators insist that, to the contrary, Mordecai is the major figure and Esther but part of the supporting cast. Both cases can be argued cogently from the text. Mordecai is the one engaged in (if not the initiator of) the story's (ostensible) central conflict, the hostility between him and Haman. (That personal antagonism, however, may be merely symptomatic of a larger racial/ethnic conflict—between Jew and Agagite, Persian and non-Persian.) Esther is but part of the resolution of that hostility. On the other hand, Mordecai might be described as a rather flat, stagnant character, saying little and revealing little, while Esther's character, which undergoes change and growth, exhibits complexity and contradiction. A telling pattern may perhaps be discerned among modern commentators: male commentators argue for the primacy of Mordecai while female commentators argue for the primacy of Esther.

Even in texts where there has been less debate about major and minor characters, perhaps the time has come to question the more conventional attitudes concerning centrality and marginality. Genesis 12–50 has often been identified as the 'history of the patriarchs', but while it is a 'patriarchal (hi)story' in the sense that it assumes a patriarchal society, many of the stories are about women, women who have their own desires, their own conflicts, their own plots if you will. Granted, the women's stories may be more mundane than those of the men who relate so directly to God, nevertheless they are still stories of relating that may, for their very interest in the common, everyday world, say more to us as modern readers who also find ourselves in a common, mundane world.

It has been argued that the length of the story has a bearing on whether its characters are flat or round. Shimon Bar-Efrat writes:

In real life not everything people do is characteristic of them, but this is not the case in a literary work of art, or at least in a short story. In this respect, the length of the work is of decisive importance: because there is no room in a short story to describe the various deeds and repeated actions of any one character, single actions necessarily serve to define the person. The short story chooses to relate the particular action which is characteristic of the individual and can exemplify what is considered to constitute the essential nature. We remember Cain as someone who murdered his brother, and Amnon as the person who violated his sister. If the author had wanted us to see them in a different light we would have been told about other (or additional) things they did.

(Bar-Efrat 1989: 80 ¶F)

It is true that one action, one speech, may not tell us much about a character. In the case of a short story, where a character may have little more than a single significant action or speech recounted, we may be inclined to treat that information on the assumption that what is narrated so selectively is also likely to be characteristic. However, we would venture to say that biblical short stories are seldom so stark in their representation. Remembering characters on the basis of one act or trait is more often the product of tradition, not of close reading. We remember Job for his patience (cf. Jas. 5: 7–11), but even a cursory reading of the book of Job tells us that such a reading is inadequate, if not plainly wrong.

Likewise, while tradition recalls simply that Cain was the first murderer, the text (Genesis 4), as we read it, presents a young man who is the first to take initiative in making an offering to YHWH, who is troubled by YHWH's arbitrary rejection of his gift and acceptance of his brother's, who strikes down his brother in an act that may not have been premeditated, and who laments being hidden from God's face. Though he sets out as a fugitive and a wanderer, he goes with God's protection. He has a family. He builds the first city. He is the father of society and culture. Cain actually becomes the epitome of a person who is rejected by God, who makes the terrible mistake of taking out his frustration on a fellow human being, and who, despite his alienation, makes a new start with considerable success.

Even the rapist Amnon is presented with a certain amount of complexity (2 Samuel 13). His obsession with his sister, his confusion between love and lust, his willingness to conspire with his friend, to lie to his father, and to deceive and violate his sister, his refusal to listen to Tamar's voice of reason or her plea for mercy builds not simply a violent character, but a character who is spoiled, who is used to getting what he wants, and who is in turmoil when he perceives that to be impossible. He is a character who cares only for immediate gratification and, though he knows that a dangerous Absalom lurks at the side of the stage, he says 'damn the consequences' and does what he pleases. The sudden transformation of his 'love' into hate, 'so that the hatred with which he hated her was greater than the love with which he had loved her' is, in itself, very telling of the great contradictions within him. The metamorphosis of desire to repulsion is precisely one of those unfathomable capacities of the human psyche.

Of course, many short stories do not provide such a vivid picture of internal struggle and motivation. Sometimes the narrator presents a character's action without having led up to it with any explicit information about the character's thoughts, values, or state of mind. Then the reader is required to work harder in order to make sense of the person's behaviour.

In the short story in Judges 4 and 5 we are introduced to the character Jael. She comes forth from her tent to greet the defeated Canaanite general, Sisera, fleeing from the Israelites. She invites him in, gives him milk to drink, and when he falls asleep, she hammers a tent peg through his mouth. Why does she do this? The answer most often given is that she sides with the Israelites (indeed most commentators assume that she is an Israelite) and is actively doing the Lord's business. She does in fact 'do the Lord's business', but outcome and motivation are two different things. So why does she ambush Sisera? The narrator offers subtle but significant clues. The text suggests that she is not an Israelite. She is identified as the wife of Heber the Kenite (4: 17), and Heber the Kenite is allied with Jabin, the Canaanite king, and Sisera, his general. His vocation (his name means something like 'Joiner the Smith') and the information that he has come far from Kenite territory to live near these Canaanites implies that he has most likely found employment working on Jabin's iron chariots. That means that Jael, by association, can also be identified as a friend of Israel's enemy. Israel's enemy, however, has just lost the battle in devastating defeat. Heber is nowhere to be found and has no doubt suffered the fate of all the others associated with the Canaanite army. Jael is in a delicate position. With the Israelite army approaching, her husband gone, and the Canaanite general in her tent, she does what any woman keen on survival might do: she shows her allegiance to the victors. She kills their enemy. One blow of the hammer, and she becomes a military hero rather than a victim of war.

Where episodes multiply, however, time is often of the essence just as in real life. We shape our understanding of a character as the narrative unfolds over time, offering further clues and, frequently, complexity.

Longer stories require more patience and a higher tolerance for ambiguity on the part of the reader. Rather than assessing a character on the basis of only one set of circumstances, readers of longer stories see characters in several situations, engaging in different relationships, and changing over the passing of time.

The character Esther is introduced by way of contrast to Ahasuerus' disobedient queen, Vashti. Vashti's rebellion and dismissal sets up a need for a new companion for the king. Using Vashti's fate as an example, the narrator sets up for the reader the expectation that the next woman will be demure and submissive. Indeed, Esther is first presented as a young woman with hardly a will of her own. She is (perhaps encouraged by her uncle Mordecai) selected to participate in the 'Miss Persia' contest. Following the instruction of Mordecai, she tells no one that she is Jewish. She immediately pleases the officer in charge of the harem. She follows his advice explicitly when the time comes for her to meet the king. And, not surprisingly, she pleases the king immensely as well.

This woman whose function and seeming sole desire is to please the men in her life, however, is destined for difficulties. Her uncle Mordecai who, unlike his niece, is less concerned with pleasing his superiors, incurs the wrath of Haman, the king's favourite courtier. When Haman schemes to destroy all the Jews, Esther is called upon to save her people. Caught between national allegiance and personal survival, between queenly duty and familial loyalty, she must make her own decisions, even if that means displeasing the men who have power over her. First we see her arguing with Mordecai over what she should do, and though she succumbs to his threat ('Do not imagine that you will escape in the king's house from all the Jews. For if you keep silent at such a time as this, relief and deliverance will come from another place, but you and your father's house will perish!'), she insists on doing things her way.

Rather than going to the king immediately, as Mordecai would have her do, Esther bides her time. She commands a three-day fast of all the Jews, even though it is the eve of Passover. She waits until the third day before making a move. When she comes unbidden into his presence, an offence punishable by death, we witness an act of disobedience every bit as severe as that of the former queen, Vashti. Where Vashti had refused to come when bidden, Esther intrudes without being summoned. She turns out to be not the opposite but the mirror of her feisty predecessor. Rather than pleading her case before the king at that moment, she delays. She invites the king to dinner—twice—before she tells him her problem. Granted, she seems to be in her pleasing mode again, buttering the king up before she makes her request, but it might also be said that by so doing, she is attempting to bolster the rather tenuous relationship between her husband and herself, to establish familiarity and trust before she reveals to him her nationality and her people's predicament.

Once Haman's plot is exposed and he is executed, Esther returns to the king to prod him into doing something about Haman's scheme which is already in effect. Since this king has consistently been characterized as a man who has an aversion to making decisions, this insistence on Esther's part shows yet another aspect of her courage. She and Mordecai, of course, are given the responsibility for taking care of the problem—which they do—by allowing the Jews to attack any people who are seeking to harm them. In the end, however, Esther turns out to be a rather ambiguous figure. Though thousands of the people of the provinces are killed at the hands of the Jews and the Jews suffer no casualties at all, Esther requests another day of warfare in the capital city. We are left wondering, is this a wise or sadistic move on her part? Is she 'dropping the bomb' to stop the war—that is, devastating the people beyond retaliation—or has power and blood gone to her head? For a woman who started her story submissively pleasing men, she ends her story playing the political game with all the independence, the shrewdness, and perhaps ruthlessness, that any man might display.

Reconstructing YHWH

One of the often remarked features of the book of Esther is the absence of God from the story. We might be tempted to say that this is as flat as a character can get, and leave it at that! But, for many readers, the story's canonical context—the way it invites comparison between Esther and Moses or Daniel, for example (see Fewell 1992: 11–17 ¶S)—invites also the possibility that we should think of an unseen God of Israel at work 'behind the scenes' in the narrative. Textual support is often claimed in Mordecai's cryptic words to Esther that if she stays quiet 'deliverance will stand up for the Jews from another place' (Esther 4: 14). This mode of reading is similar to a 'providential' reading of Ruth—so that Ruth's 'chancing to chance' upon the field of Boaz (Ruth 2: 3) is viewed not, indeed, as 'chance' but as the doing of YHWH. Yet the only action of YHWH explicitly recounted by the narrator in the whole story is YHWH's gift of conception to Ruth at the very end (Ruth 4: 13).

The pattern for these discoveries of an implicit God comes from stories such as that of Joseph in Egypt (Genesis 37–50) or the rebellion of David's son, Absalom (2 Samuel 15–20). In the latter, the narrator connects God to the human activity at only a few points, but enough for a reader to ascribe the whole grand scheme of things to the divinity's desire and deed. Thus as David retreats up the Mount of Olives and learns that his powerful counsellor Ahithophel has defected, he prays, 'YHWH, please turn the counsel of Ahithophel into folly' (2 Sam. 15: 30–1). At the summit 'where God was worshipped', Hushai, the king's friend, comes to meet him and to offer his services. In due course Hushai, at the crucial moment, persuades Absalom to disregard Ahithophel's advice and so saves David from defeat. Hushai, we might suppose, was the answer to David's prayer. The narrator intrudes a rare comment, making explicit an even larger purpose behind Hushai's activity: 'And YHWH [had] ordained to frustrate the good counsel of Ahithophel—in order that YHWH might bring evil upon Absalom' (2 Sam. 17: 14).

This talk of 'evil' may also trigger a larger connection for a reader—to Nathan's prophecy against David after his taking Bathsheba and having her husband, Uriah, killed (2 Samuel 11–12). David's action is characterized by YHWH (according to both the narrator and Nathan) as 'evil'. Moreover, since David has slain Uriah by the sword of the Ammonites, YHWH vows (says Nathan) that 'the sword shall never depart from your house' (2 Sam. 12: 10). A reader might well decide that Absalom's rebellion fits the prophetic bill—it sees the sword turned against both father and son.

Furthermore, just prior to the crucial council scene, Ahithophel advises Absalom to 'Go into your father's concubines, whom he has left to guard the house; and all Israel will hear that you have made yourself odious to your father, and the hands of all who are with you will be strengthened.' So Absalom does so, 'in the sight of all Israel' (2 Sam. 16: 21–2). Again many a reader has made an implicit connection between this scene and Nathan's prophecy: 'Thus says YHWH, "Behold, I will raise up evil against you out of your own house; and I will take your women before your eyes, and give them to your neighbour, and he shall lie with your women in broad daylight. For you did it in secret; but I will do this thing before all Israel, and in the light of day"' (2 Sam. 12: 11). Thus, despite the fact that the narrator tells us little explicitly about YHWH, we may none the less formulate a picture of divine desire and activity, in this case largely retributive, spanning the whole narrative. The picture, however, is not without its deeply disturbing ironies. We shall return to this text below.

In the Joseph story, a 'providential' reading is a product not so much of the narrator's as the characters' speech, especially the words of Joseph himself. Joseph insists to Pharaoh that God is both author and interpreter of the king's dreams (Gen. 41: 14–40). He names his sons, Manasseh and Ephraim, as expressions of God's providence in making him 'forget all [his] hardship and [his] father's house' and 'be fruitful in the land of [his] affliction'—sentiments somewhat contradicted by their own terms. He pounds home the message to his humiliated brothers that 'God sent me before you to preserve life

... And God sent me before you to preserve for you a remnant on earth and keep alive for you many survivors. So it was not you who sent me here but God' (Gen. 45: 5–7). And if he makes himself sound a little like Noah it is probably no accident. In this story, then, if we choose to believe that Joseph has got it at least roughly right we may again construct a picture of divine desire and activity, in this case largely salvific.

The book of Ruth also allows for a picture of God to be constructed from the beliefs of the characters, though these express different, sometimes conflicting, points of view.

To Naomi, the bereaved Israelite stranded in a foreign country, Yнwн seems a menacing power in her life—'it is more bitter for me than for you,' she says to her daughters-in-law, 'for the hand of Yнwн has gone out against me' (Ruth 1: 13). 'Do not call me Naomi [pleasant], call me Marah [bitter]', she tells the women at the gate of Bethlehem, 'for Shaddai has dealt me much bitterness. I went away full and Yнwн has brought me back empty' (Ruth 1: 20–1). Whether she sees herself as an innocent victim or guilty wrongdoer (perhaps for going to Moab in the first place, and being party to her sons marrying Moabite women) is at times difficult to tell, though her sense of oppression is undoubted: 'Why call me Naomi, when Yнwн has testified against [or 'afflicted'] me and Shaddai has brought evil upon me' (Ruth 1: 21). Her words, especially the forensic imagery and the use of the name Shaddai for God, remind us of Job's complaint against God—and God's dubious treatment of Job. She pointedly insinuates, by the way she words a blessing, that Yнwн might do well to show her as much loyalty or commitment (*hesed*) as her daughters-in-law had shown (Ruth 1: 8). Yet, on seeing the grain Ruth brings back from Boaz's field, she is not above blessing the man by Yнwн 'whose loyalty has not forsaken the living or the dead'—though whether the loyalty is Yнwн's or the man's is ambiguous. Naomi's God, whose reality and impact upon her Naomi never doubts, she views in terms shaped by her grief and destitution.

Boaz's Yнwн is more straightforward, constantly the subject of blessing. 'Yнwн be with you', he greets his reapers. And 'Yнwн bless you', they reply. 'Yнwн make good for you your deed,' he tells Ruth, complementing her on coming with her mother-in-law to Bethlehem, 'and let there be a full repayment for you from Yнwн, the God of Israel, under whose wings [*kanaph*] you have come to seek refuge' (Ruth 2: 12). Confronted intimately by Ruth on the threshing-floor, he again responds with words of God and blessing: 'May you be blessed by YHWH, my daughter; this last loyalty [*hesed*] you have made even better than the first, in not going after the eligible young men, whether poor or rich'—he means to say, of course, that she is to be blessed for going after *him*. Finally, in swearing to be a redeemer for Ruth, Boaz invokes (and associates) YHWH as God of life—'As YHWH lives . . .' (3: 13). Boaz's God, never doubted by Boaz, he views in terms shaped by his wealth and security.

Ruth, the Moabite woman, has the least to say about YHWH. Pressing Ruth to part at the beginning of the story, Naomi urges her to follow Orpah's example: 'Look, your sister-in-law has gone back to her people and to her gods; go back after your sister-in-law' (Ruth 1: 15). Naomi's implication is clear. Like her sister-in-law, Ruth has her own people and gods. The Moabite woman and the Israelite woman have nothing basic in common. Ruth, however, throws her words back at her: 'Do not push me to desert you, to go back . . . Your people [shall be] my people, your god, my god.' And to clinch her point that she will not let religion get in the way of her determination to accompany Naomi she invokes her new-found god, Naomi's god, in an oath—appropriately, for Naomi's god, an oath about death. 'May YHWH do so to me and doubly, if even death comes between us' (Ruth 1: 16–17). That is all she ever says directly about YHWH. Indirectly, however, she has one more word. On the threshing-floor, she challenges Boaz to do something about his pious blessing on the harvest field: 'Spread *your* wing [*kanaph*] over your maidservant, for *you* are a rescuer [redeemer]' (Ruth 3: 9). That is to say, it is all very well for the rich man to mouth pieties, however sincerely meant, about divine reward for a destitute woman's commitment. Rich men can afford to wait around for the gods to act; destitute women cannot. Is Boaz willing to make his own commitment and rescue her himself? Ruth invokes YHWH in order to spur the possibility of human *hesed*. Ruth's God, at the margins of her own belief, she views in terms of the practical business of humans getting on with their lives.

How a reader configures the character of YHWH from these perspectives is an open question. Naomi's god of emptiness is countered by Boaz's god of fullness. But is the former thereby annulled? Perhaps the narrator has the last word, characterizing Y<small>HWH</small> as in charge of life, with the simple report that Y<small>HWH</small> gave Ruth conception. Yet we might wonder if that is altogether true. Without Ruth there would be no conception, and as for life, it is not the baby boy who brings life to this story but the Moabite woman, the daughter-in-law who loves her mother-in-law, who is worth more than seven sons (Ruth 4: 15). So if she is central, what is Y<small>HWH</small>'s relationship to her? In short, the character of God in the book of Ruth is inextricably bound up with the human characters.

Readers groping for a sense of Y<small>HWH</small>'s character when the divinity is only lightly sketched in the narrative will often bring to the story a conception of God from other stories. This is often a flat character. Y<small>HWH</small> is a redeemer (*go'el*) or a helper (*'ezer*) or a god of justice (*mishpat*). From a faith position, Jewish or Christian, there are powerful traditional reasons to read for a positively construed, flat character. Yet, as we have seen in the discussion of Ruth, we can read the character of God in Hebrew narrative more elusively, positing of God the enigmatic ambiguities found in complex human characters.

Take, for example, the great account in Exodus of how Y<small>HWH</small> delivered the people of Israel from slavery in Egypt (Exodus 1–15). This is one of the paradigm stories of Y<small>HWH</small> as saviour. Yet the story can be read as more nuanced than that where Y<small>HWH</small>'s character is concerned. For one thing, it is not said that God answered the people's cry for help out of compassion or simply to alleviate suffering, though some such feeling may of course be implicit, but because he remembered his covenant with Abraham, Isaac, and Jacob (Exod. 2: 24; 3: 6–8, 15–17; 6: 2–8). His action is spelled out in terms of this 'covenant', which obliges him to see the children of the patriarchs flourish in the land sworn to them. Y<small>HWH</small>, therefore, is once again Providence, here the Provider of a future already promised in the past. The story could have emphasized the motivating power of pity, compassion, love; rather it singles out plan, promise, obligation. This depiction of Y<small>HWH</small> befits a story about mastery and control, for that is how it can be read.

Y<small>HWH</small>'s dealings with Moses are patently forceful (Exodus 3–4). His culminating anger (Exod. 4: 14) is followed by silent acquiescence on Moses' part, indicating perhaps what is to follow. YHWH is all-powerful and cannot be resisted without incurring terrible anger. Pharaoh, like Moses, holds out against reasoned appeal and ignores the message of harmless 'signs'. But where Moses succumbs in servanthood before YHWH's anger, Pharaoh continues to object, because compelled to do so by YHWH's hardening his heart, to his eventual destruction. YHWH treats Moses with some patience. Not so Pharaoh, though it will *appear* that YHWH is patient with him. Final retribution will be delayed by the prolonged sequence of plagues, each plague purporting to give him a chance to repent. Why does God treat Pharaoh like this? Explicitly, he says to Pharaoh (9: 14–16) that he will send him plagues, 'that you may know that there is none like me in all the earth'. Indeed, he goes on, he could have destroyed Pharaoh and Egypt by this time but 'for this purpose have I let you live, to show you my power, so that my name may be declared throughout all the earth'. This is, as it were, an answer to Pharaoh's (rhetorical) earlier question (Exod. 5: 2), 'Who is YHWH, that I should hear his voice and let Israel go?' The answer is that YHWH is one who will choose when Pharaoh lets Israel go. YHWH is the master of all masters, and his merciless manipulation of Pharaoh is a practical demonstration of the point. This is not to say that YHWH's self-glorification is his primary motivation for delivering Israel; but that it is, perhaps, the motivation for his treatment of Pharaoh. It is, of course, an appropriate purpose to express to Pharaoh, for the king is thereby reminded of his proper place in the scheme of things: as he has exalted himself over Israel, so YHWH has exalted himself over Pharaoh. Pharaoh is but a servant before YHWH as will be made plain not only to Pharaoh but to all his subjects and all the earth (14: 4, 18). YHWH is a jealous god, jealous of his standing as king above all kings and god above all gods.

YHWH delivers Israel—and demonstrates his mastery. By effecting the deliverance with repeated signs and wonders he elevates the belittling of Pharaoh into an event of cosmic proportions (as the first-born die and as, at the Red Sea, the civilized world reverts to chaos and then becomes dry land once again)—and thereby demonstrates his mastery. But it is not only Egypt and the nations who are to learn of YHWH and his power through the signs and wonders. It is also Israel herself. 'For I have hardened his heart . . .', says YHWH, 'that I may show these signs of mine among them, and that you may tell in the hearing of your son and your son's son how I have made sport of the Egyptians and what signs I have done among them; that you may know that I am YHWH' (Exod. 10: 1-2).

Early in the story the question arises regarding YHWH's identity (Exod. 3: 13; 4: 1; 6: 1-7). What is his name? How are the people to know that it is indeed YHWH who is their god and the god of their deliverance? YHWH's demonstration of power over the Egyptians is also bound up with his need to establish himself securely as Israel's God, the god of the covenantal promise, in the eyes of Israel. At this point a reader may detect a curious hint of insecurity in YHWH's own self, paradoxically as it may appear in the context of this massive demonstration of mastery. For what does it profit YHWH if he 'provides' but his people fail to identify their provider? YHWH needs Israel, just as Israel needs YHWH. Thus by signs and wonders YHWH also seeks to secure identity. The outcome is successful—nearly. 'And Israel saw the great deed which YHWH did against the Egyptians, and the people feared YHWH; and they believed in YHWH—and in his servant Moses' (14: 31).

We spoke above about the way a reader might begin to build a picture of YHWH in the story of Absalom's rebellion (2 Samuel 15–20) or the larger story of David in 1 and 2 Samuel. A figure of providence and retributive justice emerged. It would be easy to leave it at that—seeing a character who loyally, lovingly perhaps, sustains his chosen servant, David, even when betrayed by him (as in the Bathsheba/Uriah episode in 2 Samuel 11–12); who deals out poetic justice, evil for evil, ordaining to defeat the good counsel of the turn-coat Ahithophel in order to bring evil upon the traitor Absalom. But what if we were to rotate our point of view just a little and think of these divine predilections out of an interest other than David's? (See Linafelt 1992 ¶N.3.)

David takes Bathsheba, so YHWH takes the child born to her— without regard for either mother or child. The fathers have eaten sour grapes, so the children's teeth are set on edge. This justice has rough edges. David takes Bathsheba, so YHWH ordains, according to Nathan's prophecy, that his women will be taken by someone else. This is poetic justice—as long as the women are ignored in the 'balance'.

In one of his decidedly less than heroic moments the great King David deserts Jerusalem and leaves ten defenceless concubines to 'keep' (or 'guard'!) his house/palace which he knows will be taken by Absalom (2 Sam. 15: 13–17). The result is that the father's women, like his city, are publicly 'entered' by the son. On his return David incarcerates these betrayed women in a 'guardhouse', widows to the day of their death (2 Sam. 20: 3). (We could contrast his magnanimous treatment of Shimei who had cursed him, 2 Sam. 19: 21–3.)

Now we may easily see David's action as the callous hypocrisy of an autocratic king in a patriarchal world. The betrayer ruthlessly shifts his own shame on to the women since, as patriarchy would have it, they had been shamed by Absalom's rape. Is this then what Hannah so hopefully prayed for at the beginning of Samuel (1 Sam. 2: 10), 'May [YHWH] give strength to his king / And exalt the horn (power) of his anointed'? But, by the same token, what of YHWH who raises up evil by taking women? Ironically, Nathan's prophecy against David lays the rape of the women, in fact by Absalom and in effect by David, at YHWH's door. Again Hannah's song turns to discord. Is this taker of women the YHWH of whom she sings? Is this the one who weighs actions in the balance, who breaks the bow of the mighty and girds the feeble with armour, who raises the needy from the dust and seats them on a throne of honour?

Thus Nathan's words, that seem to weigh out just recompense, instead collapse the difference between punisher and punished. YHWH's scales are tilted. YHWH's character is deeply compromised. This God of the children of Israel seems transfixed by his chosen 'son', oblivious to his chosen 'daughters'.

Such examples of the 'dark' or 'fallible' side of YHWH could be multiplied, in this story and others. In the discussion of Abraham and Sarah in the next chapter, for example, we could shift the focus more specifically to YHWH and press to know more about the divinity's consideration, or lack of it, for Isaac (not to speak of Sarah) when tempting Abraham to sacrifice the boy. In looking at the book of Jonah in terms of plot, we shall see YHWH making a powerful case for mercy. Yet in the story of Abraham's intercession for Sodom and Gomorrah, a story that has many (inverse) points of comparison with that of Jonah, YHWH fails to find a single creature worth mercy; and even Lot's wife, for looking back (in compassion for her doomed friends, perhaps), is turned to salt, seemingly at YHWH's behest. The predicament of the God who needs recognition, even exclusive recognition (the 'jealous' God), is not confined to Exodus or even the primary history of Genesis–2 Kings. The theme is intimated in Daniel 3, for example, and we could see it played out further in Daniel 1–6 were we to read those chapters as a whole narrative. And in our final chapter, as we review some readings of the Garden story (Genesis 2–3), we could take time to consider more deeply why YHWH put the tree of the knowledge of good and evil in the garden in the first place, and failed to anticipate the outcome (cf. Gen. 3:22).

Coming to some understanding of the character of YHWH is one of the great challenges of the Hebrew Bible, not only of its narrative. Of course, we can make it simpler by treating component stories as wholly discrete so that we see not one character but many. On the other hand, as we have seen, the canonical shape of the Bible may incline us to keep looking for a single character, even if complex, mysterious, enigmatic, and quite often frustratingly elusive. Whatever the case, bound up in our search for the character of YHWH, as is true of other characters, are our decisions about what motivates a character or, put another way, what a character desires. Here we have begun talking about plot—something that may have become obvious earlier, particularly in our discussion of the stories of King David's family and the plagues in Egypt. Here, therefore, we bring our discussion of character to a close, pause for a more detailed exploration of character in a particular text, the story of Abraham and Sarah, and then turn to the question of plot.

4

Abraham and Sarah: Genesis 11−22

For some readers who have read selected stories about the first patriarch, Abraham is the man of faith, the man who obeyed God even when it meant leaving his home, even when it meant sacrificing his son. For readers who are willing to read the whole story in its final form, however, Abraham can be seen as a man of frequent surprise and great contradiction. Waffling between faith and unfaith, courage and cowardice, he meanders along supposedly in search of the fulfilment of God's promise. But what is it that truly motivates Abraham and the woman who travels with him?

Abram, the man of faith, we see at the beginning of Genesis 12:

Now YHWH said to Abram, 'Go from your country and your birthplace and your father's house to the land that I will show you. And I will make of you a great nation, and I will bless you, and make your name great, and you will be a blessing. I will bless those who bless you; I will curse whoever curses you; and by you all the families of the earth shall be blessed.'

And Abram went, as YHWH had told him . . .   (Gen. 12: 1−4)

We cannot ask for a clearer call or a more compliant response. God calls and Abram goes. We could easily take this to be an instantaneous and unambiguous revelation of Abram's character, if it were not for the fact that Abram's story does not end here. Nor, in fact, does it begin here.

The beginning of Abram's story, in genealogical fashion, lies in the middle of his father's story:

Terah took Abram his son and Lot the son of Haran, his grandson, and Sarai his daughter-in-law, his son Abram's wife, and they went forth together from Ur of the Chaldeans to go into the land of Canaan; but when they came to Haran, they stayed there. The days of Terah were two hundred and five years; and Terah died in Haran.   (Gen. 11: 31–2)

By the time God's call comes to Abram, he has already left his land and the place of his birth. Abram, along with his father, has already started for the land of Canaan. During the delay in Haran, Abram's father dies. There is nothing to hold him in Haran. God's call comes at an opportune time with an opportune content: Abram is to leave his native land, which he has already done, and his father's house, of which there is nothing left, to go to the land which is already the destination of his migration. We might ask ourselves, how much faith does it take to do what one has already decided to do?

If we should take the text's silences seriously, we might notice that Abram does not tell his wife Sarai of God's call. She is not privy to, nor seemingly included in, God's plan. And yet she is expected to follow her husband, doing dutifully whatever is necessary in order that he might fulfil God's call and receive God's promise.

When Abram brings his family into Canaan, he passes right through the land. He camps in Shechem where God tells him, 'To your descendants I will give this land.' But, seemingly unimpressed with 'this land', Abram tarries only long enough to build an altar before he heads toward the Negeb desert.

Famine strikes and Abram turns toward Egypt. The detour to Egypt suggests that we might now see an example of how other families of the earth will, through Abram, receive a blessing. Abram, however, is much less concerned with being a blessing to other families of the earth, than he is with saving his own skin. His anxiety stems from Sarai's exceptional beauty. All the Egyptian men will desire her, he fears. His worry is not about what all this unwanted attention might mean for Sarai (as we might have expected from a concerned and loving husband); rather, his worry is what it might mean for him.

'The Egyptians will see you and they will say, "This is his wife". Then they will kill me, but they will let you live. Say you are my sister, that it may go well with me because of you, and that my life may be spared on your account.'   (Gen. 12: 12–13)

Abram, with a mastery of understatement, is requesting that Sarai avail herself sexually to the male population of Egypt 'that it may go well with me because of you and that my life may be spared on your account'. His speech turns out to be doubly ironic. His life is, of course, spared; but, as the story continues, we are given no indication that his life would have been in danger. Furthermore, things go *very* well with Abram on account of Sarai because he, in essence, sells Sarai to the Pharaoh for a handsome profit: 'And for [Sarai's] sake [Pharaoh] dealt well with Abram—he had sheep, oxen, male donkeys, male and female slaves, female donkeys, and camels' (12: 16). Later we are told that, when Abram went up from Egypt, he 'was very rich in livestock, in silver, and in gold' (13: 2).

One might well wonder at this point, What does Abram think will be the outcome of this barter? Sarai is hardly being 'borrowed'—Pharaoh himself later claims that he took her for his wife (12: 19). If events are left to their natural course, Abram can hardly expect to get Sarai back. But then, perhaps he is not presuming to get her back. Certainly she is beautiful and they have been together a long while, but her value lies now in his safety and his wealth. Besides, she is barren and, if he is giving any thought at all to God's promise that *he* will be a great nation, that *he* will be blessed, that *his* name will be great, that *his* descendants will have land, he is probably of the opinion that a barren wife is hardly going to be any help. He can always find another woman, a younger, fertile woman, preferably —perhaps one of the Egyptian servant women given to him by Pharaoh.

Consequently, Abram sacrifices his wife for his own physical and economic security. And as far as God's call and promise goes, it is clear that he sees himself to be the sole recipient. If God is interested in blessing *him*, then he must be the one to succeed. Sarai is expendable.

God, however, has a rather different perspective on things. In God's point of view, Sarai is not expendable.

But YHWH afflicted Pharaoh and his house with great plagues because of Sarai, Abram's wife. So Pharaoh called Abram, and said, 'What is this you have done to me? Why did you not tell me that she was your wife? Why did you say, "She is my sister", so that I took

her for my wife? Here now is your wife. Take her and be gone!' And
Pharaoh gave his men orders concerning him and they set him on the
way, with his wife and all that he had. (Gen. 12: 17–20)

So Abram leaves, blessed with wealth, but hardly having been a
blessing to other families of the earth. And as for Sarai's value, he
seems to have learned nothing. Though God continues to reassure
Abram that he will become a great nation (13: 14–18; 15: 1–21), ten
years pass, and Abram has yet to share with Sarai any mention of
YHWH's call and promise. And, in the mean time, Abram's actions,
by contrast to the events in Egypt, further devalue Sarai's worth.
When his nephew Lot is kidnapped by the enemies of Sodom,
Abram wastes no time mustering the men of his household in order
to save him. The reader might ask why the capture of Lot inspired
such courage and risk on the part of Abram when the taking of Sarai
by Pharaoh did not.

Furthermore, when he brings back the people and their possessions to Sodom, he spurns the offer of wealth from the king of
Sodom.

Then the king of Sodom said to Abram, 'Give me the persons, but take
the possessions for yourself.' But Abram said to the king of Sodom, 'I
have sworn to YHWH, God Most High, maker of heaven and earth, that
I would not take a thread or a sandal strap or anything that is yours, lest
you should say, "I have made Abram rich".' (Gen. 14: 21–3)

Where was such pride when Abram was in Egypt? He certainly had
no qualms about Pharaoh's sandal straps.

Sarai takes center stage in Genesis 16. She, too, would like to have
children, though she knows nothing of God's promise to Abram of
many offspring. Frustrated by her infertility, she offers to Abram
her young Egyptian maid Hagar as a surrogate. She does this not for
Abram's sake, but for her own.

Look, YHWH has prevented me from bearing children. Go in to my
maid. Perhaps I shall be built up through her. (Gen. 16: 2)

Abram accepts the proposition without hesitation. Using Sarai's
desire for a child to fulfil his own desire for a mighty lineage, he

eagerly takes the young Egyptian woman as a second wife. Hagar conceives, but Sarai's plan backfires. For when the young woman learns that she is pregnant, she makes the most of her newly elevated status. Sarai finds herself further devalued and proceeds to blame Abram. Abram, surely pleased about the pregnancy but obviously unconcerned about the young woman Hagar, leaves her to Sarai's harsh treatment.

Just as Hagar threatened Sarai's importance in the family, she temporarily usurps her place in the narrative's spotlight. Hagar runs away, but an angel of YHWH finds her and instructs her to return. But although she must return to an oppressive mistress and an indifferent master, she goes with a divine promise. Abram is not the only one destined to have a mighty lineage. God has listened to her affliction, and she will bear a son and name him 'God hears'. Indeed when the time comes, she does bear a son to Abram who names him Ishmael, 'God hears'.

Thirteen years go by, and God appears to Abram to establish a covenant. God renames him Abraham, father of a multitude, and promises that his lineage will produce nations and kings. Abraham, in true piety, listens with reverence, acceptance, and no doubt pleasure, to the promise of greatness and to the call to covenant. When, however, God announces that Sarai is also to receive a new name (Sarah, 'princess') and that she is to be included in this call and promise, Abraham balks.

God said to Abraham, 'As for Sarah your wife, you shall not call her Sarai, but Sarah shall be her name. I will bless her, and moreover I will give you a son by her. I will bless her, and she shall give rise to nations. Kings of peoples shall come from her.' Abraham fell on his face and laughed and said to himself, 'Can a son be born to someone who is one hundred years old? Can Sarah, a woman of ninety years, give birth?' And Abraham said to God, 'May Ishmael live in your sight!'

(Gen. 17: 15–18)

God cannot be serious, thinks Abraham. Sarah is not capable of this. How can she ever be the mother of nations and kings? She is too old. Besides, her participation really is not necessary. I already have a son. 'May Ishmael live in your sight!'

God, however, is resolute. The promise includes Sarah. It is not enough that the child is Abraham's. The child of promise must be Sarah's. As for Ishmael, he is also to be blessed, but it is Sarah's son Isaac with whom God will renew the covenant.

Abraham falls silent before God. We might think this symbolizes acquiescence if not for the fact that Abraham is also silent before Sarah. Even after hearing directly from God of Sarah's importance to the promise, even after her name has been changed to symbolize that importance, Abraham says nothing to her of her role in God's plan.

Consequently God returns to reiterate Sarah's part in the promise (Genesis 18), and Sarah, this time listening to the announcement, cannot believe what she hears. She laughs. It is a small wonder. This is the first she has heard of any divine plan, the first time she has considered that she might have a part in a call from God. Years of living with Abraham have conditioned her response to be much the same as his: 'After I am withered, shall I have pleasure—and with my husband so old?' Abraham, so protective of his own special standing with God, shows no confidence in Sarah, and Sarah, unaware of her own importance and potential, shows no confidence in herself. Like Abraham before her, she cannot believe that God is serious. It must be a joke. She is too old. She is not capable of such a thing. But though surprised and amused, she is also intrigued. Could it just be possible?

God's move to include Sarah is left hanging without closure, while her husband debates with YHWH over the fate of Sodom. YHWH has decreed destruction for Sodom and its brother city Gomorrah if the outcry against them can be substantiated. Abraham bargains for the lives of ten hypothetical righteous people and YHWH concedes that if ten righteous are found there, the city of Sodom will not be destroyed. Abraham's rhetoric, however, is in vain. Not even ten righteous are found in the city. In spite of that, God remembers Abraham and delivers his nephew and his nephew's daughters from the midst of the overthrow.

In chapter 20 the story turns its attention back to Abraham and Sarah. While we might expect the last visit from God to have finally made an impact on their vision of themselves and each other, we are to be disappointed. Not even a word from God can change who they are and how they think.

From there Abraham journeyed toward the territory of the Negeb, and dwelt between Kadesh and Shur; and he sojourned in Gerar. And Abraham said of Sarah his wife, 'She is my sister.' And Abimelech, king of Gerar, sent and took Sarah.   (Gen. 20: 1–2)

Although God again intervenes and Sarah is returned to her husband, the episode clearly tells us that, for Abraham and Sarah, the lesson never seems to end. The nephew Lot may be worth a show of courage on Abraham's part, but Sarah still is not. In Abraham's point of view, Sarah continues to be dispensable, especially when his security is at stake. And as for Sarah, she allows herself, in characteristic silence and passivity, to be sacrificed for the safety of the 'chosen one'.

Abraham, the man to bring a blessing to all the other families of the earth, fails again. If anything, his deceit brings affliction on the innocent. The only one to receive a 'blessing' is Abraham himself:

And Abimelech took sheep and oxen, and male and female slaves, and gave them to Abraham, and restored his wife Sarah to him . . . And to Sarah he said, 'Look, I have given your "brother" a thousand pieces of silver; it is compensation for you before all who are with you. With all, you are set right.'   (Gen. 20: 14, 16)

But while her 'brother' continues to acquire more wealth, in the larger scheme of things, Sarah is not exactly 'set right'. Being returned to Abraham is no guarantee that she will not be wronged again by a husband who views her to be expendable. It is not until she herself is visited by God that she can finally view herself as a rightful participant in God's call and promise. She bears the child that she thought she was incapable of bearing. For Sarah there is laughter: 'God has made laughter for me; everyone who hears will laugh over me!' Having accomplished the seemingly impossible, she begins to see her own value. She has a special place in her family and in God's plan. 'Who would have said to Abraham that Sarah would nurse children? Yet I have borne him a child in his old age.'

From Sarah, however, laughter is not the last sound we hear. Comfort and privilege breeds a narrower vision. Security becomes a thing to be guarded. She, like Abraham before her, sets limits on who is to be included in God's promise.

Abraham made a great feast on the day that Isaac was weaned. But Sarah saw the son of Hagar the Egyptian, whom she had borne to Abraham, playing. So she said to Abraham, 'Cast out this slave woman with her son; for the son of this slave woman shall not inherit along with my son Isaac.' (Gen. 21: 8–10)

Abraham is unhappy with Sarah's demand, but God's response, surprisingly, indulges Sarah's exclusivity.

'Do not consider this to be evil on account of the boy and on account of your servant woman. Listen to whatever Sarah tells you, for it is through Isaac that offspring will be named to you.' (Gen. 21: 12)

For the ethically sensitive reader such response is troubling: a god who shows arbitrary favouritism is a god who cannot be trusted. But perhaps God deserves a bit more credit. God is rather limited by the cast of human characters. The jealousy and competition between these two women spells inevitable strife. Perhaps the gesture is intended to avert more tragic hostility between these women and their sons in the future.

God understands and works around Abraham's limitations as well. The partiality most men in patriarchal society feel toward their first-born son might also bias Abraham in years to come, thus thwarting God's whimsical desire to use and bless unlikely candidates. The thing was 'exceedingly evil' to Abraham, says the narrator, 'on account of *his son*.' God nudges him to see that the woman as well as the boy should be of concern: 'Do not consider this to be evil on account of the boy *and on account of your servant woman*.' God knows better, however, than to push the point. For Abraham, women will never rate the way sons do. And so God continues to address what is, for Abraham, the major concern: 'As for the slave woman's son, I will make a nation of him also, because he is your offspring.'

While God panders to Abraham's constricted vision, God also acts to prevent human frailty from gaining the better ground. Moreover, as the rest of the story soon reveals, God can make up for human failure. As Abraham and Sarah circumscribe their divinely blessed family, God envelops Hagar and her son in blessing and promise as well.

The fact that Abraham has sacrificed his first wife Sarah to strangers on two occasions, has sacrificed his second wife Hagar first to affliction and then to ostracism, and has sacrificed his first-born son Ishmael to the wilds of the desert, casts an ambiguous shadow on the testing of Abraham in Genesis 22. While some commentators, in trying to reconcile Genesis 22 with the preceding episodes, have suggested that, in Genesis 22, the man of unfaith has reached a pinnacle of ultimate faith, a reading attentive to consistency of character might conclude otherwise. Abraham is a man who has shown that he has no problem sacrificing members of his family. Granted, he has not volunteered nor has he been called upon to do violence personally to any of them. He has, nevertheless, given their bodies over to certain suffering.

With that in mind we read that 'It was after these things that God tested Abraham'. The test, we discover, hinges on God's command to Abraham to offer up his son Isaac as a burnt offering. We are not told what God wanted or expected to find in Abraham's performance. Most readings assume that what Abraham did met with God's approval. Abraham, on account of his radical obedience, becomes an exemplary character. Such a reading, on the other hand, leaves the character of God in a rather sticky situation. At the very best one might assert that God is simply unfathomable; at the worst, God is deranged and sadistic.

Suppose, however, that God is well aware of Abraham's tendency to forfeit his family to danger and uncertainty. What if the test is really designed to see just how far Abraham will go? To begin with, we might ask, what is the unspoken alternative? If Abraham refuses to do this thing, what will happen to him? Disobedience usually results in punishment. Might not Abraham hear in the silence a threat, an unstated 'or else . . .'? Abraham, as we have seen, is rather sensitive when it comes to his personal safety.

How far will Abraham go when self-preservation is at issue? Perhaps God needs to see if there is ever a point where Abraham is willing to sacrifice himself rather than his family. He has sacrificed the other members of his household; will he go so far as to sacrifice this son of promise? Will he go so far as to implicate himself in the violence?

What might we have heard from an exemplary Abraham? 'Take me! I am old. The boy has his whole life in front of him.' Or might we have even heard the Abraham of old (cf. Gen. 18: 25): 'Far be it from you to expect such a thing, to want to bring death upon the innocent as if they were guilty. Far be that from you! Shall not the Judge of all the earth do what is just?' But whereas the Abraham of old would dare to challenge God for the sake of people he did not even know, this Abraham says nothing on behalf of his own son. Whereas the Abraham of old argued for the deliverance of what turned out to be an irredeemably violent and perverse city, this Abraham risks nothing for this innocent boy.

Instead, we get nothing but silent obedience, with commentators through the ages injecting profundity into each mute movement. Abraham makes every effort to go through with the sacrifice of his son. Only God's intervention keeps him from murder. Here we have a rather sudden revelation of character: God is not willing to have the boy killed. But Abraham is. In the final analysis, God says no. Why doesn't Abraham?

Perhaps it is because God has been sending Abraham the wrong signals all this time. Every act of familial sacrifice performed by Abraham has been met with God's intervention. God has restored Sarah twice and saved the lives of Hagar and Ishmael when Abraham had sent them to wander in the desert. And in the midst of all this, God continues to renew his call and promise to Abraham. God keeps trying to set right what Abraham makes go wrong, but the final outcome of this is that Abraham is relieved of responsibility. And Abraham is always the one who wins. Abraham has been conditioned to bank on his chosen status.

God's response to Abraham is impossible to decipher. 'Now I know that you fear God.' For most commentators, this spells triumph for Abraham: he reveres God for God's sake. Tone, however, is an elusive thing, and 'fear' can mean more than reverence. God could be saying that, at the very least, Abraham has shown that he fears God, indeed for his very life. He may not have much backbone or compassion, but at least he fears God. Or perhaps, God is saying, 'Now I know that you fear God as much as you do other human beings. You have given in to your fear of me in the same way that you have given in to your fear of others—the Egyptians (ch. 12), the men of Gerar (ch. 20), even Sarah (chs. 16 and 21).'

Abraham, ironically, names the place 'YHWH will see'. YHWH has, in Abraham's point of view, 'seen' to the sacrifice, substituting a ram for a son. But what has YHWH actually seen? On the mountain, YHWH sees a man who fears, a man in need of grace.

A messenger of YHWH called to Abraham a second time from the heavens. 'By myself I have sworn', declares YHWH, 'that, because you have done this thing, you have not spared your son, your only one, indeed, I will bless you and I will make your offspring as numerous as the stars of the heavens and as the sands of the seashore. Your offspring shall possess the gate of their enemies. Through your offspring all the nations of the earth will be blessed because you have listened to my voice.'   (Gen. 22: 15–18)

Whether or not Abraham has passed the test, we do not know. We fear not. What we do know is that God chooses to bless him anyway. Although Abraham has been busy reducing his family, YHWH will work even harder to expand it. And because Abraham has listened to God's voice, the voice that said 'Do not raise your hand against the boy or do anything to him', Abraham's offspring (at least this particular offspring) will have the chance to multiply and do what Abraham has been unable to do—be a blessing to other families of the earth. But then that is another story in the story.

5

Designs on the Plot

Reading for the plot: desire for order

> 'Reading for the plot', we learned somewhere in the course
> of our schooling, is a low form of activity. . . . Plot has been
> disdained as the element of narrative that least sets off
> and defines high art—indeed, plot is that which especially
> characterizes popular mass-consumption literature: plot is
> why we read *Jaws*, but not Henry James. And yet . . . [plot]
> is the very organizing line, the thread of design, that makes
> narrative possible because finite and comprehensible.
>
> (Brooks 1985: 4 ¶A)

Plot is the organizing force or principle through which narrative
meaning is communicated. There must be events for there to be
story; not random events but events that are connected, events that
have design, that form a pattern—events that are in fact 'plotted'. It
is this plotting of events that allows narrative to communicate the
temporal nature of its message. For the meaning of narrative is not
static, like that of a painting, but something that is developed
through time—the time of the characters living out the events of
their narrative lives and the time of readers as they enter and 'live
out' the lives of the characters they read.

Plot provides a time continuum, but it is a continuum that relies
upon the reader's sense of design. Plot is constructed through different and incomplete sources—the voice of the narrator, the speech
and actions of characters. As Peter Brooks puts it, 'narrative stories
depend on meanings delayed, partially filled in, stretched out' (1985:

21 ¶A). Relations between events are not always apparent, but our propensity for order drives us to make sense of what we read.

This is particularly apparent in the reading of Hebrew narrative. Most events, even whole stories or episodes, are simply connected with 'and' (most often in a construction called the *vav-* or *waw-*consecutive). Readers, however, usually following the lead of translators, variously interpret the 'and' to mean 'when', 'then', 'now', 'so', 'but', and so forth. Hebrew narrators provide the events, but often the relationships between and among events are not explicit. The reader infers the chronological order or the system of cause and effect. It is as though the text provides a kind of map and the readers are left to chart a course. We plot our way, connecting events, often without thinking, in a way that makes the most sense to us.

Presuming that every element of the story has a purpose and is somehow connected to every other element of the story, we are constantly organizing and amplifying the fragmented but potentially coherent information, striving in the process to forge meaning and a sense of the whole. We read 'in a spirit of confidence, and also a state of dependence, that what remains to be read will restructure the provisional meanings of the already read' (Brooks 1985: 27 ¶A).

Structure

Plots may be charted most simply with three basic categories which correspond perhaps to Aristotle's famous 'beginning, middle, and end'. The *exposition* sets up the story world and initiates the main series of events. The situation presented in an exposition is usually characterized by incompleteness, disorder, or unfulfilled desire, from which develops a subsequent *conflict* or complication. The conflict, which may be internal to a character or an external one, between characters, moves through various phases until a climax gives way to some degree of *resolution*.

Plots, based on this understanding, have clear beginnings and clear endings. Often they are patterned after natural experiences, the span of a life, for instance. For many stories that focus on individuals, birth marks the beginning, death marks the end. Human aspiration is another common model. A quest that must be undertaken, a goal that must be attained introduces the incompleteness and structures the complication and resolution.

While they may be structured around real-life experiences, literary plots differ from real life. Whereas, in real life, events often seem random, narrative shapes events into meaningful patterns. Even clear beginnings and endings are not apparent in real life. Death is hardly the end to the biological process, and one need only listen to the abortion debate to be reminded that birth is hardly the very beginning. Our lives, even particular episodes in our lives, do not have the distinct parameters that we find in literary plots. Nor, for that matter, are they commonly accorded obvious meaning. Consequently, while plots must be similar enough to real life so that we can understand and relate to them (i.e., mimetic, in Aristotle's terms), they must also be different in order for us to appreciate them. We see enough disjointedness in everyday life. When we read, we expect to see significance.

The simple model of exposition, conflict, climax, and resolution is, of course, merely heuristic where many biblical narratives are concerned. The book of Esther's exposition (the introduction of Esther to the court) has its own exposition (the deposing of Vashti). The book of Jonah has no exposition at all. The exposition might become a lengthy prologue that sets the stage for the kernel of the story and ties the story to a broader literary tradition. Although it seems like merely a list, 1 Chronicles 1–9 is a genealogy that takes the reader back to the very beginning of Israel's story. If one knows the stories of Genesis–Judges, the very names function as allusion. It is the tradition in shorthand. The genealogy also communicates that the Chronicler's story is a story about community. The genealogy represents all Israel. Even the attention to David is one that takes in the larger community and shows David to be a public, community figure rather than the private individual who is found in the books of Samuel.

There may be more than one conflict and more than one climax. Longer stories are characteristically plotted this way. The story of David and Saul in 1 Samuel includes a whole series of episodes in which Saul seeks to kill David or have him killed. After David's victory over Goliath, Saul becomes angry at the praise David receives from the welcoming women. Under the malignant influence of God's spirit he hurls a spear at him but misses (18: 6–11). Saul removes him from the court and makes him a field commander, no doubt hoping for him to be killed in battle. To Saul's frustration David becomes a great success (18: 12–16). Saul then attempts to snare him by offering him his daughter in marriage at the price of a hundred Philistine foreskins, again without success, so that David ends up marrying Michal (18: 17–29). Afterwards equilibrium appears to be established through the efforts of Jonathan, acting as a go-between, but is destroyed once more by YHWH's evil spirit prompting Saul for a second time to try to spear David (19: 1–10). At this point David flees from court, starting a new series of pursuits and escapes which only reach a resolution in chapter 26 with Saul publicly acknowledging that he has done David wrong, urging him to return, and concluding, 'Blessed be you, my son David. You will do many things and will succeed in them' (26: 25). Yet even here the reader may feel cheated of a truly final resolution since, as the verse brings the scene to a close, it makes abundantly clear that (like Esau and Jacob in Genesis 33), despite the pacific words, a deep division still lies between the two men: 'And David went his way, and Saul returned to his place.'

With Saul's death on Mount Gilboa in battle against the Philistines (1 Samuel 31) a reader may suppose that this conflict is finally brought to a close. Even beyond that point, however, the shadow of Saul hangs over David. We may see it, for example, as he wages war against the northerners who support Saul's son, Ishbosheth (2 Sam. 2: 8–5: 3), as he is the butt of Michal's bitter scorn (6: 16–23), as he seeks to take care (or is it custody?) of Saul's descendant, Mephibosheth (2 Samuel 9; see also 16: 1–4, 19: 24–30), as he confronts the hostile Saulide, Shimei, who curses him on his retreat from Jerusalem in the face of Absalom's rebellion (16: 5–13; even that rebellion reminds us of Jonathan's siding with David against his own father), and, finally, after he has defeated Absalom, as he faces further rebellion by the northerners who had earlier supported the house of Saul (19: 41–20: 22). In other words, the conflict established near the story's beginning governs numerous points of tension and climax in a narrative encompassing a large part of the two books of Samuel.

Reading for the ending

Recent theoretical work on plot has drawn an analogy between readers' experience of this classic plot pattern and Freud's pleasure principle. The implication of this model is that plots, and the reading of plots, are goal-oriented: we read to get to the end because the end will make sense of what has gone before. 'The reader proceeds forward under the thrust of expectation to the conclusion which provides a vantage point from which the story is seen as a whole' (Ricoeur 1975: 44 ¶C). The end represents meaning, fulfilment, completion, and closure.

When we are reading a Bible story for the first time, the obsession with the end is often operative. The unfulfilled desire in the story's beginning creates desire in the reader. We want to know how order will come from disorder, completeness from incompleteness, and the further we become immersed in the conflict, the obstacles to resolution, the more captured we are by our desire to know how it will all end. The end, we trust, will not only bring resolution to the story's action, but also resolution to the reading process—for the end offers us a 'promise to bestow meaning and significance on the beginning and the middle' (Brooks 1985: 19 ¶A).

The idea that endings will bring resolution and will clarify all that has come before is, however, too simplistic. Plot endings, whether signalled by a closing formula or by the fact that the words on the page simply stop, do not always make sense. Genesis–2 Kings, for instance, ends with Jehoiachin, king of Judah, in exile, but sitting daily at the Babylonian king's table. Certainly the end tells us that the entire story has been pointing to the possibility, perhaps the inevitability, of the nation's exile. The image of the Judaean king (of the line of David) dining at the foreign king's table, however, is an ambiguous one. Does his political servitude spell a pessimistic ending? Or does his release from prison and his receipt of a regular allowance indicate hope for the nation?

Some endings, like that of the book of Jonah, bring no closure at all. As YHWH's final speech ends in a question—'Should I not be concerned about Nineveh, that great city, in which there are more than a hundred and twenty thousand people who do not know their right hand from their left, and also many cattle?'—so the reader, too, finishes the story with questions. First and foremost, What is the point of the ending? Of course YHWH should be concerned, but what happens to Nineveh? And what happens to Jonah? And what does our knowledge of the eventual destruction of Nineveh tell us about this final revelation of God's concern?

Some endings provide resolution, but the resolution may be hardly satisfactory. The book of Job, for instance, has a tidy ending in which God replaces all that Job has lost. He is given health, new wealth, and even a new batch of children. The resolution may strike many of us as absurd—its very neatness going against our sense of reality—and it offers us very little with which to make sense of what has gone before. God may have 'restored' Job, but the divine sense of justice and balance in this ending is not one that brings every reader much comfort.

Familiarity

While a drive toward the ending may capture the nature of some of our reading experiences, it far from captures the nature of all. People who read to pass the time may be by no means anxious to reach the end of a story. In fact many readers feel a certain sadness when they have finished a good story. It is as though they have lost a companion. Some people, too, are much happier in the midst of ambiguity and uncertainty, in the process of discovering meaning, than they are in having the final answers, knowing for sure how it all turns out. Then there is the problem of familiarity. What if we have read the story before?

Scholars have often praised the story of Abraham's attempt to sacrifice his son Isaac as a masterpiece of suspense. From the beginning of the story, when God calls Abraham to offer up his son, we are left wondering what Abraham will do. The tension gradually mounts as we see him prepare for and take the journey, guide his son up the designated mountain, build an altar, and bind his son upon it. Then, at the last minute, when he lifts the knife to kill his son, a voice from heaven stays his hand and the boy is saved. If the story is new to you, the building of suspense can have a powerful effect, but what if you have heard the story before? You can hardly be pulled by a desire to know what you already know.

Reading for the plot is more complicated than simply being pulled toward an unknown end. Perhaps the fascination of reading lies in the journey, not the destination, even if it is a journey we have made before. Knowing the end merely throws us back to reconsider the significance of the beginning and middle. Hopefully, with each rereading we discover something we did not notice before and we find ourselves constantly re-evaluating how beginnings, middles, and ends relate.

For those who love biblical literature, reading a biblical story is not a one-time event. Rather, it is a relationship renewed and revitalized each time we open the text. Some of us reread the Bible because it represents some sort of authority for us, however that authority might be construed. But at the least, we reread biblical stories because we see something of our own stories in them. As we gain new perspectives on the Bible, we gain new perspectives on ourselves. And often we do not have to wait until the end to acquire these new insights.

Even biblical narrators understand the power of familiarity. Within the larger narrative of Israel (Genesis–2 Kings), some stories, like musical themes, echo again and again, each time with a slight variation, but each time recognizable.

Repeated stories remind us that neither plot nor the reading of plot is always linear. Plots do not always move neatly from problem to complication to resolution. They are not always oriented toward some final goal. Meaning is not always the product of cause and effect or of chronological ordering. Meaning sometimes emerges through association—and association is often in the eye of the beholder. Like a needle returning to pick up thread, a plot can loop around and reconnect, stitching intricate patterns of meaning. The reader, attentive to similar colours and textures, may be able to see the larger design.

In Genesis 26 Isaac goes to Gerar in Philistia and lives there. There follows a familiar story:

When the men of the place asked him about his wife, he said, 'She is my sister'; for he feared to say, 'my wife', thinking, 'lest the men of the place should kill me on account of Rebekah because she is attractive.' (Gen. 26: 7)

After a while, Abimelech, king of the Philistines, sees Isaac 'fondling' (a word-play on Isaac's name) Rebekah, and remonstrates with him:

'Look here, she is your wife; how could you say, "She is my sister"?' Isaac said to him, 'Because I thought, "Lest I die on account of her".'

(Gen. 26: 9)

Abimelech protests that this deception could have caused one of his people to commit sin unknowingly and warns all his people against touching either Isaac or Rebekah. Subsequently Isaac is blessed by YHWH and becomes very wealthy from his farming at Gerar, so much so that Abimelech presses him to go away. At first he camps in the valley of Gerar, only to have his herdsmen and those of Gerar quarrel over some wells. But eventually he digs a well 'over which they did not quarrel', and so names the place Rehoboth (meaning 'Room', for, as he says, 'now YHWH has made room for us . . .'). Finally, having moved on to yet another place, he receives there a peaceful delegation from Abimelech and his chief advisers and makes a covenant with them. The narrator concludes by recounting how that very day his servants discover another well and come to tell him, 'We have found water' (26: 32). Hence the name of that place is 'to this day' Beer ('well of')-Sheba.

The story has no immediate connection with the preceding incident involving Jacob and Esau's birthright (Gen. 25: 27–34). Nor does it flow into the next episode, which reverts to the rivalry between the brothers (Gen. 26: 34–28: 9). Its significance does not lie in its linear placement.

Yet, when we look back over the larger expanse of narrative through which we have been travelling, we recognize the story. We can see Isaac playing out the same role in the same plot as his father Abraham in Egypt and Gerar (chs. 12 and 20). The text provides us with any number of indicators to those earlier stories. It starts, like the account of Abram in Genesis 12, with the same situation: 'Now there was a famine in the land' (12: 10, 26: 1). It tells of YHWH appearing and urging him not to go down to Egypt—as Abram had done—but to stay in the land and be the recipient of the promise of blessing made to Abraham (12: 1–3; 26: 2–5). It uses a similar phrase to explain why Isaac claims that his wife is his sister—he feared for his safety because she was good-looking (12: 11–14; 20: 2, 11–13; 26: 7, 9). So, too, the language relating the king's aggrieved response on discovery of the truth (26: 10) is but an echo of what has been said before, first by the Pharaoh of Egypt (12: 18–19) and then by King Abimelech of Gerar (20: 9–10). In turn, we are reminded explicitly that some of the wells Isaac dug in the valley of Gerar were first dug by Abraham (26: 15, 18). Furthermore, the covenant between patriarch and Philistines is implicitly reminiscent of Abraham's earlier covenant at Beersheba with Abimelech who is both times accompanied by Phicol, his army commander (21: 34; 26: 26–31).

Isaac's story of trickery and self-preservation at the expense of his wife firmly ensconces him as Abram's own son. On the other hand, we also see him, like his father, coming to know the political and financial benefit of peaceful, covenanted, coexistence. Later on, as we encounter deception and strife amongst Isaac's own sons, we may recognize these elements of conflict from their father's story and be hardly surprised to encounter them again. We may also wonder whether his sons, too, might see the possibilities of covenanted reconciliation. In such terms we watch as Jacob cheats his brother of his father's blessing, as he struggles with Laban to gain wealth and a wife (an ironic contrast, since Isaac, like his father, tried to lose his), and as he makes uneasy but necessary covenants with family members who are to become foreigners (Esau = Edomite; Laban = Aramean).

In other words, the reader, seeking order among these plots, is discovering associations among them and making retrospective connections. Thus the perceived repetitions begin to create a sense of design to what otherwise might be considered random, indeed rambling, stories. Each generation, at least to some extent, relives the plot of its predecessor. The larger story of the family is not simply linear, but frequently coils around to pick up bits of the past—failures as well as successes. Every generation essentially provides the same kind of 'stuff' from which God is to build a 'great nation'. Yet there is always variation—as the 'wife–sister' story makes clear—and always possibilities for change and movement into a new story. And with each new story and each new generation we look for the character and the event that will fulfil God's desire for relationship and blessing for the world.

Repeated plots are, of course, not always so obviously similar. The same sorts of events may take place, but the cast of characters or the setting may differ. As we have seen above, associated plots often reveal character. Sometimes, however, the repetition of similar plots works to construct a theme. The first biblical plot in which human beings have a significant role (Gen. 2: 4–3: 24) is one that involves family division. When the first couple eat from the tree of the knowledge of good and evil they become, not divine as the serpent had promised, but truly human. True humanity from that point on is characterized by an alienation from other humans, from the natural world, and from God. There is, from this point on, a distrust of difference and a self-consciousness that elevates a concern for self-preservation beyond any other obligations. The result and manifestation of the primeval divisions in the Garden ('original sin'?) is family division, a division which in the larger story continually subverts the 'great nation' that YHWH has in mind. The original human drive toward unity ('the two become one flesh') is overpowered by the force of fission.

Consequently, just as we see in the Garden the man, in a desperate effort to protect himself, lay responsibility on the woman, so we continue to see Abraham and Isaac abandoning their women in similar acts of self-protection. Furthermore, the fraternal conflict between Cain and Abel that follows the eviction from Eden in Genesis 4 finds its voice more than once in the larger story of Israel. Isaac and Ishmael, Jacob and Esau, Joseph and his brothers all vie for favour and blessing. Abimelech and his brothers, Jephthah and his brothers, Absalom and Amnon, Solomon and Adonijah fight and kill over matters of honour and place in the family. So, too, the tribes compete with each other for pride of place or 'line of battle' honours, or for any number of other reasons: Deborah and Barak castigate Gilead and other tribes for not joining the fight against Jabin, king of Hazor; the Ephraimites abuse Gideon for not summoning them to battle; Gideon flays the elders of Succoth and slays the men of Penuel; the men of Gilead slaughter the men of Ephraim at the Jordan; David's nation is split by civil war; at the war's end, the men of Israel split with the men of Judah to follow Sheba ben Bichri; at the end of Solomon's reign north splits with south, permanently. Nor does the fighting stop until the northern kingdom is destroyed and there is no tribe left to fight but Judah. Repeated competition, hostility, violence, and even expulsion haunt the story of this 'great nation'. The family that is to bring blessing to the other families of the earth is a family that is too busy grasping for its own blessing to be of benefit to others.

Shifting boundaries

Familiarity is a problem that biblical literature poses not only for recent plot theory. While literary theorists since Aristotle have spoken confidently of beginnings, middles, and ends, biblical stories often have shifting boundaries. It is easy enough to determine what marks the beginning or the ending of narratives like the books of Ruth, Esther, or Jonah. But what if we are reading in Genesis or Samuel? Often one story's end is another's beginning or a whole story is but a larger story's middle. This complication stems from the fact that many biblical narratives are constructed from a number of seemingly separate plots, a feature which has often led scholars to postulate the presence of originally independent sources.

Irrespective of their origins, however, these plots, while having their own beginnings, middles, and ends, may also be seen as sub-plots or episodes within a larger plot. Thus the stories of Abram and Sarai in Egypt (Genesis 12), Sarai and Hagar (Genesis 16 and 21), or the wooing of Rebekah (Genesis 24) can be read in and of themselves or as episodes within the larger story of promised land and nationhood. Within the family story of Jacob (see Genesis 37: 2), Genesis 38, as we have seen, offers us a complete 'plotting' of Tamar's dealings with Judah. In the wider view of things, however, the story becomes a sub-plot within a larger plot which deals primarily with Joseph but where, in the fraternal struggle for ascendancy, Judah also plays a prominent role.

Defining the boundary of a single narrative is as much a product of the reader's desire for reconstruction as it is the product of the narrator's art. Where the story begins and ends will drastically affect what the story can mean. Biblical literature's natural fluidity means that narrative boundaries are constantly shifting and the reader is challenged to reinterpret accordingly.

For example, the story of the succession to David in 1 Kings 1–2 can be viewed as a self-contained plot. The exposition establishes that the king is old and senile and that the oldest son, Adonijah, desires and expects to succeed to the throne. Conflict materializes in a rival party backing Solomon, and a climax is reached when Nathan and Bathsheba make a successful pre-emptive strike on Solomon's behalf. The king yields the throne to the younger son. Resolution follows in stages with the king's death and the eventual execution of Adonijah.

One might just as easily understand this plot to be but the concluding episode in the larger plot of David's story (starting at least at 1 Samuel 16). In that case the significance of the story shifts from Israel's need for a new king and Adonijah's failed ambition to one last example of violence and division in David's house, the lingering prophecy of Nathan finally satisfied.

On the other hand, one might also see this as the introduction to Solomon's story, an episode that contrasts Solomon's sudden gain of power with his father's careful and ambitious procuring of kingship, and that forecasts a ruler who will eliminate anyone who poses a threat.

Plots and points of view: Judges 10–12

There is another common reason why plots are not simple matters of situation, complication, and resolution. Because most stories involve more than one character, it is not uncommon to see several desires, often in conflict, working themselves out. There may be several climaxes and several resolutions. How we see the plot structured may depend upon which character's point of view we perceive to be predominant in the narrative as a whole or, alternatively, which point of view, dominant or not, we bring into focus. The story of Jephthah and his daughter well illustrates the complexity.

We might begin the story in Judges 10: 6 where we are told that the people of Israel again did what was evil in the sight of YHWH, worshipping foreign gods and abandoning the god of Israel. The word 'again' alerts us to the fact that beginning the story at this point might be a rather arbitrary decision, because even though what follows can be read as a self-contained story, the word 'again' solidly connects this story to what has gone before. Choosing to read this story as an individual story rather than as a small episode in the whole Judges narrative could very well affect what meanings we see emerging.

YHWH's anger is kindled against Israel so that the people are sold into the hands of the Ammonites who oppress them cruelly for eighteen years. The Israelites cry to YHWH confessing their sin of apostasy, but the divinity is not so easily persuaded. 'I have delivered you from your enemies over and over again, yet you have abandoned me and worshipped other gods. I will deliver you no more. Go and cry to the gods you have chosen. Let them deliver you in your time of distress.' The Israelites are insistent: 'We have sinned. Do to us whatever seems good to you, only deliver us this time!' They put away their foreign gods and worship the god of Israel again. YHWH's response to this is ambiguous. The NRSV says that YHWH 'could no longer bear to see Israel suffer'. The Hebrew is much more enigmatic. It says something like 'YHWH grew short [or impatient] with Israel's troublings'.

This can mean either that YHWH grew impatient with those who were troubling Israel or that YHWH grew impatient with the troubler Israel. The second reading makes more sense if we see this story as part of the middle of a much larger story. Throughout the book of Judges we can see the same kind of behaviour from the Israelites. One could easily imagine Israel's god growing tired of Israel's fickleness. If, however, we see the story beginning here in Judges 10, the divinity's impatience is rather surprising and it is much easier to read YHWH as ready to come to the rescue.

The situation with the Ammonites comes to a head with the Ammonite army gathering to fight at Gilead and the Israelites attempting to muster forces at Mizpah. The people of Gilead, since they are in closest proximity to the enemy, are obviously the most threatened. They begin to cast about for a leader. 'Whoever will begin the fight against the Ammonites', they promise, 'shall be head over all the inhabitants of Gilead.'

Thus chapter 10 ends. Judges 11 begins with information about a particularly able fighter named Jephthah. Many people would like to begin the story here, thus making the background information about

Jephthah the exposition of the narrative. If, however, the reader understands the beginning of the story to fall elsewhere, whether in chapter 10 or Judges 1, this information is but the narrator's aside.

Jephthah the Gileadite is an able warrior, but he is the son of a prostitute. His father, the narrator tells us, is Gilead, which is an ingenious way of saying his father is anybody's guess—he could have been any man in the town or tribal area of Gilead. His fellow men of Gilead, who are, under the circumstances, all potentially his brothers, drive him away because he is illegitimate. He leaves Gilead and becomes the leader of a band of 'empty men' like himself.

When the Ammonites make war on the Israelites, the elders of Gilead seek to bring Jephthah home. 'Come be our commander', they urge him, 'that we may fight against the Ammonites.' Jephthah's response is what we might expect: 'Are you not the very ones who rejected me and drove me out of my father's house? So why do you come to me now when you are in trouble?' Jephthah's attitude is much the same as God's had been in the exposition, and indeed his speech encourages the reader to see the similarity between the two events. Just as the Israelites had rejected God only to call upon God again when they were in dire straits, so, too, the people of Gilead had rejected Jephthah only to summon him back when it was deemed convenient. The elders of Gilead, like the Israelites before them, are persistent. 'Nevertheless', they say, 'we have now turned back to you, so that you may go with us and fight with the Ammonites, and become head over us, over all the inhabitants of Gilead.' Jephthah, unlike God in the exposition, is willing to negotiate. 'If you bring me home again to fight with the Ammonites, and YHWH gives them over to me, I will be your head.'

Thus the two parties strike a deal that suits their individual desires. The elders of Gilead, knowing that Jephthah is a rough and ready warrior, now have as their leader a man who knows how to fight. He is a man who is also, from their point of view, expendable. In the event that Jephthah falls in battle, there would be no great loss to the community. In fact, if he has done his job in defeating the Ammonites, his death in battle would be a great relief since they would not have to deal with him as a permanent political leader. The reader may be justified in wondering if the elders ever really intend to allow Jephthah to remain their leader once the war is over.

For Jephthah, the deal struck is one that, in his point of view, reinvests him with a sense of worth. There is something he can do better than anyone else, and he is in much demand because of that. Furthermore, he is not only being accepted by those who once rejected him, he is able to rub their noses in their past mistake. He has made them beg. They had first offered him the command of the army; he holds out until they offer him leadership of the entire community.

Jephthah takes over his command immediately. He sends messengers to the king of Ammon in an attempt to negotiate a settlement. The Ammonites claim that they are fighting over a piece of land that, upon their entry into Canaan, the Israelites had taken from them. Jephthah responds with a different story. The territory had not, at that time, belonged to the Ammonites but to the Amorites, and the God of Israel had told the Israelites that they could have it. At this point, Jephthah commits a diplomatic *faux pas*. In his rhetoric to defend Israel's taking of the land, he asks Ammon 'Would you not possess what Chemosh your god gives you to possess?' Chemosh is not the name of the Ammonite god, but that of the Moabite god. Jephthah goes on to compare Ammon and Moab, totally confusing his history. 'Are you any better than King Balak of Moab?' he asks. 'Did he ever enter into conflict with Israel, or did he ever go to war with them?' In actuality, Balak had tried; he just had not been successful. And since then Moab had been at odds with Israel, as the story of Ehud in Judges 3 attests. The Ammonites, understandably, are not impressed with Jephthah's rhetoric. They no doubt realize that they are dealing with an uneducated man.

As Jephthah prepares himself for battle, the spirit of YHWH comes upon him—the first clear sign that God supports his efforts. Jephthah, however, is either not content with or is unsure of the significance of this divine token and, being eager for glory and acceptance, he makes a vow to God to insure his victory. 'If you will give the Ammonites into my hand, then whoever [or whatever] comes out of the doors of my house to meet me when I return victorious shall be YHWH's, to be offered up by me as a burnt offering.' We are not told if the vow was made publicly or privately, though it would be easy to see (and indeed we have evidence from the later Saul story) how such a religious gesture could imbue the troops with confidence and zeal. We are also not told explicitly where Jephthah makes this vow, though the text leads us to assume that Jephthah made it in his home town of Mizpah.

Jephthah goes into battle and, with the help of YHWH, inflicts a massive defeat on the Ammonites. If Israel's oppression by the Ammonites is, for the reader, the problem that has initiated the plot, then this plot has reached a climax and a resolution. If we understand Jephthah's expulsion from Gilead to be the initial problem, then here, too, we might locate the climactic point of the story at this turn of poetic justice.

The story, however, does not end here. Jephthah returns to his home in Mizpah, and who comes forth from his house to greet him with timbrels and dancing, but his only daughter. She is the one to fall under the curse of her father's vow. And as if to ensure our sympathy the narrator emphasizes that she was his only child; besides her he had no other son or daughter. When he sees her, he tears his clothes and says, 'Alas, my daughter, you have brought me very low. You have become one of my troublers. I have opened my mouth to YHWH and I cannot take back my vow.' If the primary plot is, for us, the story of a Jephthah who was abused as a child and who grew up deprived of family and community, then this moment functions as the climax of a tragic plot. The cycle of loss and abuse has come full circle when he comes to the realization that he, by his own hand, will destroy what little family he has.

The daughter takes the news calmly. In fact she seems to know already the content of the vow. 'My father, you have opened your mouth to YHWH. Do to me according to what has gone out of your mouth. After all, YHWH has given you vengeance against your enemies.' While some assume that she stumbles unwittingly into her father's vow, it is just as likely that she had heard her father make the vow in Mizpah (Fewell 1992 ¶M). While Jephthah may have thought the public vow would have warned his daughter not to appear first, she perhaps took it upon herself to make sure that no one else would fall victim to her father's reckless oath. Perhaps this was her way of showing her father how thoughtless and cruel such a vow could be. If so, she does indeed become one of her father's troublers. She becomes his judge, and the sentence is a bitter one.

She does, in the same speech, request a temporary reprieve which not only shows her, as a negotiator, to be her father's daughter but also reveals that she, upon setting foot out of the house, knew her fate. She asks to go away for two months to grieve with her female companions. This, too, is a judgement upon her father. She opts to spend her remaining days, not with the father who is obsessed with status and glory and violence, but with other young women who will be with her, who will grieve her fate, and who will, in the end, remember her. It is as though, for a brief moment, the daughter's plot usurps the father's. If our sympathies lie with her fate or our admiration with her courage, then we might see the climax of the story culminating with her decision to step forth from the house or, if we see her as an unwitting victim, we might identify the climax with her acceptance of her father's vow.

For her the resolution is a swift one. When she returns from the mountains to her father, he does to her what he had vowed to do. Not even the narrator seems able to articulate the horrible nature of the event. For the narrator, that is the end of her tragic story. The women, however, do not forget. A tradition is born. For four days every year the women of Israel, young and old, would go out to recount the story of the daughter of Jephthah.

The story has yet another episode (ch. 12) that apparently takes place while the daughter is away with her companions. The Ephraimites rise up against Jephthah because, they claim, they were not included in the battle against the Ammonites. Since the Ephraimites were hardly likely to have waited two months before bringing this complaint, we must conclude that this episode is a flashback of sorts. The Ephraimites threaten to destroy Jephthah's house, and though they are referring to his dwelling place, the double-edged word 'house' carries with it a certain irony. Jephthah has, through his vow, already destroyed his house.

Jephthah responds with the claim that he did call the Ephraimites, but they did not come. 'When I saw that you would not deliver me', he says, 'I took my life in my hand, and crossed over against the Ammonites, and YHWH gave them into my hand.' Jephthah's defence carries yet another irony. In the end it was not his life that he took in his hand, but the life of his daughter. Jephthah waits for no further talk, but rallies the Gileadites to fight with Ephraim. The men of Gilead defeat the Ephraimites because, the narrator reports, the Ephraimites had called them 'fugitives from Ephraim'. And here we have another story of rejection that ends in violence.

The Gileadites take the Jordan River and when any of the deserters from the Ephraimite army come to cross back into their territory, the men of Gilead ask them if they are Ephraimites. They, of course, say no, but they are required to submit to a test. 'Shibboleth' is the pass-word, but the Ephraimites pronounce it Sibboleth and thus expose their identity. The remaining Ephraimites are picked off one by one. Forty-two thousand Ephraimites die.

The end of this story shows Jephthah trapped by his ambitious words. Despite their intensity and impact on the story world, Jephthah's words throughout the story never quite produce the desired effect. On the contrary, his long 'diplomatic' speech to the Ammonites (11: 14–27) is not heeded (11: 28) and in fact produces an effect opposite to its ostensible purpose. His vow (11: 30–1) grants him victory, but costs him the life of his only child. In this final episode involving Jephthah's conflict with the Ephraimites (12: 1–6), the test of pronunciation (*sibboleth* versus *shibboleth*) throws further into relief the power of language to shape the world. Here a single word, not unlike Jephthah's vow, becomes a matter of life or death. Just as his vow led to the destruction of his own family, here his words lead to the destruction of fellow Israelites.

And for all Jephthah's desire to have a family and to occupy a prominent place in the community, he dies soon after, bereft of family, and is buried in the same obscurity in which he was born. 'Jephthah judged Israel six years. Then Jephthah the Gileadite died, and was buried [somewhere] in the cities of Gilead.' His story comes full circle. (And in a final irony the narrator observes briefly of the next judge, Izban of Bethlehem: 'He had thirty sons; and thirty daughters he gave in marriage outside his clan, and thirty daughters he brought in from outside for his sons'; Judg. 12: 8.)

In this story the desires of Israel, Jephthah, the daughter, and God have all been intertwined. Israel's dilemma is satisfactorily resolved, at least for the time being. But how crucial is that to the reader? How involved are we in Israel's struggle, if we have watched Israel time and again bring trouble on themselves by 'doing evil in the sight of YHWH'?

So, too, our involvement with Jephthah probably depends upon several factors. How far do we allow our understanding of his origins to temper with sympathy our view of his later actions? Given his background of rejection and abuse, some might see his craving for acceptance as poignant and his vow, accordingly, as more desperate and tragic. His desire for poetic justice may or may not appeal to us. In part that will depend upon whether or not we are aware of and angry about the hypocrisy of the male society that begets him by a prostitute and then, because he is a prostitute's son, casts him out. How we perceive his motivation will also affect our emotional involvement. Is he driven by insecurity? Does he crave power? Does he want revenge? Will he do anything to get what he wants? Our attachment as readers may be determined by how we answer those questions.

In turn, when the daughter's plot subverts and takes over her father's story, we may find that our emotional involvement in her predicament alters our engagement with Jephthah. Her innocence may help the reader form a picture of the innocence of a younger Jephthah and so be more sympathetic to him. Alternatively, her innocence may cause the reader to resent Jephthah's ambition and the vow it has driven him to make. As for the daughter, if we see her as an unwitting victim motivated by her desire to please her father, we may lament her lack of control, we may admire or condemn her submissiveness, or we may respect her attempt to make the best out of her situation. If we see her as a decisive agent, one who chooses to be the object of her father's vow rather than let someone else be destroyed, we may honour her courage and her vision that stands so diametrically opposed to her father's. In either case we may be caught between our hope for her survival and our fear that her fate has been settled by a patriarchal system and a limited religious world-view over which she has no control (Fewell 1992 ¶M).

And what about Yʜᴡʜ's desire? Israel's god so quickly slips from sight in this story, that it is rather difficult to stay involved in the divine predicament. God desires recognition. The divine complaint at the beginning is that the people worship the wrong gods; they do not recognize the true deliverer of Israel. Yʜᴡʜ's plot seems to have no climax and no resolution. Yʜᴡʜ is not consulted when the crucial decisions have to be made. Rather the god of Israel is called on when it is a matter of convenience—when a battle has to be won or authority has to be claimed. By the end of the story, Yʜᴡʜ is forgotten again.

Fracturing the plot: the codas to Judges and Samuel

God's plot in Judges 10–12 could be the plot of the book of Judges in microcosm. At the end of Judges, too, YHWH is hardly in evidence, consulted only as a matter of convenience when the crucial decisions have already been made. With the end of Samson's story the familiar plot pattern—Israel turns from YHWH; Israel's god brings oppression on Israel; Israel seeks deliverance; a saviour defeats the oppressor—has completely disappeared. Instead we find a collection of narratives that scholars have often called a 'supplement' and viewed as a later addition to the book proper (Judges 17–21). Yet with the final shattering of the pattern that has held together, however tenuously, the component stories in a larger story, the book comes to a fitting end—though it is hardly a resolution.

Like the plot, the very nation is shattered. The story that began with God telling Judah to go first against the Canaanites to take possession of the promised land (Judg. 1: 1–3) ends ironically with God, asked only as an afterthought, telling Judah to go first to fight Benjamin—and be defeated (Judg. 20: 18–21)! Holy war against Canaanites gives way to the slaughter of Laish, 'a people quiet and unsuspecting' (Judg. 18: 27–31); tribal co-operation to possess the promised land (Judg. 1: 1–3) turns to tribal alliance to engage in civil war and the mass rape of Israelite women by Israelite men (Judges 20). Achsah's arrival on an ass to ask for a life-giving gift from her father (Judg. 1: 11–15) is cruelly parodied in the story of the Levite's woman who is raped to death (perhaps), dumped on an ass and taken home to be divided limb by limb and sent out as a message for war. The story that begins with divine concern about false gods (Judges 2) ends with Micah resolved that his security is ensured because he has graven and molten images (made from stolen silver and 'consecrated' to YHWH!), a private shrine, and his son as a priest. When an actual Levite comes along and can be hired, Micah knows he has it made: 'Now I know that YHWH will make things good for me, because I have a Levite for priest!' (Judg. 17: 13). When read with an eye to the ironies of these actions and attitudes, the 'supplement' becomes more like a 'coda' or 'epilogue', intimately connected with the preceding plot yet distinct from it.

Punctuating these final chapters (like a refrain) is the narrator's comment: 'In those days there was no king in Israel; every man did what was right in his own eyes' (Judg. 17: 6; 18: 1; 19: 1; 21: 25). As noted above (Chapter 3), whereas some interpreters take this to be a strong word in favour of the monarchy, we might do better to think of it, like the rest of the coda, as ironic in tone—directed precisely against those who might imagine that a king could solve people's propensity for apostasy and violence. And later, in view of YHWH's comment to Samuel (1 Sam. 8: 7) that the people had rejected him, YHWH, from being king over them, we might look back at the Judges coda and consider that there was, indeed, 'no king in Israel' in those chaotic events. YHWH might as well not have existed.

Another so-called 'supplement' is found at the end of the books of Samuel. Like Judges 17–21, 2 Samuel 21–4 may be thought of as a coda which invites the reader to reflect on what has preceded and to discover thematic and often ironic associations. What can look like a random collection of fragments can also be seen as a subtle disruption of any tendency the reader may have to read David's story triumphally. With the suppression of Absalom's rebellion and the separatist Sheba ben Bichri assassinated, the plot of Samuel, seen from David's point of view, appears to have come to a resolution. His kingship and kingdom are secure. The coda provokes reconsideration of what plot we have been following and what we have learned of David.

Though no longer continuing in chronological fashion the central plot line of YHWH's gift of the kingship to David, 2 Samuel 21–4 draws some of its characters from previous parts of David's story, and in this and other ways is closely linked to the preceding episodes in David's life. It soon becomes clear that the events recounted do not all occur in sequence after the events of chapter 20—the section encompasses the whole of David's life.

The first episode (21: 1–14) deals with Rizpah and the sons of Saul. In response to a long famine David consults the divine oracle ('sought the face of YHWH'; 21: 1) and receives what is to the reader a puzzling response: there is 'blood-guilt' on the house of Saul 'because he put to death the Gibeonites' (v. 2). We know nothing of such an event. The narrator, however, hastens to explain, reminding us of the story of the Amorite (Canaanite) Gibeonites' covenant with the Israelites (Joshua 9), and informing us that Saul had indeed attempted, 'in his zeal for the people of Israel and Judah' (v. 2), to wipe out the Gibeonites—plainly without success. Ironically, in seeking to implement what the Israelites had originally been commanded, Saul now stands condemned for violating their subsequent oath, made through deception.

A moment's reflection reveals the issues of 'guilt' and justice here to be highly complex. When does one covenant (or promise or commandment) override another? For how long must 'blood-guilt' haunt a house? If Saul's house has blood on its hands, what of David's?

David's response is to allow the Gibeonites to name their compensation. Their request, obliquely, is for blood (v. 4). The king takes them up with alacrity: 'What are you saying [exactly]? I will do it' (v. 4). So seven sons of Saul are given into the hands of the Gibeonites for execution, and, once again, conveniently for David, the house of Saul is reduced, and the blame laid at another's door (cf. 1 Samuel 31; 2 Samuel 1–4).

The story is troubling. Does the oracle require the deaths of the sons or does David only get from it the answer that he wants in the first place? (We see something similar, perhaps, in Judg. 20: 18–28 in the civil war following the murder of the Levite's woman.) It is the Gibeonites, not the oracle, who determine that only blood will compensate for blood, and David who encourages them in their demand.

Against Gibeonites and David—and YHWH?—is set Rizpah. Against blood-guilt that traverses generations and swallows up the innocent is set a mother's care. Rizpah's loyalty traverses death as she fends off from her dead kin the ravening wildlife, the counterpart of the human world that consigned the sons to death. Her name captures, with some irony, something of her spirit: she is 'glowing coal', daughter of 'falcon'.

At the beginning of the book Rizpah was the voiceless pawn in a man's quarrel (2 Sam. 3: 6–11). At the end she is still voiceless and still a pawn, as she watches her sons destroyed in another quarrel between other men. Yet she succeeds in exercising power through the only action open to her—her mourning and her defiance of the gratuitous humiliation by exposure that was part of the execution

(Antigone acts in similar fashion in Sophocles' play, *Antigone*). Her action shames David into bringing the bones of Saul and his sons home, into their family tomb, in their own land.

The narrative now breaks off into some anecdotes of the Philistine wars—anecdotes of fights against descendants of giants. First we read of a tiring David rescued by his nephew Abishai—of whom we have earlier heard him exclaim in exasperation, 'What is there between you and me, you sons of Zeruiah?' (16: 10, 19: 22; cf. 3: 39). Among the items that follow, one is startling: Elhanan of Bethlehem slew Goliath of Gath, 'the shaft of whose spear was like a weaver's beam' (21: 19). That is exactly how the Goliath whom David slew is described in 1 Sam. 17: 7. So who did slay Goliath?

The narrative of 2 Samuel invites a reader to question characters' actions, to probe behind their speech, and to find so often that what appears is not what it seems to be. Now it seems that even the narrator may not have all the 'facts' of the plot reliably arrayed. Perhaps the 'truth' of the narrative lies beyond the mere ordering of 'facts.' Meaning is found when what is important to the reader and what seems important in the text interact. The narrator reminds us here that this is not a 'story brought live' but a story of life woven out of many strands of information and many perceptions of value. There will be many times when we cannot make it all 'fit'.

The song in chapter 22 is found also in the Psalter as Psalm 18, with small variations. Its position here at the end of the books of Samuel links it to the song of Hannah at the beginning (1 Sam. 1: 1–10), which is also in psalm form. Hannah's song not only reflects her own situation but foreshadows the subsequent plot about kingship; it ends with the expectation that YHWH 'will give strength to his king, and raise the horn [i.e. exalt the power] of his anointed' (1 Sam. 2: 10). David's song is related to a specific occasion ('on the day when . . .') though in fact it celebrates occasions of deliverance throughout his life, including escape from Saul. It, too, reaches its climax with 'YHWH's anointed', now specified as David himself (2 Sam. 22: 51).

The opening imagery of YHWH as rock (vv. 2–3; cf. vv. 32, 47) is apt for one who found refuge at the Rock of Escape (1 Sam. 23: 24–9). The psalmist then recalls his cry in his distress, his enemies like waves sweeping over him, and the coming of YHWH in lightning, thunder, and clouds of a storm (vv. 4–20). In the central section (vv. 21–8) the psalmist reflects on his own righteousness, the reason, as he sees it, for his reward. The focus then shifts back to God but in order to speak of what the psalmist can do through God's support (vv. 29–51). As noted, it comes to rest on David and his descendants (v. 51).

Distress, theophany, and rescue are described in graphic terms. Participants, emotions, situations, actions—all is heightened into extremes. So, too, are the protestations of righteousness and achievement. In the psalter, in the context of much similar poetry, this characteristic might slip by the reader unnoticed. In the present prose context it may well stop the reader short: 'I was blameless before [YHWH],' proclaims David, 'and I kept myself from guilt' (v. 24). One effect of this lengthy self-adulation, therefore, is to proclaim not righteousness but self-righteousness, not piety but hypocrisy. That is a reading which is hard to resist.

So it is, too, with the 'last words of David' (23: 1–7). As David's (non-levite) sons had become priests, so now the king transforms himself into the divine oracle: 'The spirit of YHWH speaks by me' (23: 2). David speaks of ruling justly and being rewarded for it. 'For a lasting covenant [YHWH] has made with me, ordered in all and secure' (v. 5). These are confident words, yet hedged about with questions: 'For is it not thus, my house, with YHWH? . . . Will he not cause [all my deliverance and desire] to spring forth?' These are rhetorical questions, of course, but they invite scrutiny.

The poem shifts focus to the field (cf. v. 4), to threatening thorns and the 'weapons' of those who root out the forces of chaos (cf. vv. 6–7). The vision is like that of David's psalm (ch. 22). Good arms itself for battle with evil, a David against a Goliath. (But, we might wonder, was it not Goliath who armed himself with iron and the shaft of a spear?) So the poem dissolves into a listing and telling of this weaponry—of the anointed's mighty men and their deeds (vv. 8–39).

In the centre of the chapter is one of those great stories of David (vv. 13–17). In an unguarded moment he buys water at the price of other men's blood. We see the man who commands intense loyalty and who is alert to providence as he refuses to drink the water, pouring it out to YHWH, blood upon the ground. That reminds us of the

David who would not reach out against Saul, YHWH's anointed (1 Samuel 24 and 26), or who turned Abishai's sword back to its sheath when Shimei cursed him and called him a 'man of blood' (16: 5–13; cf. 19: 21–3).

In turn, however, to think of David as a 'man of blood' raises disturbing recollections of other occasions—recollections of the slaughter of the priests of Nob (1 Sam 22: 11–23; especially v. 22), or the murder of Uriah (2 Samuel 11), or the execution of the seven sons of Saul in the story of Rizpah (ch. 21).

In fact the tale of the water of Bethlehem is surrounded by recollections, for the chapter is full of names. As we recognize them we bring the whole story into review. David's psalm speaks only of himself, of his God, and of his righteousness. The lists of mighty men tell a different story. They tell of a house secured by many, with blood and pain and not always with righteousness.

The narrator reminds us of Abishai (v. 18) who, we recall, saved David from the giant (21: 15–17). Within a verse or two (v. 24) another name, Elhanan from David's home town, has resurrected that unsettling anecdote of Elhanan and Goliath (21: 19). Asahel takes us back to the civil war and Joab's killing of Abner (chs. 2–3); Benaiah takes us forward to Solomon's ruthless disposal of Shimei at David's behest (1 Kgs. 2: 36–46)—Shimei of whom the king said, 'You shall not die', and gave him his oath (2 Sam. 19: 23).

The list in verses 24–39 is particularly rich in allusion to the Bathsheba story. Names jump out: Eliam (Bathsheba's father? cf. 11: 3), Nathan, Zobah and the Ammonites (ch. 10), Joab (chs. 10–12). Finally (v. 39) it comes to rest upon none other than Uriah the Hittite! We might hear other oracular words: 'Why have you despised the word of YHWH, doing what is evil in his sight? Uriah the Hittite . . . you have slain with the sword of the Ammonites; so now a lasting sword will not turn aside from your house' (Nathan, in 12: 9–10). Is the psalmist blameless before YHWH? Is his house secure?

David's story has a way of shifting out from under us. It is a story that refuses to be tamed, secured, or neatly ordered.

Finally we come to chapter 24, a short account of a plague that strikes Israel. The plot takes some curious turns. Why YHWH's wrath is kindled against the nation in the first place we are not told, but it is plainly worked out through David. As in the Rizpah story (ch. 21) he appears to be a ready champion of the divine message (again, perhaps, an oracle or a decision by lot, with the questions put by the inquirer). Here it is an instruction to conduct a census. But having taken the census he is struck with guilt, confesses that he has sinned, and asks for forgiveness.

What exactly is wrong with the census is unexpressed, though in the eyes of YHWH (and the prophet Gad) it is perhaps its potential for military aggrandizement at the expense of trust in the power of YHWH. To number the people is to number the army (the same word in Hebrew). A census is a tool for centralizing power; its purpose is usually to raise taxes and an army. David makes no attempt to question the command. Rather, ironically, it is Joab, the power broker at the center of this centralized government, who protests against the action (vv. 3–4). We may be reminded of the early chapters of 1 Samuel and Samuel's speech about the grasping ways of kings, when the people first ask for a king (1 Sam. 8: 10–12). There YHWH, perceiving that he has been rejected by the people, tells Samuel— perhaps ironically, intending to demonstrate kingship's weakness —to give them a king. That decision sets the larger plot of kingship firmly in motion. Its first phase ends much later with Saul, the people's choice, defeated and dead on Mount Gilboa. Here YHWH's anger at the nation issues in a command, again perhaps ironic, to do something that would further entrench the power of the king. David indicts himself by failing to recognize the test until too late. He could have said 'no'. By presenting David with a choice of punishments YHWH again puts the people's fate in the hands of the human king they wanted.

The plot is now at a turning point. Given a choice, David opts for a plague. His reasoning is couched in pious terms: 'Let us fall into the hands of YHWH, for his mercy is great; but let me not fall into human hands' (v. 14). Yet by choosing the plague he eliminates the crucial second option, that he flee three months before his foes— the only option where he is the focus and where the spread of death might be contained. So once more a question hangs over our reading. Is the king who promoted the census unwilling still to relinquish power in the interests of his people? Is he unwilling to return to his roots, houseless, living by his wits, pursued by Saul in the wilderness? Instead he bequeaths on Israel the deaths of seventy thousand people (v. 15).

Here the plot forks, giving us (at least) two endings, so that even the plot ends in ambiguity. The narrator disturbs the temporal sequence of the narration, much as the coda as a whole has done to the larger plot. According to verse 16, as the angel of plague is about to destroy Jerusalem YHWH repents of the evil (reminding us of the book of Jonah, as we shall see) and tells the angel to stay his hand. Then we read of David seeing the destroying angel, confessing his sin again and interceding belatedly with YHWH on behalf of the people: 'These sheep, what have they done? Let your hand be against me and my father's house' (v. 17). God instructs him to build an altar on the threshing-floor of Araunah, which he does in quintessentially Davidic fashion, receiving from Araunah an extraordinarily gracious and generous offer of help and responding with memorable words: 'No, but I will certainly acquire it from you for a price; I will not make burnt offerings to YHWH my God for nothing' (v. 24). He offers burnt offerings and peace offerings. The story ends: 'And YHWH was entreated by/for the country; and the plague was stayed from Israel' (v. 25).

We have several options for constructing a temporal sequence here. We can take verse 16, YHWH's change of heart, as a summary statement preceding a detailed explanation of precisely how that change took place—in response to David's supplication. The final clauses then sum up: so this is why the plague was stopped—YHWH heeded David's offerings. Alternatively, David's willingness to take on himself the punishment is, ironically, too late. God has already made the decision to stop but instructs him to make offerings none the less. In that case, the last clause may be read not as a consequence of the penultimate clause—YHWH was entreated, *so* the plague was averted—but as an additional summary statement—in this fashion two separate things happened, (*a*) YHWH was supplicated for the country (rather than for David himself), *and* (*b*) the plague was stopped. (Yet another possibility exists: the preposition used after 'was supplicated' normally indicates the worshipper, in this case the country—so is the narrator impishly telling us that what YHWH heeded were *other* people's supplications?) These alternative endings are, of course, full of irony directed at David's self-importance. But however we read the end, there is irony in this story. For all along, while David thinks that he is the cause of the plague, and that the expiation of his sin is the key to everything, we know that it is primarily Israel that is the object of God's anger. David has been merely God's unwitting tool in the expression of that anger.

A reader might sense Saul haunting this last episode of the book, like the first. David, so different from Saul, is yet so alike. David, induced by YHWH to offend, reminds us of Saul, driven by the spirit to fits of jealous rage. Though both stand at the focal points of their stories, YHWH's action pushes us to see that they are not the ultimate focus of YHWH's concern. Rather they facilitate YHWH's dealings with the covenant community. At heart, we could decide, the plot is about God and the people.

Our discussion of plot has taken us from the simple construction of a situation, complication, and resolution, through the manifold operations of desire, the pleasures of familiarity, into shifting beginnings and endings, multiple points of view, and complex deconstruction by a coda. Again we have been unable neatly to separate out our analytic categories of plot (order), character, and point of view, to name a few. In our reading of the book of Jonah in the following chapter, the interdependence of narrative elements will also be obvious, though our focus will be, as in this present chapter, on plot.

6

Jonah and God: the Book of Jonah

Now the word of YHWH came to Jonah ben Amittai, saying, 'Arise, go to Nineveh, that great city, and call out against it; for their wickedness [evil] has come up before me.'   (Jonah 1: 1–2)

Setting the plot in motion YHWH summons Jonah to a mission. The story breaks the rules right from the start—there is virtually no exposition. Nineveh's evil has confronted (affronted?) YHWH who has decided to do something about it by means of Jonah. Who is this Jonah? Where and when does he live? The narrator tells us nothing, though the sentence has a decidedly prophetic ring to it—reminding us perhaps of Jeremiah's commissioning (Jeremiah 1) or Isaiah (Isaiah 6). And, indeed, a prophet of this name has appeared before, Jonah ben Amittai ('Dove, son of Faithfulness'), in 2 Kgs. 14: 25. There he announces the restoration of (northern) Israel's borders, in the time of King Jeroboam ben Joash, several decades before the Assyrians finally destroy the northern kingdom. So, although nowhere in the story is the term 'prophet' used, we may decide that Jonah is an Israelite prophet.

What is this mission, precisely? To many readers it will sound as though YHWH desires Nineveh's destruction and is telling the prophet to proclaim the evil city's doom. If so, the plot's end, a first-time reader might well imagine, is likely to come with the fulfilment (or possibly failure) of the prophecy.

Almost immediately we meet a complication. Prophetic calls, like those of Isaiah and Jeremiah, as well as of Moses (Exodus 4) and Gideon (Judges 6–7) among others, often elicit an objection on the part of the one summoned. Jonah, however, does not wait even to argue the point. 'The word of Y<small>HWH</small> came to Jonah . . . And he arose . . . to flee to Tarshish from the presence of Y<small>HWH</small>.' Jonah takes to his heels. So this story of a prophet is going to be no ordinary story—this is a prophet who kicks over the traces. Jonah's response thus fills out the shape of Y<small>HWH</small>'s plot by apparently blocking Y<small>HWH</small>'s desire. But it also raises the possibility of another plot, Jonah's own. The initial situation seems to be Jonah's special relationship with Y<small>HWH</small> which the divinity proceeds to disrupt by demanding that he call out against Nineveh. Resolution for this plot could come in several ways—by Jonah successfully escaping from the relationship, for example, or by Y<small>HWH</small> relenting, or by Jonah overcoming his own objection.

Where we think this latter plot is headed is bound up with what we think is Jonah's reason for refusing the commission. What is wrong with calling out against Nineveh? We seem to have so little to go on at this point in a first-time reading that we can do hardly more than guess. For many readers, he is simply frightened at the prospect of venturing with a hostile message into the heart of Assyria, a feared imperial power.

So Jonah gets up . . . and goes down. He goes down to Joppa, embarks on a ship to distant Tarshish, and as a storm breaks, goes down into the 'innermost part' of the ship. He falls into a 'dead sleep', and even when wakened can say little. Thrown into the sea by the sailors, his path continues downward, down under the sea, to the roots of the mountains, the belly of Sheol, the Pit of Death. Only at the door of death does he find words to pray. His flight could be read as a retreat into the womb, a metaphor of a psychological or spiritual journey towards personal eclipse.

But let us not leave the ship quite so soon. While Jonah is being dragged back from his death-sleep by the captain anxiously demanding that he get up and call upon his god, the fearful sailors attempt to find out what plot they have stumbled into. They hasten to determine (divine) the cause of their trouble. And, unerringly (because the divinity so wills? or because the sailors are good diviners?), the lot falls upon Jonah. To the rush of questions thrown at him, Jonah replies with the barest of answers. Yet it can be interpreted as an answer that reveals much: 'I am a Hebrew; and I fear Y<small>HWH</small>, the god of heaven, who made the sea and the dry land.'

To the sailors, the profession of the 'fear' of YHWH is more than a stock profession of faith ('I *worship* YHWH'), but a clue to the ghastly truth. They see this runaway Hebrew as 'afraid', not of his mission as we earlier surmised, but of his god. That makes them 'exceedingly afraid'. Plainly, these men, too, are god-fearing. Their worst fears are confirmed. The man has committed some offence against his god, and the storm is indeed divinely inspired. 'What is this that you have done!' they exclaim.

To the reader, Jonah's use of this well-worn liturgical phrase to describe his god may seem more than a little ironic. YHWH, affirms Jonah, is the creator of the world, heaven and earth, the sea and the land. Such a god, initiator of the plot of humankind, might well be considered the controller of every individual human's plot, wherever in the world it might be enacted. And yet here is Jonah attempting to flee from him! Already, therefore, many a reader may be inwardly reciting, for Jonah's benefit, another liturgical favorite which could equally have been on this god-fearing prophet's lips :

> Where shall I go from your spirit [wind!]?
> Or where from your face shall I flee?
> If I ascend to heaven, there will be you!
> Or I bed down in Sheol, behold—you! (Ps. 139: 7–8)

With their passenger's 'confession' giving them the clue to their predicament, the desperate sailors attempt, like their captain, to extricate themselves from Jonah's story. What can they do to Jonah, they ask him, to quiet the storm (1: 11). The plot now offers to take what is for many readers a surprising turn. Without hesitation Jonah offers them a way out: they should take him up and throw him into the sea. And he acknowledges again, this time explicitly, that he is the cause of their trouble: 'for I know that it is because of me that this great storm is against you' (1: 12). All of a sudden the plot may look as if it is coming to a resolution, though not the one that either YHWH or Jonah earlier desired. His character also may take on a new hue: this man is willing to die to save others.

Surprise succeeds surprise. The sailors disregard Jonah's invitation. They try to row back to shore. Again plot has implications for character. Why not take up Jonah's offer? Typically, the narrator leaves us with a teasing ambiguity. The sailors' reluctance to take

Jonah's life is usually credited to their humanity. But what if the choice before them is less than clear-cut. Are they still afraid for their own lives? After all, they know that Jonah is fleeing from his god. To throw him into the sea—might that not be Jonah's final escape from the god? The sailors then would become Jonah's accomplices and so equally the direct objects of the god's wrath. Better, then, to return Jonah to the place he came from, reverse the flight, reverse the plot. But, in turn, seen in that light, Jonah's invitation itself needs to be rethought—as more of a challenge than a profound gesture of generous self-sacrifice.

Whatever Jonah and the sailors desire, however, YHWH insists on controlling this plot. The reader recognizes that return in this fashion is not what YHWH desires. The storm rages even more, the rowing is frustrated, and the sailors themselves understand that the god has closed their options—they will perish if they continue ('We beg you, let us not perish for this man's life'). Their only remaining move now is to hurl Jonah overboard, coerced by the divinity ('and lay not on us innocent blood'). For YHWH has brought matters to a head ('for you, YHWH, have done as it has seemed good to you').

So Jonah is hurled into the sea and, as he sinks to the bottom, the sea ceases to storm—the 'proof' to the sailors of their worst fear, that all has been the act of the god. Thus the calming of the sea produces as much fear as the raging of the storm. And in their fear they make the appropriate (conventional) religious response: 'So the men feared YHWH exceedingly, and they offered a sacrifice to YHWH and made vows.' From god-fearing, these men have moved to being specifically YHWH-fearing. Inadvertently, and ironically, the reluctant prophet has played a key role in 'converting' these 'pagans' to the worship of his own god. (As we shall see, this turn of events foreshadows, and more, what is to come in chapter 3.) For the sailors this is the end of their plot!

Now comes the second great miracle:

And YHWH appointed a great fish to swallow up Jonah; and Jonah was in the belly of the fish three days and three nights. And Jonah prayed to YHWH his god from the belly of the fish, saying, 'I called to YHWH, out of my distress . . .'   (Jonah 1: 17–2: 2 [2: 1–3])

Surprise is a familiar element of plot, and the plot of Jonah is no exception. Indeed so frequently does this plot take an unexpected turn that we would probably be surprised if, as we read on, we were not surprised. While the fish could be wholly unexpected on a first reading, most of us today have known of Jonah and the whale before we ever read the book! Perhaps more surprising, then, for many readers, is that Jonah prays at last to YHWH. When asked to do so by the sailors his answer had been silence. And if his challenge to the sailors to throw him into the sea was after all a gesture of defiance, a willingness to seek death rather than meet God's demands, why now a prayer?

An answer might lie in what has happened in the mean time. Just as the sailors are forced to understand that the god YHWH wishes Jonah to be thrown into the sea, so, too, with Jonah. As he is hurled into the waves he knows that he has not managed to escape from YHWH. He is forced to give up his own plot. His spirit of defiance is undermined. At last distress begins to break in on him.

His prayer in chapter 2 is from the belly of the fish. He has moved from one enclosure (the innermost parts of the ship) to another, via a fleeting visit to that ultimate of enclosures, the belly of Sheol. He sought comfort in the first (the ship), found comfort in the second (the fish), but recoiled from the third (death). Yet the innermost parts of the ship and the belly of the fish are in one sense but analogues of death. There is irony here, too. Reading with James Ackerman (1981 ¶P), we see Jonah seeking security in 'enclosure'. Psychologically speaking, we could say that he wishes to escape the challenges and—as we shall see—the contradictions of the 'real', the 'outside', world. He seeks to be fenced around with certainties. Yet when faced with the security and certainty of death, he recoils. He cannot see that there is a dark side to 'enclosure'. We shall come back to this theme.

His prayer from the fish takes (largely) the conventional form and language of a psalm of thanksgiving, modified to allow it to contain a story within it, a flashback. For many a reader the plot here suddenly becomes a jumble. Instead of events neatly narrated in sequence, time is rearranged, collapsed even. Perhaps the compression of time imitates Jonah's experience as he is confronted with his moment of truth. Certainly the inversion of sequence tempts many

of us at first to see the fish as yet a further occasion of distress for
Jonah and to wonder whether God will yet take pity on him. Then,
surprised, we become aware of the flashback. The psalm is itself
subsequent to another prayer—the prayer of distress uttered as
Jonah sinks into the Pit of Death. The belly of Sheol is the cause of
distress, the belly of the fish the cause of gratitude. The fish is the
answer to Jonah's prayer. In the fish he acknowledges himself
rescued—and glad after all to be part of YHWH's plot!—and prays
to his god now a hymn of thanks (that is, a Psalm of Thanksgiving). What we may have taken to be oppression turns out to be
deliverance.

Historical critics have made a practice of ignoring the psalm-
prayer as a later addition to the tale. They read right across it,
moving directly from Jonah's being swallowed up and praying (1:
17–2: 1) to YHWH's command to the fish to disgorge him (2: 10). And
indeed, in terms of plot, pure and simple, the psalm might not seem
necessary. Yet the arguments about originality can be countered on
their own terms, and, in any case, here we have the story with the
psalm in place as it has been for the last two thousand years or so.
Reading the psalm as integral to the story can make a significant
difference to how we interpret the story as a whole. It gives us
an extended interior monologue from Jonah, something that so far
we have not had. In the prayer we may begin to discover some of
Jonah's motivating values and to learn something more of his
relationship with YHWH, the relationship that seemed to underlie his
original predicament. While the psalm may seem to be superfluous
to the plot viewed simply as a sequence of events, it may be important in offering us possible ways of interpreting key elements in the
plot, such as Jonah's flight in the first place and, in due course, his
behaviour at Nineveh.

He called to God, he tells us, from the belly of Sheol, 'For you
cast me into the deep . . .' (2: 3 [4]). Some readers see here an ironic
touch. Jonah is only too ready to 'blame' God for his misfortune and
to forget that he himself invited the sailors to throw him overboard.
But we could also accept that what Jonah says is in some measure
true: it was indeed YHWH who threw Jonah 'into the deep' in the
sense that it was God who called Jonah in the first place and then
forced the sailors into casting him overboard. In that case, Jonah

may not so much be blaming YHWH (though he may be doing that too) as acknowledging that he, Jonah, is aware that his flight has failed. Following this interpretation, however, we could develop a reading of the psalm which also sees it in an ironic light, harbouring implicit criticism of its speaker.

With Jonah's recognition of failure, what seem like the irrevocable consequences of his act bear in upon him:

Then I said, 'I am cast out from your presence; How shall I again look upon your holy temple?' (Jonah 2: 4 [5])

A deep desire emerges. Whether we see him now as simply grieving his loss or (less generously on our part) trying to ingratiate himself again with God, it seems that his belief in YHWH is deep-seated. He 'fears' YHWH in every sense. His flight notwithstanding, he desires to stand again before that 'presence' that is in the centre of his world.

His flight has become his casting out, his disowning, by YHWH, and for Jonah YHWH's presence is bound up, above all, with the temple. ('Holy temple' may even be taken as a metaphor for the divinity itself.) Thus, face to face with spiritual as well as physical death—'as his soul faints within him'—he 'remembers' YHWH. He recapitulates his former life of faith. His prayer of distress breaks out and comes, he knows, to God, 'into your holy temple' (2:7). This talk of the temple may strike some of us as odd and prompt some questions, not easily answered. Why is this northern prophet talking thus of the temple, the place where YHWH 'caused his name to dwell' (as Deuteronomy puts it) in Jerusalem, in the southern capital? Is he after all a southerner? Or has his faith long since traversed and trivialized these geopolitical divisions? And what other relationship does this story have to the story of the building, destruction, and rebuilding of the temple in Samuel–Kings and Chronicles–Ezra–Nehemiah? Does it, for example, like that story, imply perhaps a Judaean audience, of people who, like Jonah, have placed the temple at the centre of their faith?

From YHWH's 'holy temple' (v. 7) Jonah turns to sacrifice and vow-making (vv. 8–9). The shift is not wholly unexpected if we understand that psalms of thanksgiving may have accompanied sacrifices and vows at the temple. The conventional institutions of religion are ingrained in Jonah. Indeed, his point is that his religious loyalty (*hesed*) to YHWH is ingrained, so that he can be relied upon to maintain his religion, unlike others whose habitual regard is for 'vain idols' and who will therefore readily forsake their true loyalty (*hesed*), namely to YHWH. Jonah, like many a psalmist, is quick to assert his religious rectitude over against the unreliability (or, in the psalmist's case, enmity) of others. In this psalm, in this context, these unreliable 'forsakers' may look to a reader like a reference specifically to the foreign sailors who feared YHWH and went on to offer sacrifices and make vows (although strictly speaking, of course, Jonah did not witness the latter actions). True *hesed* (loyalty), Jonah seems to be saying, knows truly the fear of God; true *hesed* is a product of established worship; the *hesed* produced by ephemeral fear will itself prove ephemeral—the sailors will never know the presence of YHWH in the temple. In short, Jonah is ready to believe that he has been delivered by virtue of his own faith, his own *hesed*, the quality of his religious life, which has prompted his prayer and thereby prompted God.

It is thus doubly ironic that Jonah ends his thanksgiving by ascribing deliverance to YHWH (v. 9). One critic jokes, 'It is no wonder that immediately after Jonah shouts, "Deliverance belongs to Jahweh!" the big fish throws up!' (Holbert 1981: 59 ¶P). But whatever we think Jonah intends by his concluding exclamation we could also translate it 'Victory is YHWH's!' YHWH has won the first round. YHWH is firmly in charge of the plot.

So Jonah is vomited out on to the dry land (v. 10), the world he tried to flee. Immediately the plot begins again. YHWH's desire seems not to have changed. The divine word confronts Jonah a second time (3: 1-2) and this time we read, as we might have expected in the first place: 'So Jonah arose and went to Nineveh, according to the word of YHWH' (v. 3). Whatever the reason for Jonah's desire to avoid this mission, God appears to have circumvented it.

A day's journey into the 'exceedingly great city', and Jonah forecasts the plot's outcome, calling out: 'Yet forty days, and Nineveh shall be overturned!' (v. 4). We should not let these few words slip by us. For one thing, we might detect a note of petulance still: the prophet gives no credentials, offers no clue to the author of the overthrow. We hear no typical prophetic, 'Thus says YHWH . . .' Furthermore, the words interpret, explicitly for the first time, what

God desired of Jonah at Nineveh. 'Call out against ['*al*] it' is all that God had specified at the beginning (1: 2). 'Call out to ['*el*] it the proclamation [the 'calling out'] which I am telling to you' was the second commission (3: 2). Two points are worth noting in the divinity's word choice.

First, the changing of '*al* to '*el* makes our translation of '*al* as 'against' less than certain, for the preposition can also mean 'concerning'. Are we so sure, as Jonah seems to be sure, that YHWH is intending judgement? We have interpreted YHWH's desire in terms of the narrator's report that Nineveh's evil came to the divinity's attention, together with a notion that YHWH presides over a just universe where evil is punished and good rewarded. But what if YHWH does not respond in this way to evil? Which brings us to the second point. What is it precisely that YHWH wants called out?

'Proclaim the proclamation which I am speaking to you.' But what YHWH is speaking to Jonah beyond the fact that he is speaking to him we are never told. If the first commission is cryptic, the second is doubly so. We have several options for interpreting this strange speech. For example, we can suppose an ellipsis: YHWH goes on to tell Jonah something which the narrator omits. Or YHWH simply has difficulty communicating well. Or YHWH, having deliberately left the interpretation of his wishes to Jonah the first time around, this time makes his desire so enigmatic that he might think Jonah bound to ask for clarification.

But Jonah seems to see no difficulty in the speech and certainly asks no questions. He is intent on conveying the message he wishes that YHWH wishes him to convey: Nineveh is doomed. So Jonah's desire includes the destruction of the evil city. On the other hand, God's desire, which first set this plot in motion, has been rendered less obvious. That hint of ambiguity in turn masks the likely direction of the plot. We assumed that its resolution would be found in the fate of Nineveh. But if YHWH's words to Jonah are vague deliberately, it is conceivable that the plot is primarily concerned with the relationship between Jonah and his god and will find its resolution there.

So Jonah proclaims Nineveh's overturn, and once again the plot itself takes a surprising, miraculous—or even absurd—turn. Without so much as a whisper of disbelief, 'The people of Nineveh believed in God' (v. 5). Indeed, the scale of this repentance reaches epic proportions, as from the greatest to the least, including the king, they proclaimed ('called out') a fast and put on sackcloth. And even this extraordinary turn-about is not sufficient. The scene is capped with a proclamation by the king decreeing a ritual of penitence which involves not only the people but the very beasts. To a person they turn from their habitually evil ways, put aside the violence that is in their hands, and cry mightily to God (vv. 6–9).

And God is impressed: 'And God saw what they were doing, that they turned from their evil way, and God repented of the evil which he planned [literally 'said'] to do to them; and he did not do it' (v. 10). So now we know that God had indeed intended judgement against the city, although whether he had told that to Jonah explicitly remains unclear—the relevant expression may mean 'promised himself' or 'planned' (as we have translated), rather than literally 'said [to Jonah]'. That leaves God's intentions *vis-à-vis* Jonah still unclear.

But there is another point of interest to us here. The narrator is quoting exactly Exodus 32: 14, from the story of the golden calf: 'And God repented of the evil which he planned to do to his people.' The only difference is that the object of the planned evil in that story is not evil Nineveh but evil Israel, worshipping the golden calf even as Moses was receiving the law on the mountain. As regards Jonah, however, there is a larger contextual difference—whereas God's repentance over the Ninevites follows upon their repentance, in Exodus the yet unrepentant Israelites are spared because of Moses' impassioned intercession on their behalf. Moses asks for mercy, Jonah pronounces judgement.

God repents of the evil he was planning to do to Nineveh. But, the narrator continues (4: 1), 'That was evil to Jonah, exceedingly evil!' And Jonah is angry! Without hesitation this time, he prays to YHWH:

'Surely, YHWH, is not this what I said when I was still on my own soil? This is why I hurried to flee to Tarshish; for I knew that you were a gracious God and compassionate, slow to anger and abounding in steadfast love [*hesed*], and you repent of evil. So now, YHWH, take my life from me, please, for it is better for me to die than to live.'   (Jonah 4: 2–3)

So here at last is Jonah's stated reason for fleeing from YHWH in the first place. It was not that he had feared the evil of the Ninevites (or if so, he is not admitting it) but that he had feared that YHWH would not render them the evil that was their due. To Jonah, Nineveh is like Sodom and Gomorrah (Genesis 18–19), whom YHWH 'over-turned' (the word Jonah uses of Nineveh) on account of their evil. And sure enough, here is YHWH taking notice, not of their habitual evil, but of some superficial rituals of repentance. It is the situation of the sailors writ large. To Jonah such divine behaviour strikes at the basis of right religion and justice. How can God expect the faithful to persevere with religious rectitude and justice when evil escapes punishment merely because of a moment's convenient 'repentance'?

He quotes Exodus again—perhaps unconsciously, since the allusion does not reflect well on him. The problem is that YHWH is a God compassionate and gracious, slow to anger and abounding in *hesed*, and forgiving iniquity and transgression and sin (Exod. 34: 6). The Exodus passage comes from YHWH's self-revelation to Moses after the golden calf episode and again contrasts the two prophets. Whereas Moses intercedes for the sinning people (and Abraham at Sodom intercedes for the righteous), Jonah condemns the city out of hand. Whereas Moses' anger is directed at the wayward people on account of their sin (Exod. 32: 19), Jonah's anger is vented at YHWH on account of God's accepting the people's repentance.

It is easy for a reader to be smug about Jonah. He is only interested in preserving his reputation as a prophet—since, if the criterion of true prophecy is fulfilment (cf. Deut. 18: 21–22), God's sparing the city marks out Jonah's prophecy of its overthrow as 'false'. (Of course, the irony is that 'overturn' is precisely what does take place, only in a very different sense from the 'destruction' that Jonah preaches!). Or, it might be said, he represents an allegedly 'narrow' post-exilic religion which is unwilling to recognize that gentiles as well as Jews merit God's gracious mercy—an interpretation in terms of 'universalism' versus 'nationalism'. Or he fails to respond in love to the repenting gentiles: he is so obsessed about a just world that he is not prepared to allow that love and mercy are the true hallmarks of God—an interpretation in terms of 'love' versus 'justice'. Our present reading has been in line with this last interpretation, aligning with 'justice', however, notions of 'order' and 'right religion'.

Yet is it so clear that Jonah's frustration at God's change of mind is totally unwarranted? He can affirm that YHWH is a god of *hesed* (steadfast love), but borrowing from his psalm he might also ask, How long will it be before those repenting Ninevites 'forsake their true *hesed* (loyalty)'? A good question, especially when we reflect again on that repentance scene. We read it almost as a farce. Why? Because it *is* a farce! It is ludicrous! The overnight conversion of the whole of evil Nineveh—including the animals? We do not have to be ancient Israelites to recognize Nineveh and respond, 'Unbelievable!'

So perhaps Jonah sees only 'skin-deep' repentance, produced, like the conversion of the sailors, by the 'fear' (terror, not awe) of the moment. It will prove ephemeral. So why should YHWH compromise his role as the just creator and ruler of the universe, in order to offer *hesed* (mercy) to those who will profess *hesed* (loyalty, worship) today but forsake it tomorrow? Jonah has a point.

We have reached another turning-point in the plot. When we reflect on what has happened so far, we could decide that YHWH's plot, conceived in terms of his desire regarding Nineveh, has reached resolution. We surmised that YHWH planned to punish the city for its evil after first having his prophet announce the judgement. A complication arose when Jonah refused the commission. And then came a further complication—at the announcement the people turned to YHWH. Resolution came when YHWH accepted their repentance as transcending his desire for judgement. Character shapes plot: God's *hesed* displaced his desire for order, redirecting the plot that was set in train by his instinct for justice. When we wondered at the beginning of chapter 3 whether we had perhaps wrongly anticipated YHWH's intention to punish Nineveh we were both wrong and right. We were wrong inasmuch as he went on to make clear that his initial intention was judgement. We were right inasmuch as our questioning of conventional correlations of evil and judgement turned out to anticipate the subversive power of God's *hesed* which allowed a resolution such as we could hardly have imagined at the story's outset.

On the other hand, when we follow Jonah's plot, or if we take YHWH's plot conceived in terms of Jonah, we are plainly at an impasse. Jonah's desire to see Nineveh reap its just reward has been frustrated by YHWH's incorrigible propensity to be, as Jonah sees it, a soft touch. And what YHWH's desire for Jonah might be is still unclear. The two are estranged. We are still looking for a resolution to their differences.

So the plot takes another turn (4: 4–5). YHWH initiates it with no more than a question. Jonah protests about the value of life in the face of this patently undeserved exercise of divine mercy: 'take my life from me . . . it is better to die than to live' (v. 3). (Moses, on the other hand, offers to be blotted out of God's book in atonement for the people; Exod. 32: 32.) Shrugging off Jonah's protest, God says simply, 'Do you do well to be angry?' (Aaron frames a similar question to an angry Moses at the site of the golden calf; Exod. 32: 22.) Jonah refuses to answer. Instead he goes out of the city and makes a booth for himself there. (Moses, too, would go out of the camp to the tent of meeting, to encounter God; Exodus 33.) Once again he encloses himself. For he needs a secure, ordered world, a world with certainty built around it. Unable to sit in the comforting surrounds of his familiar temple, while he looks out on a chaotic world of evil and shallow repentance, he makes a substitute temple—a booth. The booth cools him and his anger. There is strength as well as weakness in Jonah's religion.

He sits in the booth in the shade, 'till he should see what would happen in the city' (v. 5). Given our reading so far, let us suppose that he is looking for a change of mind, first on Nineveh's part, and then on YHWH's. Come the forty days and no destruction—maybe much earlier—and all will be back to normal. Then evil will meet with judgement.

But God will not give up the initiative. The plot takes yet another curious turn:

And God appointed a plant and made it go up over Jonah, to be a shade over his head, to save ['deliver'] him from his discomfort ['evil']. And Jonah was happy about the plant, exceedingly happy. (Jonah 4: 6)

Already, like the ship, the booth has proved inadequate. The plant, then, is to the booth, as the fish was to the ship. It is the plant that will save Jonah from his 'evil' (RSV, NIV translate 'discomfort'). Jonah's one supreme conviction has been that 'evil' is something he finds elsewhere; 'evil' is what others do. We remember the ironic undercurrent of self-righteousness in his psalm: 'others will forsake you, but I will remain your faithful worshipper.' For a brief moment the plant is the tree in the Garden, the tree of the knowledge of good and evil. Jonah partakes of its fruit—its shade. The tree delivers him from evil. The question is, what knowledge of good and evil will he learn from it? What revelation will bring this plot to a close?

Jonah's pleasure in the plant is short-lived. God gives the plot another turn of the screw. This tree, like the one in the Garden, has a worm.

But God appointed a worm at the coming of dawn the next day and it attacked the plant, so that it dried up. And when the sun rose, God appointed a sultry east wind, and the sun beat upon the head of Jonah so that he was faint; and he asked that he might die, and he said, 'It is better for me to die than to live!'   (Jonah 4: 7–8)

The great fish had secured him, ensconced him, been the occasion of thanksgiving, and then, after only three days, had vomited him up upon the dry land. Now the plant has shaded him, been the occasion of his rejoicing, and then, in the space of a day, left him 'high and dry' again. The 'enclosures' provided by God (God's response to Jonah's religious needs?) echo those chosen by Jonah himself in their offer of security, but their intention is not security or comfort but to be a gateway back into the world, the dry land, the world where YHWH makes demands and subverts good order. The reality with which Jonah (and all of us?) must live lies outside the well-ordered garden, beyond the pleasant shade of the tree, in the struggle against the chaos of brambles and thistles. Perhaps God's whole point has been to make this indubitably religious person uncomfortable. Perhaps God *is* the worm.

But God said to Jonah, 'Is it good to be angry on account of the plant?' And he said, 'It is good for me to be angry, angry enough to die!'

(Jonah 4: 9)

The last time YHWH had asked Jonah about his anger at YHWH's 'repentance' over the Ninevites, Jonah had not replied. Now when the question is turned towards his anger over the plant, he replies emphatically, out of growing frustration. We could decide that he resents the death of the plant because it results in his own personal discomfort—for his assertion that death is preferable to life follows upon his feeling faint (4: 8). Yet YHWH's response to him—'you pity the plant . . .' (4: 10)—suggests that we, too, might see in his anger a dimension of pity and compassion. That the plant should grow, serve a high purpose (shading him, Jonah, the prophet of YHWH), and then be so suddenly and (apparently) mindlessly destroyed is inimical to his sense of good order, elicits his pity for the vulnerable plant, and (as the sun beats down upon him!) provokes his anger.

Of course, his response to the plant's destruction is undercutting him. His new-found pity is misplaced. The moral is obvious. YHWH presses the point home:

'You, you pity the plant over which you did not labour or make it grow, which came into being in a night, and perished in a night. But I, may I not pity Nineveh, that great city, in which there are more than 120,000 persons who do not know their right hand from their left—and also much cattle?' (Jonah 4: 10)

The final phrase is the *coup de grâce*. If Jonah, who pities one plant, cannot find compassion for more than 120;000 people, at least let him not grudge God's pity for those countless cattle!

The plant has turned into a parable. It is rather like the parable of the rich man and the poor man's ewe lamb, told by the prophet Nathan to David (2 Samuel 12)—a parable that elicits self-judgement from (and upon) the hearer. David angrily condemns the rich man 'because he showed no compassion' (2 Sam. 12: 6), and so condemns himself. In his anger over the plant, Jonah, the prophet of judgement, elevates the quality of mercy and judges himself. Thus the story ends on an ironic note.

Yet there is, of course, a striking difference between YHWH's parable and Nathan's. Nathan's accusation comes with an unambiguous indicative, 'You are the man!' YHWH's comes at a tangent, with a question, 'May I not pity Nineveh . . . ?' And where David's response to the revelation is given us—'I have sinned against YHWH'—Jonah's response is missing. The plot that forms around the relationship between YHWH and Jonah finds potential resolution in a revelation, but no formal closure. Whether Jonah recognized, let alone accepted, YHWH's point of view, we can only conjecture, not know.

This plot has the ending the reader, and Jonah, gives it. At the beginning of the story we saw Jonah's plot in terms of his relationship with YHWH being disrupted by the divinity's demand that he speak to Nineveh. Now at the end, Jonah has been unable, indeed unwilling, to escape the relationship, YHWH has not relented over his demand, and whether or not Jonah has reached an understanding of, and accepted, YHWH's action and attitude remains an open question. Some readers may have found acceptable resolution in the parable of the plant. For them the plot may be over. For others, resolution may be less obvious. For Jonah, it all depends on how he responds beyond the story.

As for YHWH's plot, inasmuch as it has become a plot of relationship with Jonah, again we are left with various possibilities. If God has been wanting Jonah to learn to accept him for who he is, including all that problematic *hesed*, then it is not clear that Jonah has done that by the end. On the other hand, many a reader may have been convinced by what may not have convinced Jonah. Yet again, however, others may be less persuaded that the plot is truly resolved.

Although Jonah's response to God is not known, the story's ending can bear a little further reflection. For one thing, we might consider whether YHWH's interpretation of the plant parable is the only one possible. What, for example, if the plant is a paradigm of Jonah himself? The plant's purpose was 'to save [*hassil*—deliver] Jonah from his discomfort [evil]'. Jonah's purpose was to pronounce doom (evil) on evil Nineveh, but by doing so he delivered the city from its evil. The plant, however, proved ephemeral. Did the deliverance Jonah effected prove ephemeral too? That certainly seems to be what Jonah considered most likely, as he sat sceptically watching the city, waiting for its relapse. Reading this story in the context of Israel's 'primary story', we know that within a few decades Nineveh would destroy Jonah's (northern) Israel and within a few generations would be destroyed itself. So did YHWH, the compassionate God, destroy those more than 120,000 persons who did not know their right hand from their left—and also much cattle?

When Jonah quoted YHWH's self-characterization to Moses—YHWH is a gracious God and compassionate, slow to anger, abounding in steadfast love, and repenting of evil ('forgiving iniquity and transgression and sin')—he omitted what came next: 'but who will by no means clear the guilty, visiting the iniquity of the fathers upon the children and the children's children, to the third and fourth generation' (Exod. 34: 6–7). Jonah's omission is ironic, for here is all the judgement he could want. This is judgement with a vengeance— visiting the fathers' evil upon the children's children. What price pity? we might ask. YHWH's self-revelation to Moses is deeply para- doxical. And Moses could appreciate the paradox—despite his apparently successful intercession on the people's behalf (Exod. 32: 7–14), despite his efforts to discipline them himself (vv. 25–9), and his further attempt to make atonement for them (vv. 30–4), YHWH still struck them with a plague anyway (v. 35). Viewed in this broader context, then, Jonah's characterization of YHWH as simply of *hesed* and mercy, slow to anger, is something of a caricature. Jonah and YHWH have more in common than either seems ready to admit. We have sought a resolution to the plot formed about the relation- ship of Jonah and YHWH, and framed our search in terms of Jonah learning something of himself from YHWH. The question could be turned, however. Did YHWH learn anything from Jonah?

As a postscript to our reading of the book of Jonah let us do some- thing we could also have done at the beginning, when considering the exposition. The brief account of Jonah ben Amittai in 2 Kings 14: 23–7 could be taken as a story to read in conjunction with our larger story. What does reading it do to our reading of the book of Jonah?

We learn that Jeroboam ben Joash, king of Israel, whose reign exceeded the proverbial forty years, did evil and sustained Israel's evil. Yet as YHWH's agent he restored the nation, in alliance with the word of Jonah, YHWH's servant. Here we read of no repentance on the part of king or people, no fasting, no crying mightily to God, but rather of 'sin' and 'evil'. Yet because Israel in affliction has no helper, YHWH restores its boundaries and rescues its name. And Jonah proclaims salvation—though whether in gladness or protest, and whether before or after Nineveh, we can only guess.

This little story in Kings has some familiar plot elements: YHWH responds to an evil king and people by determining to save them rather than blot them out; and Jonah speaks·the prophetic word that leads to their salvation. It is as though history repeats itself—after a fashion. Here we glimpse again the paradox of a god who wishes to sustain justice, order, and loyalty (*hesed*), and yet 'be sorry for' the afflicted or ignorant, 'repent' ('change his mind') about evil, show compassion and mercy (*hesed*). On the other hand, if we read these texts together, our understanding of Jonah may be further nuanced, if not complicated. For example, is his protest against YHWH a product in part of his already having seen YHWH ignoring (as Jonah might term it) evil 'on his own soil'? Or is his promotion of his own loyal 'temple' religion rendered doubly hollow by our being told that the condition of Israel in his time was 'evil'? One effect of such a reading is to make us more attentive to the way the book of Jonah relates to Israel's story, not just Nineveh's or even Jonah's personal story. The relationship governing the story is not just that between YHWH and Jonah, or between YHWH, Jonah, and Nineveh. It is between YHWH, Jonah, Nineveh, and Israel—God and human, outsider and insider, oppressor and oppressed, saviour and saved. Perhaps the book of Kings makes us more aware that the plot of the book of Jonah could have involved Jerusalem or Samaria instead of Nineveh—and stayed the same.

7

The Lure of Language

The search for narrative significance is the scrutiny of words. The story world—with its setting, its events, its characters—is a verbal construct, a world made of words. In narrative, life is language. Words create the narrative world, and words hold the key to the significance of that world. Hence to suggest, as this chapter does, that the study of narrative language can be neatly separated from the study of character or plot is misleading. We have, in fact, been working with words all along.

There are, however, other dimensions to the linguistic texture of narrative besides character and plot. All sorts of meanings and messages are found in the network of a text: theological and ideological themes, subtleties and polemics, social structures, symbols, metaphors, allusions. As words are woven into narrative discourse, they connect to form patterns that are both contained within the text and extend beyond it. Furthermore, the multivalence of language creates a 'thick' texture, where words often participate simultaneously in more than one pattern. Another metaphor we could use is the lure: language lures us—allures us—from one word to another, from one meaning of a word to another, from the literal to the metaphorical, from one part of a text into another, from one text into another. We can think of the text luring us, or we can think of ourselves as readers selecting and casting the lure. We read by trying out specific language as baits for meaning, testing where this or that word or word cluster will take us, what meaning we may 'catch' with it. What we choose and where we cast are crucial to what meaning we end up with. In the present chapter we cast around our narratives, seeking significant words, and lured by words. Put prosaically, we look selectively at certain of the machinations of repetition, a device much favoured in Hebrew Bible narrative, at allusion and intertextuality, dialogues between texts, and at some ways in which metaphoric reading exploits language's capacity for multivalence to enlarge meaning.

Repetition and variation

Whereas English prose composition eschews repetition, so that we are constantly looking for synonyms as we write, ancient Hebrew prose enjoys it. The verbatim repetition of a word, phrase, sentence, or set of sentences, or even the recurrence of words falling into the same semantic range can function to structure the story, to create atmosphere, to construct a theme or a character, to emphasize a certain point to the reader, or to build suspense. A repetition might exaggerate and thus be a humorous ploy or a means of ridicule, thus turning what otherwise might be construed as a straightforward account into one that mocks a character, an attitude, or an idea. Reappearing words and phrases, then, often guide the reader in understanding the narrator's rhetoric.

If meaning, as many say, essentially depends on difference, then sorting out similarity and difference is a central operation of close reading. Repetition creates rich possibilities of variation, and variation creates new meaning. Repetition can first lull the reader into false expectations and then, through sudden variance, can introduce an element of startling surprise. Repetition and variation can equate and contrast events or characters or even whole other texts through association, inviting the reader to consider the significance of similarities and dissimilarities.

Tamar and Amnon (2 Samuel 13)

In the story of Tamar and Amnon, a series of familial and political terms connect the characters and construct a world in which the personal and the political are inextricably intertwined.

And it came to pass after this that Absalom son of David had a beautiful sister whose name was Tamar, and Amnon son of David loved her. And it was distressing to Amnon, to the point of making himself sick, on account of Tamar his sister, for she was a virgin and it was impossible in Amnon's view to do anything to her. (2 Sam. 13: 1–2)

This harrowing story of incest, rape, and fratricide introduces its characters in terms of familial relationships—son, sister, and, by implication, brother. As the tale unfolds, the narrator loads it with these reminders of family connection: 'And Amnon had a friend, whose name was Jonadab, the son of Shimeah, David's brother . . . and he said to him, "Why are you so low, king's son? . . ." And Amnon said to him, "I love Tamar, my brother Absalom's sister".' The redundancy is relentless. After Amnon has set in motion Jonadab's plan to gain access to Tamar, we read: 'Then David sent word to Tamar at home, saying "Go to your brother Amnon's house, and prepare food for him." So Tamar went to her brother Amnon's house . . .'

And right at the point of crucial interchange between the two, the sibling words are there. Moving to 'do something' to Tamar, Amnon perversely exploits the ambivalence of the term 'sister', pressing it into service as language of courtship and affection: 'Come lie with me, my sister.' ('Open to me, my sister, my love, | my dove, my perfect one', one lover entreats the other in the Song of Songs (5: 2).) Tamar, however, refuses to hear it thus and resolutely names the act: 'No, my brother, do not rape me . . .'

Amnon's reiteration of 'sister' makes the word's subsequent absence from his speech all the more striking. Having done what he desired, his 'love' exposed and expended as lust, he cannot be rid of her fast enough: 'Get up and get out!' She is no longer 'my sister' but nameless. And though Tamar perseveres with the familial language ('No, my brother . . .' (v. 16, reading a widely accepted emended text)), desperately seeking to tap the bond of responsible relationship, Amnon cannot abide to be reminded. His language now matches his behaviour, treating her as a disposable object. 'Put this [woman? thing?] out of my presence, and bolt the door after her.'

But try as he might he cannot wholly obliterate his brotherly connection with her. That relation rapidly re-enters the story through

Absalom's perspective, though, just as quickly, this brother seems to marginalize the matter. 'And her brother Absalom said to her, "Has Amnon your brother been with you? Well then, my sister, keep quiet about it; he is your brother; do not take this thing to heart." So Tamar dwelt, desolate, in the house of Absalom, her brother' (2 Sam. 13: 20).

That this is not the end of the matter, however, becomes apparent in the narrator's additional comment, one that forms a transition to the subsequent, fratricidal episode: 'But Absalom spoke to Amnon neither good nor evil; for Absalom hated Amnon, for he had raped his sister Tamar.' This time the term 'brother' is oddly absent. Conveying Absalom's perspective, the word choice shows him now suppressing his sibling connection with Amnon (as earlier Amnon had attempted with Tamar), but unsuccessfully. The ambiguous possessive pronoun 'his' connects 'sister' with both men, marking them as brothers yet again. In due course, when hating Amnon turns into killing him (vv. 23–9), we may understand why Absalom has attempted to suppress his fraternal connection.

The ambiguous possessive—prompting the question, 'Whose sister?'—may set in train another line of observation about possession and competition. 'Absalom son of David', the story begins, 'had a beautiful sister whose name was Tamar, and Amnon son of David loved her.' Tamar starts her narrative life as a possession, competed for. Absalom son of David has something that Amnon son of David wants—Tamar. The men are clearly brothers yet the narrator refrains from using the term, identifying them instead, in repetitive symmetry, as sons of David. The genealogically attentive reader may remember that Amnon was David's first son, born to Ahinoam of Jezreel, and Absalom was David's third son, born of Maacah, daughter of King Talmai of Geshur (2 Sam. 3: 2–3).

As the story progresses we see David pulled into its purview, as David, as father, and especially as king. In relation to Amnon, except in Jonadab's speech, David is repeatedly, even redundantly, presented as king. 'And when the king came to see him, Amnon said to the king, "Let my sister come, please . . ."' (v. 6); 'So now [says Tamar to Amnon], please speak to the king; for he will not withhold me from you' (v. 13); 'And as for King David, he heard of all these things and was very angry, but he would not punish him, for he loved him for he was his first-born' [v. 21, following the ancient Greek translation (LXX) and the Qumran text of Samuel; cf. NRSV]. So, too, in the account of how Absalom persuaded David to send Amnon to the fatal sheep-shearing feast at Baalhazor and in the relating of the murder's aftermath. Additionally we may notice that the princes are always referred to collectively as 'the king's sons', even when the story has switched to Absalom's point of view (vv. 23–9) where we might have expected instead to find '['Absalom's' or 'his' or 'my'] brothers'.

The insistent reminder that these men are sons of David and the frequent naming of David as 'king' remind a reader of the political dimensions to this story. That Absalom is next in line to the throne is a factor that should not be overlooked in assessing his motivation for murder. His desire to possess the kingdom is likely mixed with, or may even outweigh, his desire to avenge his sister.

The avalanche of familial and political connectives pull other stories of rape into view. Shechem's rape of Dinah in Genesis 34 is the violation of an Israelite woman by a foreign man. It is an episode that results in war. The rape of the Levite's wife in Judges 19 involves intertribal violence. Men of Benjamin violate a woman from Bethlehem. This event ends in war between Benjamin and the other tribes of Israel. By the time we come to 2 Samuel 13, we have moved to rape within a family—not just any family, but the first family, the royal family. Tamar's protest that 'such a thing is not done in Israel' becomes hauntingly ironic. Such a thing *is* done in Israel. It is done in David's own household. It fractures the family and eventually fractures the nation.

Jehoshaphat (2 Chronicles 17–20)

The Chronicler's account of Jehoshaphat, king of Judah, is one that employs repetition and word-play to construct character and advance a particular ideology. According to the Chronicler, Jehoshaphat is a deeply pious man, active in promoting YHWH's cause in the south against the depredations of an impious northern kingdom. While it contains, parallel to 1 Kings 22, the extended narrative of Jehoshaphat's abortive expedition to Ramoth-Gilead with Ahab, king of Israel, it frames that ambivalent episode with unambiguous

God-fearing activity and sentiment. Indeed, the narrator has shaped the account so that in the centre we see Jehoshaphat's behaviour as the very epitome of his name: 'YHWH judges (*shaphat*).'

Jehoshaphat [*Yeho-shaphat*] lived in Jerusalem; and he went out again among the people . . . and brought them back to YHWH, the God of their fathers. He appointed judges [*shophetim*] in the land in all the fortified cities of Judah, city by city, and said to the judges, 'Take care what you do, for you judge [*tishpetu*] not for humankind but for YHWH who is with you in your word of judgement [*mishpat*] . . . And also in Jerusalem did Jehoshaphat appoint some of the Levites and priests and heads of families for Israel to implement YHWH's judgement . . . And he commanded them, saying, 'Thus shall you do in the fear of YHWH, faithfully, and wholeheartedly . . . Be strong in your dealings, and may YHWH be with the good!'

(2 Chron. 19: 4–11)

This central episode, like the major opening and closing episodes in 2 Chronicles 17 and 20, is unmatched in Kings. Here in Chronicles the rhetoric centres our attention upon the essential harmony of identity and activity in this character. It does so by strategic place-ment of an elaborate word-play (which has a parallel in Joel 3: 2 [Heb. 4: 2]—YHWH will bring the nations to the valley of Jeho-shaphat, and 'enter into judgement [*nishpatti*] with them there'). In this way the Chronicler's narrative reads typically as promoting a clear-cut vision of the world, with dissonances submerged or sidelined (like Jehoshaphat's alliances with Ahab (2 Chronicles 18) and Ahaziah (2 Chron. 20: 35–7)), and YHWH unambiguously siding with and rewarding the good (cf. 2 Chronicles 17 and 20: 5–12, 25–30).

Solomon and Adonijah (1 Kings 1–2)

The story of how Solomon, rather than his older brother Adonijah, came to be king in succession to David (1 Kings 1–2) revels in the phrases 'be king after [David]' and 'sit on [David's] throne'. The words travel from character to character, threading the narrative like a musical motif in a Wagner opera.

They form first on the lips of Nathan the prophet, already subtly aligned by the narrator with the party backing Solomon. Intimating to Bathsheba that Adonijah has seized the throne and pressing her to save herself and her son Solomon from him, Nathan tells her to go in to King David and say to him, 'Was it not you, my lord the king, who swore to your maidservant, saying, "Solomon your son shall be king after me, and he shall sit upon my throne"? So why is Adonijah king?' Following this, he assures her, he will arrive and confirm her words. And so it happens. Having urged David that he had sworn to her 'by Yhwh [his] God' that Solomon his son was to be king after him and sit upon his throne, Bathsheba indicts Adonijah as a usurper, and claims that all Israel is waiting for David 'to tell them who shall sit on the throne of the king after him'. Her fate, she suggests, and that of her son rest on his words. In turn Nathan arrives and disingenuously asks, 'My lord the king, have you said, "Adonijah shall be king after me, and he shall sit upon my throne"?' Amplifying Bathsheba's indictment of the usurping Adonijah, he plaintively ends, 'Perhaps this thing is my lord the king's doing and you have not told your servants who shall sit on the throne of my lord the king after him.'

In the circumstances it seems almost inevitable that finally David himself should give voice to this refrain: 'As I swore to you by Yhwh, the God of Israel, saying "Solomon your son shall be king after me, and he shall sit upon my throne in my stead," even so I will do this very day.' He gives instructions that Solomon be anointed king and 'come and sit upon my throne; for he shall be king in my stead'. Even Benaiah the military leader gives obsequious (or is it ironic?) echo: 'As Yhwh has been with my lord the king, even so may he be with Solomon, and make his throne greater than the throne of my lord King David.'

Word now travels by messenger to where Adonijah and his guests are celebrating: 'Solomon sits upon the royal throne . . . And the king also said, "Blessed be Yhwh, the God of Israel, who has granted this day one of my seed sitting upon my throne in the sight of my own eyes".' With trembling Adonijah's party dissolves and we are told that 'Adonijah feared Solomon'. Finally, with David's death, the narrator concludes: 'So Solomon sat on the throne of his father David.'

But the story has not yet ended. Adonijah's fear is well grounded. Allowed to live by his younger brother, he goes to Bathsheba with a request. Reminding her that she knew well that 'the kingdom was mine and that all Israel was looking to me to be king', he nevertheless acknowledges his brother's position as ordained by YHWH, and urges her to ask Solomon to let him have for a wife Abishag, the young woman who had been David's companion over his last days. Solomon is rent with suspicion. Is Adonijah perhaps seeking a witness to what transpired between Bathsheba, Nathan, and David on the fateful day of Solomon's accession? Or is he, by claiming his father's concubine, seeking to reclaim his father's authority? Solomon responds without hesitation: 'Now, then, as YHWH lives, who has established me and caused me to sit on the throne of David my father . . . Adonijah shall be put to death this day.' And so it happens. Adonijah is murdered at the king's command.

As we follow these words of succession through the story we may find them acquiring some unexpected freight. When Nathan the prophet first speaks of Adonijah becoming king we may easily miss the tenuous quality of his words. 'Have you not heard that Adonijah son of Haggith has become king and our lord David knows not of it?' The words fall in the shape of a question. Moreover, we cannot be sure that their implication (that Adonijah *has* become king) is even true. Certainly the narrator has presented Adonijah in terms that are highly reminiscent of that earlier rebellious son, Absalom (1 Kgs. 1: 5–10; cf. 2 Sam. 13: 23–9, 14: 25, and 15: 1). But the narrator nowhere confirms Nathan's words, neither those to Bathsheba nor those (replete with conveniently damning circumstantial detail) to David. Adonijah may simply be throwing a feast for his supporters.

As Nathan puts the requisite words about Solomon as successor in Bathsheba's mouth and arranges his own arrival so that he can offer what will appear to be independent confirmation of the promise, our suspicions can only be further aroused. For nowhere, either, has the narrator ever mentioned this alleged promise. Is it then a lie, framed at an opportune moment to galvanize a senile old man into pre-emptive action? Once voiced, that suspicion is not easily shaken off. And though Adonijah agrees before Bathsheba that YHWH has given Solomon the throne, we might wonder whether he can safely say anything else, given the *fait accompli*. That Solomon should claim that the throne came from YHWH should not surprise us. Power-takers are wont to make such claims. Again the narrator fails to confirm the assertion and we are left wondering. Even more telling, Bathsheba makes no attempt to deny that she did indeed know that the throne was Adonijah's.

Thus we may find that these words of succession, kingship, and the throne of David belong to a rhetoric of grave dubiety. Moreover, they readily produce fear—Adonijah's response and probably that of both Nathan and Bathsheba (1 Kgs. 1: 21)—and they incite to murder. As we enter this story of succession we might expect that the key phrases about being king and sitting on the throne of the great King David would intimate exhilaration and celebration. Instead we find by the end of the story that something quite other has happened. These words carry ominous overtones of power struggle, duplicity, and paranoia. David's throne is no different from the thrones of a myriad other monarchs.

Multivalence, ambiguity, and metaphor

The heartbeat of language's allure is its resistance to determinacy. No word (sign or signifier) is ever in an absolutely fixed relationship with meaning (what is signified) but is always dependent upon its relationship to other words. A word is defined by its relation to other words in the language stock, those, for example, that stand in relations of opposition or similarity. Only in distinction can singularity begin to emerge. Another way of putting the point is to say that meaning is difference. More to the point for narrative discourse, a word's meaning will be dependent upon the other words in its context, whether immediate (say a phrase or sentence or paragraph) or broad (a book, perhaps, or a genre or kind of discourse).

The process of establishing meaning is never complete, since the meaning of one word is always dependent on that of another, in an infinite cycle. Likewise the possibilities of context are potentially infinite, since recognizing a text's context is not only a matter of locating words in a text but also of locating the reader, crucial to the process of making meaning, in a personal and social context. The meaning of words is therefore in constant deferral. Together, difference and deferral produce the instability of language which, depending on its form, we call ambiguity, or multivalence, or metaphor.

Multivalence, the potential for words to have more than one meaning at once, offers a rich resource for making meaning in narrative. It offers, for example, the possibility of verbal ambiguity. Sometimes two or more meanings of unequal force may be present in a single word or phrase. Often the more obvious meaning will be literal, the other(s) figurative. An attentive and imaginative reader may recognize the interplay of both (or several) meanings, while the characters may perceive only one. Thus we have already seen how in Genesis 38, Tamar, disguised as a prostitute, bargains with an over-eager Judah for his cord, seal, and staff as a pledge of payment for her sexual services. Judah understands her to be referring to the staff that he is carrying in his hand and he willingly leaves it along with the other articles in her care. We noted, however, that the Hebrew word for staff also means 'tribe', and we might muse over the fact that Tamar, in the course of the story, indeed controls the future of Judah's tribe. The phallic shape of the staff also allows sexual connotations to play in an already sexually loaded story. Tamar is essentially bartering for a phallus that will bring her children and security and, with Judah's staff in her possession, she is able to emasculate him publicly when he attempts to have her burned for harlotry.

Once we move beyond the surface meanings of words to symbolic or theological ones, we enter the realm of metaphor. Here, through multivalence, the everyday discourse of the story world becomes imbued with larger meanings, particular constructs of experience or world-view.

In Ruth 1, words like 'cleave to', 'forsake', 'go after' are used by the narrator and by Ruth. The primary meaning reflects the context of the physical and verbal interchange between the characters: Ruth 'cleaves' to Naomi. She promises not to 'forsake' her or to return from 'going after' her. On the surface of the narrative, the words point to Ruth's physical commitment to Naomi: she is determined to accompany her back to Bethlehem. However, because they are often used to describe the relationship between Israel and YHWH, the words also carry theological impact. Israel is to 'cleave' to YHWH, and not to 'forsake' YHWH by 'going after' other gods. Consequently, the secondary connotations of this language invite the reader to view Ruth's commitment to Naomi as one with theological implications.

When meanings of equal force are carried in the same word or phrase, the multivalence may be recognized by the characters as well as by the reader. Moreover, it may be seen either as simple multivalence, where several meanings are pertinent, or as ambiguity, where multiple meanings offer alternatives from which a reader may choose. Ultimately, the recognition of multivalence or ambiguity and the resolution of ambiguity is for the reader to determine. For example, in Ruth 2 Naomi exclaims upon seeing the grain Ruth has gleaned from Boaz's field, 'Blessed be he by YHWH whose *hesed* [loyalty and kindness] has not forsaken the living or the dead!' It is unclear from the construction whether Naomi is referring to the kindness of YHWH, or that of Boaz, or perhaps deliberately leaving the possibility of both. A reader's decision on this will probably depend, for one thing, on how far he or she thinks Naomi has come from her earlier invective against YHWH (as responsible for her griev-ous plight). On the other hand, a reader may decide that, even if Naomi intended no ambiguity, the blessing may indeed be read as having a double subject, thereby underscoring a major theological point of the book of Ruth, namely, that divine and human action are often indistinguishable. Boaz's *hesed* is thus an expression of the *hesed* of God.

Whole stories can become metaphors that point to particular ideas or experiences. When such stories recur, like verbal repetitions within a text, one can assume that important meanings are at work. The telling of a story, the writing of a text, is often an attempt to control—to influence an attitude, to reinforce a world-view, to reconfigure (and thus render acceptable or understandable) a critical experience. We might see the story of Ruth, for example, as counter-ing a prejudice against foreigners, or the story of Jehoshaphat as supporting the divine ordination of Judah's monarchy.

The Babylonian exile is a crisis which plays through much of biblical literature. It marks the end of the Genesis–2 Kings corpus and provides the central hinge to Chronicles–Ezra–Nehemiah. It is the event without which Esther and the stories in Daniel have no mean-ing. The loss of home, of native place, and in some cases, of family was such a traumatic experience in the life of Israel, that it became, in Israel's literature, the critical characteristic of the human con-dition. The expulsion from the garden in Genesis 3, the banishment of Cain in Genesis 4, the scattering of the builders of the tower of Babel in Genesis 11, and the sequels of family strife throughout Genesis–2 Kings inscribe the event as a threat to every generation. The smaller stories of exile, along with the explicit warnings of exile on the parts of God, Moses, and Joshua, plague the larger story with impending loss. The fate of the nation is acted out by individuals—Abraham, Jacob, Joseph, Jephthah, David, Absalom, to name a few—individuals who, seemingly, are attempting to attain security, to promote themselves at the expense of others, or to grasp something that does not belong to them. As these stories of individuals are linked to explicit warnings of exile, we find again and again that God's promise cannot be traded on. The land is a gift; its loss is judgement. With each repetition, Israel attempts to deal with its trauma, seeking to make sense of its tragedy.

Reading for the metaphor: Judges 1

Just as words are defined in relation to other words, both in the common language stock and in their immediate context, so too the significance of stories often emerges in relation to other stories. Sometimes the connection is made in the immediate context; at other times, different contexts are juxtaposed. A series of stories in Judges 1 connect with each other and with other stories to produce a metaphor of the larger story of Israel.

Judges 1, set 'after the death of Joshua' (Judg. 1: 1), both recapitulates and recasts the story of Israel's taking possession of the promised land. Some of its elements we have met first in the book of Joshua, some are new. Joshua's sprawling story of success and failure, fulfilment and non-fulfilment, is now represented in a single chapter as a prelude to the first phase of Israel's living in the land. The account starts with success, as Judah defeats the Canaanites, and ends with a swelling list of compromises and failures to fulfil the divine injunction to possess the land and dispossess its inhabitants and their gods. By the beginning of chapter 2 an angel of YHWH is accusing them of having broken their covenant with YHWH.

If we seek the moment where things begin to go wrong for Israel, we may perhaps come to rest on a verse in the middle of the chapter, as the account of Judah's achievements draws to a close.

And YHWH was with Judah, but they took possession of the high-lands [only], for they could not dispossess the inhabitants of the plain, for they had chariots of iron. (Judg. 1: 19)

So despite YHWH's presence Judah does not take the whole of its promised allotment. Yet Judah's campaign is prefaced with YHWH's assurance, 'Behold, I have given the land into [Judah's] hand' (1: 2), and before that the assurances of success have been more than plentiful. YHWH, for example, has promised Joshua, 'Every place where you set foot is yours: I have given it to you as I promised Moses' (Josh. 1: 3, REB), and Joshua has specifically reassured Ephraim and Manasseh, 'You shall dispossess the Canaanites, though they have chariots of iron, and though they are strong' (Josh. 17: 18).

The question arises, then: is it the narrator's view that Judah was 'unable' to take the low country because of the iron chariots? Given the space the narrator has devoted to those reports of divine assurance and to the extraordinary story of Jericho's capture, for example, that seems doubtful. More likely the narrator presents here Judah's point of view. In that case, Judah's failure, perhaps a paradigm for understanding the other failures, is a failure of vision. In the real world of Judah's soldiers, the iron chariots are as tanks to infantry. They appear as an insurmountable obstacle. In this vision of what constitutes power, YHWH's words, Moses' words, Joshua's words, all those wonderful words of empowerment cannot overcome chariots of iron. And so the compromise is effected—the highlands, unfriendly to chariots, are taken and the lowlands abandoned.

Thus those strategically placed chariots of iron represent in this chapter a vision of reality opposing that conjured by YHWH's words.

Compromise in the 'real' world marks the little cameo story that follows within a verse or two. Here the iron chariots are a city's walls, denying entry to the invading Israelites.

The house of Joseph went up, they too, against Bethel; and YHWH was with them. And the house of Joseph spied out Bethel, the name of which used to be Luz. And the spies saw a man coming out of the city, and they said to him, 'Show us a way into the city, and we will deal loyally [*hesed*] with you' [or, capturing the implicit threat, 'we will see that you come to no harm,' REB]. So he showed them the way into the city; and they put the city to the sword, but they sent away the man and all his family. And the man went to the land of the Hittites and built a city, and named it Luz, and that is its name to this day. (Judg. 1: 22–6)

The spies' covenant with the man of Bethel—'dealing loyally' is the language of covenant—reminds us of Jericho (Joshua 2–6). We recollect the Israelite spies at Jericho and Rahab the prostitute who hid them, enabled them to escape, and extracted from them a promise to spare her and her family. But there are significant differences between the stories.

One difference is that Rahab's covenant, though in contravention of YHWH's instructions, grew out of her profession of YHWH's invincible presence among the Israelites. We hear of no such recognition by the man of Bethel. This covenant is a simple trade. The spies get the information they want, and the man makes his escape. Another difference is that, whereas the house of Joseph takes the city by means of this covenant-breaking covenant, Israel took Jericho by walking around its great walls and blowing trumpets! Jericho's walls could have been chariots of iron for Joshua. Instead he chose to see through them, beyond them. A third difference is that, where Jericho was put to the ban and left in ruins, Bethel is left both standing and displaced—for Canaanite Luz springs up again elsewhere!

By comparison, then, the present story shows a failing vision. It fits well, placed where it is, with the falling tone of the chapter's second half. Joseph's success is subtly marked with failure: Luz lives!

Earlier in the chapter, in counterpoint to Luz and the chariots of iron, is another image, of springs of water.

And Caleb said, 'Whoever attacks Kiriath-Sepher and takes it, I will give him Achsah my daughter for his wife.' And Othniel the son of Kenaz, Caleb's younger brother, took it; and he [Caleb] gave him [Othniel] Achsah his daughter for his wife. When she came [to Othniel], she urged him to ask her father for a field.

And she dismounted from her ass, and Caleb said to her, 'What's the matter with you?' She said to him, 'Bring me a blessing! For the land of the Negeb you have given me; so give me also springs of water.' So Caleb gave her the upper springs and the lower springs.

(Judg. 1: 12–15)

Like the story of YHWH giving the promised land, the story in which
it is embedded, this little anecdote tells of a gift. Like the story of
the taking of Bethel, it tells of a deal. Like the story of Adoni-Bezek
which precedes it, it tells of equity and excess.

Achsah is introduced as the object traded for the city. (The
equivalence of city—feminine in Hebrew—and woman reminds us
of another story, in 2 Samuel 11–12, where the siege and taking
of Rabbah frames the story of David's taking of Bathsheba.) Yet
suddenly she takes the initiative. Her father has given her to Othniel
in fulfilment of the deal. Achsah now urges her husband—apparently
inconveniently reticent when not attacking cities—to ask for more.
Let Caleb make a true gift. The young couple need land. The
narrator abruptly jumps us to a subsequent scene. Achsah now
confronts her father herself. Her arrival must have been unexpected
and her dismounting urgent, for Caleb immediately demands to
know what the problem is. Now, as she makes her request, we
discover that the field has been asked for and given. Caleb has
indeed given land, but it is land in the wilderness (the Negeb). We
can only imagine Achsah's confrontation with her husband. What we
see is her action. She confronts her father and asks for what she
must have if she and her family are to have life: land without water
is land without life. 'Give me also springs of water!' The response to
her request is simply narrated and, in its simplicity, powerful. 'And
Caleb gave her the upper springs—*and* the lower springs'!

For Achsah the dry land is a chariot of iron. But she does not
settle for what she has. She has a vision of a land that is a blessing.
So she asks for the water that will transform the dry land. She asks
for something that will support a family and fruitful existence in the
land. She asks for life itself—and receives it in double measure.
Caleb gives not one spring but two. Unlike Caleb, perhaps, she
knows that the two of them cannot live fruitfully on their own. They
need that gift. And Caleb, asked, immediately recognizes this truth
and blesses them with a gift that goes beyond the asking. Caleb's gift
overflows.

The parable is not hard to recognize. Achsah asks for water in the
dry land, just as the people of Israel have earlier asked for water in
the wilderness, and for a new land of freedom in place of the old of
slavery and oppression. Judah now confronts its opportunity in the

land. A new land is what they have sought. Now it is given them, theirs for the taking. Yet they hesitate and nervously compromise, though YHWH is with them. The bride sees springs of water and life. She acts. She asks. And somehow we doubt that Achsah would have capitulated to chariots of iron.

There are three developed anecdotes in Judges 1, each cameo size but with individual characters and dialogue. We have looked at two, the stories of Achsah and the taking of Bethel. The third, the story of Judah's defeat of Adoni-Bezek at the outset to the chapter has often intrigued commentators. Why is it told?

Adoni-Bezek fled; but they pursued him, and seized him, and cut off his thumbs and his big toes. And Adoni-Bezek said, 'Seventy kings with their thumbs and their big toes cut off used to pick up the scraps under my table; as I have done, so God has repaid me.' And they brought him to Jerusalem and he died there. (Judg. 1: 6–7)

The Canaanite king speaks of equity. His understanding of divine justice is familiar to the reader of the story so far—an eye for an eye, as the law of Moses would have it, or a thumb for seventy thumbs, in Adoni-Bezek's version. But if this reader should agree readily that the king's punishment is just, even more than just (given the disparate one for seventy), some consequences follow.

Talk of kings at tables reminds us of other texts subsequent to this one: Mephibosheth, heir of King Saul, found himself eating out his days at the table, and by the favour, of the usurper, King David (2 Sam. 9: 1–13); so, too, Jehoiachin, king of Judah, of the house of David, ended his days eating at the table of his captor, the king of Babylon—an anecdote that brings to a close the whole great story of Genesis–2 Kings. The nation devastated, Jerusalem destroyed, and the people scattered, the story of Israel ends at a captor king's table (2 Kgs. 25: 27–30) (Miscall 1986: 22 ¶N; see further Granowski 1992 ¶O.2).

The dispossession of Israel has been, so the narrator has insisted, divine punishment. Given this ending, then, Adoni-Bezek's story may be recognized as a parable of Israel's relationship with YHWH. As Israel constantly breaks its covenant with its God what is its just requital? A thumb for a thumb would have brought the story to a grinding halt, before the very chapter were out. As it turns out, the larger story begins to seem more like Adoni-Bezek's version of equity, a thumb for seventy thumbs.

The parable makes another point. In the parable Adoni-Bezek is Israel. The Canaanite is an Israelite. Not such a strange thought, from Jehoiachin's point of view since, in the event, YHWH had the Assyrians and Babylonians do to the Israelites—dispossess them —just what the Israelites in this part of the story are enjoined to do to the Canaanites. As the angel in Judges 2 observes, the issue *is* YHWH—the difference between being an Israelite and a Canaanite is the difference between serving YHWH and serving other gods. As the story proceeds, it becomes clear that the reason Israelites are Israelites and not Canaanites is because of YHWH's kindness/loyalty (*hesed*). For YHWH has a way of offering two springs of water instead of one, and requiting one thumb for seventy.

Allusion and intertextuality

Context is not the only connector of stories. Allusion can invite other texts into play. Allusion can be effected through the choice of identical or similar words, similar grammatical arrangement, or similarly constructed narrative situation. Allusion to other literature can enrich a narrative in several ways. Allusions can foreshadow; they can help the reader fill gaps in terms of character motivation, for example, or of social expectation. Allusions reflect the larger text or context of literary expression and give the reader a sense of both the commonality and the uniqueness of the work in question.

Stories, we have said, attempt to control. Allusions can provide support for social, theological, or political claims; allusions can also be parodied or disclaimed in a story's attempt to promote a different message. In the larger corpus of biblical narrative, some connections are more apparent than others. Recognition of associations depends upon the degree to which the reader is familiar with the whole of the biblical text, the extent to which the parallels are thought to be explicit, and the willingness of the reader to consider certain narratives in conjunction with others.

In the book of Ruth, for example, awareness of the symbolic value of Moab in other stories—the story of Lot and his daughters

(Genesis 19) and the sin of Baal-Peor (Numbers 25), as well as the law singling out Moabites as prohibited from entering the assembly of YHWH (Deut. 23: 3–6 [4–7])—enables a reader of Ruth to align his or her point of view for a moment with that of the Israelites in the story or its implied ancient Israelite reader and detect ethnic and religious prejudice against Moab. Throughout the story, Ruth is constantly called 'the Moabite woman', whether by the narrator or the characters. We *know* she is a Moabite woman from the beginning of the narrative and hardly need to be reminded. Yet we are, redundantly, reminded. The repetition sends us to other texts about Moabites. The result is constructive. Negative allusions to Moab as the son of incest (compare the connotation of the term 'bastard' in English today), or to Moabite women as those who snared Israelite men who came to eat and drink in Moab (patriarchy habitually blames the women), make Elimelech's foray into Moab to find food a move likely to invite severe condemnation from many in Bethlehem. Could Naomi, especially when accompanied by a Moabite daughter-in-law, hope to escape such criticism herself? How could Boaz, a pillar of Bethlehem society, even consider marrying a Moabite woman? The narrator's insistent naming of Ruth's nationality pushes this issue of prejudice into the foreground and helps us to see it as a, perhaps *the*, major complication to the plot, once Boaz has noticed and admired (desired?) Ruth. Allusion helps make this meaning possible.

The exposition of the book of Ruth describes a situation structurally reminiscent of the exposition to the Judah and Tamar story in Genesis 38. There is separation from family/homeland, a sojourning elsewhere, marriages to foreign women, deaths of two sons and spouse. In the Genesis story, as noted above, Judah suspects Tamar the Canaanite widow to be the cause of the death of his two eldest sons. Without openly accusing her, however, he urges her to return to her father's house. Naomi's attitude towards her daughters-in-law is not openly declared by the narrator, but she, too, urges return— each to her mother's house. Struck by the analogy between the stories, a reader might well wonder whether Ruth has become to Naomi what Tamar was to Judah, namely, an albatross around her neck. The reader seeking to understand Naomi's motives is thus prompted to scrutinize her speech and actions with a degree of suspicion instead of taking them simply at face value.

Likewise, the depiction of Naomi sending Ruth down to the threshing-floor at night to lie with Boaz calls to mind not only the way Tamar deceived Judah in order to get a son, and how Lot's daughters got pregnant, but also how Laban tricked Jacob into marrying Leah rather than Rachel (Genesis 29). And again the allusions inculcate suspicion on the part of the reader so that entrapment comes into focus as an explanation for an enigmatic episode. That these connections with other texts are not arbitrary is perhaps established when, at the end of the story, the people and elders at the gate invoke Rachel and Leah, and the house of Perez 'whom Tamar bore to Judah', as models for Ruth and Boaz (Ruth 4: 11–12).

Intertextuality, a term coined by the French theorist Julia Kristeva, differs from allusion. In the case of allusion, markers in the text itself (words, phrases, motifs, etc.) point to other texts. Intertextuality, on the other hand, is a relationship that might exist between any two texts. The reader, rather than the text, makes the connections. Connections can, of course, be arbitrary, but most readers do not bother to associate texts which have nothing in common. Dialogue is the goal, and for dialogue to take place texts must have a common subject.

Historical critics have been unwilling to view narratives in conjunction unless they were considered to be by the same author, in the same literary trajectory (that is, chronologically placed in the history of tradition), or obviously alluding to a literary precedent. Recent theorists have realized that many texts compete, whether or not they have had historical contact. It is this competing of texts that makes intertextual reading an enlivening, if unsettling, process.

Intertextuality plays upon the notion of control. Literary traditions are built by texts attempting to outdo each other. Texts endeavour to rewrite other texts, to usurp their power, to displace their authority. In the Hebrew Bible, there are many texts competing for rhetorical power. Two such texts are the Genesis–2 Kings and Chronicles–Ezra–Nehemiah narratives.

Reading between words and stories: the house of David

In our final reading of the chapter we bring into play some of the language lures about which we have been speaking. We start with a word-play, a simple case of repetition in the story of David in 2 Samuel, observing a powerful metaphor at work, and extend the metaphor into Kings beyond the account of David himself. Then we use it to configure a contrastive reading of Chronicles, Ezra, and Nehemiah.

We start in the aftermath of David's taking of Bathsheba and murder of Uriah. Confronted by Nathan the prophet, David acknowledges his sin. The prophet casts YHWH's reproach at him. 'I gave you', says YHWH, 'your master's house . . . I gave you the house of Israel and of Judah' (v. 8). Why then has he done evil? 'So now', says the prophet, 'a sword will not turn aside from your house, a lasting sword . . . Thus says YHWH: Behold, I am raising up evil against you from your house . . .' (2 Sam. 12: 10–11).

The house of Israel and the house of Judah. The house of Saul and the house of David. 'House' is the nation, the kingdom; 'house' is the dynasty; 'house' is the extended family. David's political and private lives are correlates, mirroring each other and curiously intertwined (especially in 2 Sam 10–20; see Gunn 1975 or 1978: 87– 111 ¶N.3; Gros Louis 1977 ¶N.3). The point comes to expression particularly in the ambiguity of Nathan's phrase 'your master's [adonai's] house'. Does that mean house of Israel (Saul's kingdom), or house of Saul (Saul's family—Michal and Jonathan, Ishbosheth and Mephibosheth), or dynasty (the right to succeed to Saul's throne), or God's (Adonai's) own house (the whole of Israel and Judah), or all of these? The houses have a way of giving expression to each other. They are integral parts of the organism that is 'all Israel', the people of YHWH. What happens privately in David's own house (palace and family) will have an impact on the nation.

From the roof of the palace ('the king's house') David sees Bathsheba and sends for her. When she sends word of her pregnancy, David sends for her husband, Uriah, and commands him to go down to his house. Wittingly or unwittingly, Uriah refuses to go (see 11: 8–9 and the reiteration of 'house'). He is therefore no party to the corruption in the king's house, though his forbearance will cost him his life. But this is only the beginning of the violence. In the following story of Amnon and Absalom, both family and nation will be torn apart (chs. 12–20).

Why does this pivotal Bathsheba/Uriah episode come where it

does in David's story? One reason might be that here above all the king is on the point of securing his house. All surrounding enemies have been defeated. War against the Ammonites is the final phase, the seizure of the Ammonite capital, Rabbah, spelling completion. The city is then for David the crown of empire. Victory is imminent. David need not even go out to battle. Internally, the house of Saul is subdued, Michal (Saul's daughter) and Mephibosheth (Jonathan's son) assimilated into the new king's house (2 Samuel 6 and 9).

Dynasty, the 'house' which eluded Saul, is promised by oracle of YHWH through Nathan (2 Samuel 7). Validation has also come through the cult in another way, for now the ark, too, like Mephibosheth, dwells in Jerusalem (2 Samuel 6). David even wants to build a house for it to match his own ('And when the king dwelt in his house and YHWH gave him rest from all around, from his enemies, the king said to Nathan the prophet, "Consider: here am I sitting in a house of cedar but the ark of God sits in the midst of a tent" [7:1]). Chapters 5–10 spell consolidation of power, legitimacy, security (Flanagan 1983 ¶N.3). They also bring to completion a story which began even before David, before Saul and the feuding years, back in the opening chapters of 1 Samuel. There the issues confronting Israel were the threat from external enemies, the cult in disarray and bereft of the ark of God, and priestly leadership that had failed, giving rise to the cry for a king 'like other nations'. With David these issues are all resolved. The kingdom is secured. So the king, comfortable in his cedar house in Jerusalem as his men go out to seize Rabbah, seizes Bathsheba. As one house (the house of Israel) is secured, another (the house of the king) begins to crumble.

Kingship—God-given or not—is no talisman, we might decide, remembering the warnings by Moses and Samuel in Deuteronomy 17 and 1 Samuel 8. On that reading, then, our story would retell a story told and retold in Genesis–2 Kings: YHWH alone is sovereign, YHWH alone offers security; and even then the people of YHWH cannot secure that security or fashion it their own way (and Saul, pathetically pious, YHWH's loyalist to the end, epitomizes that last point).

Thus King David here embodies the nation that is given the land, but falters in the very realization of the gift. Solomon, too, plays his part in this iconoclastic story. Established on David's throne, secure in the gracious promise of a house/dynasty (2 Samuel 7; cf. 1 Kings 8), he does what his father considered. He builds further security, a house for Yʜwʜ. We are dazzled by the description of it (1 Kings 5–7), swayed by the rhetoric of prayer and proclamation (1 Kings 8), pushed by both subject-matter and style to recall the elaborate description of the building of the tabernacle, back in that formative, prescriptive period at Sinai and in the wilderness (Exodus 35).

There are some differences, though. The tabernacle was modest in size and moved with its tent. The new house of God is huge and anchored. The tabernacle was the gift and work of the congregation of Israel, 'all whose hearts stirred them, whose spirit moved within them' (Exodus 35). The temple is built by forced labour, tens of thousands who quarried the stone and hauled the cedar purchased from King Hiram of Tyre (1 Kings 5–6), and its bronze is cast by another Hiram, brought especially from Tyre.

The glory of Yʜwʜ's house, moreover, soon gives way (1 Kgs. 7: 1–12 and chs. 9–11) to the expanding glory of Solomon's own house (via, ironically, his God-given gift of wisdom)—the house of David will not suffice. The house of Yʜwʜ takes seven years to build, the king's house thirteen. A reader might well decide that this whole elaborate narrative edifice harbours no little ironic comment on the king. Such a reading seems to be confirmed when the king's grandiose indulgence in house-building finally gives way to an account of an extraordinary devotional failure incubated within his own house (1 Kings 11; the thematic parallel with David's failure, 2 Samuel 11–12, is striking). Solomon, secure in the glory of the house of Yʜwʜ (not to speak of his own), serves other gods!

So the house of Yʜwʜ is no talisman. The larger story (Genesis–2 Kings) ends with it ruined, the people dispersed. Neither does the house of David hold out absolute security. We are hardly surprised to find the story take a sudden turn in the very next chapter. The house of Israel is torn from Solomon's house, leaving only Judah. Though the relationship between Yʜwʜ and David (2 Samuel 7) is given as the reason for at least part of Yʜwʜ's forbearance towards Judah-Israel and its kings (cf. 1 Kgs. 2: 4; 8: 22–6; 9: 4–5; 11: 30–9; 15: 4; 2 Kgs. 8: 19), by the end the house of Judah, like the house of Yʜwʜ and the house of Israel, has disappeared. The erstwhile king of Judah, of the house of David, eats, like Mephibosheth of the house of Saul (2 Samuel 9), at the usurper's table!

The ambivalence of the promise of a house (dynasty) to David, conditional or unconditional, is perhaps a theological rather than a historical question. God offers grace that is lasting—grace to Abraham, to Moses, to David. But God cannot be taken for granted. A banal comment, a truism, yet one that catches the story of the nation, from entry into the land to exit. The promise of a 'house' is grace—ordered, institutionalized. Yet that is a paradox, for grace confounds order and institution—as Jonah knew and resented. No institution secures, no institution is secure. The promise, suggests our reading of this story, cannot be presumed upon; it is not a crutch but an invitation to share in God's grace for the future.

The search for David's house also has intertextual dimensions. The Chronicles–Ezra–Nehemiah corpus is also preoccupied with the building of a house. Just as we found repetition and variation to produce meaning within a text, here we find that similarity and difference can also generate meaning between texts.

Addressing Solomon in Chronicles, David explains why he will not himself build a house to YHWH's name: 'There came upon me the word of YHWH, saying, "Much blood have you shed and great battles have you waged; you shall not build a house to my name; for much blood have you shed upon the earth before me"' (1 Chron. 22: 7–8; and cf. 28: 3). Yet despite a label which we can hardly fail to recognize from Samuel and Kings (Shimei was not all wrong when he hurled at David: 'Away, away, you man of blood . . .'; 2 Sam. 16: 5–13), if we seek David the murderer of Uriah in 1 Chronicles we will not readily find him. Here the man of blood will give place not only to a sweet psalmist (2 Chron. 29: 30), but above all to a great patron of liturgy and the music of worship, and a planner of institutions, indeed of *the* institution, the house of YHWH.

It is not that the warrior is gone: in 1 Chron. 11: 4–9 the taking of Jerusalem is recounted, and later come summary accounts of wars against foreign foes to recall the glory of empire (18: 1–13). Yet these have, by and large, a rather aseptic character, at least as far as David is concerned. The Ammonite war is there (19: 1–20: 3), but no longer framing a story of adultery and murder. Bathsheba and Uriah have vanished. Complementing this cluster of battle reports is the story of Elhanan slaying not Goliath (cf 2 Sam. 21: 19), but Lahmi, Goliath's *brother* (1 Chron. 20: 5).

Tamed also is the story of the census (1 Chronicles 21; cf. 2 Samuel 24, which we looked at above, Chapter 4), inasmuch as Satan now stands between David and total culpability, though Joab's remonstration with the king (more vehement than in Samuel) prevents a total idealization of David. The Chronicler, too, knows that there is no perfection in humankind. Yet even this strange story is deftly woven back into line, for Ornan's threshing-floor (where the story ends) becomes the site of the temple. The census story thus issues in praise to God's name—for the house of God in Chronicles is above all the building of praise and thanksgiving.

When, therefore, we review David's story from its narrative inception in chapter 10, the death of Saul, we see that the concerns of peace have enveloped and permeated the accounts of war. The divisions of north and south, house of Israel and house of Judah, are bridged as all Israel gathers. The mighty men gather, a muster transformed into a congregation, to hear Amasai (a fortuitous reconciliation of 2 Samuel's rebel Amasa and aggressive Abishai!) shout 'Peace!' (12: 18). Battles against the Philistines are encompassed by a greater purpose for the congregation, namely the bringing of the ark to Jerusalem. It is in ordering and activating the great praise due to God that David finds life in the Chronicler's narrative.

As the ark story in chapters 13 and 15–16 envelops the Philistine battle accounts in chapter 14, so the celebrations of chapters 15 and 16 at the installation of the ark and the intimations of house-building in chapter 17 eventually envelop the campaigns of chapters 18–20. Though death touches Israel itself in the pestilence of chapter 21, nevertheless there is, by the end of the chapter and throughout the remainder of David's reign, a rapid shift from repentance to mercy and the promulgation of worship in the building of YHWH's house.

The issue of succession is digested in a verse (23: 1), swallowed up by more important issues. Charges have to be made ('Be strong and build!'), leaders assembled, divisions established (divisions for harmony!). The organizing of divisions for temple and community (chs. 23–7) lies within a frame of ordering speech that is typical of the Chronicler: David's charge to Solomon and the leaders (ch. 22) leads to an assembly (ch. 23), while after the details of the divisions there follows a newly constituted assembly (ch. 28) and a resumed charge to Solomon and the whole assembly. The focus of all the organization is upon the sustenance of YHWH's house: priests and levites, musicians and gatekeepers, commanders of this, chief officers of that, all are ordered to such an end.

The very style orders our understanding. It is processional, like its subject-matter; it is comprised of lists and careful descriptions, prayers and exhortations; it is above all monologue rather than dialogue. It harks back to Leviticus and Deuteronomy, to Samuel's sermon (1 Samuel 12) and Nathan's prophecy (2 Samuel 7). Rather than creating 'gaps', ambiguities, openness, in the text—as in so much of David's story in Samuel–Kings—it closes around us and marches us towards 'plain' understanding. We become less attuned to those ironies and paradoxes that inhabit Samuel–Kings. It is, in other words, monologic rather than dialogic (and 'serious' rather than 'rhetorical'; see above, Chapter 1). There is a deliberate, measured quality about this material. The reader has to march with it, mark time, develop stamina even. This is the style of commitment.

It also has the effect of turning us away from David, to the task, the many actors, and the community. Indeed, before we ever start into the narrative proper (ch. 10) we become enmeshed in the web of community through the extensive genealogical lists. Again, it is striking that the hymn of chapter 16 is no longer David's (compare the 'I' of 2 Samuel 22–3) but appointed by David to be sung by the appropriate leaders for the worshipping community.

At the centre of the community is the house of YHWH, not David's house, nor even Jerusalem. Thanksgiving is fundamental. Giving is fundamental. David's purchase of the site of the house is paradigmatic. The whole community can contribute, beyond those who directly serve in the house. In this way the act recovers the construction of the tabernacle in Exodus and sharply differentiates the account from the building of Solomon's temple in 1 Kings. The narrative moves towards an exhortation to give (ch. 29); and in the context of this inexorable knitting together of a myriad persons, all with their allotted role, who can stand aside from the call to commitment?

The end of Kings is a gaping hole which, when we peer into it, loops us back to Deuteronomy, to where we stand 'today' before

Moses, 'outside', pondering the invitation to enter and participate in a new gift. The end of Chronicles bridges that gulf surely, converts desolation into a sabbath (2 Chron. 36: 21), and marches us resolutely towards an unambiguous goal—to build YHWH a house. Cyrus' decree (36: 23; Ezra 1: 3) strikingly resumes David's charge to Solomon (1 Chron. 22: 6, 18–19).

Invited into the books of Ezra and Nehemiah by the resumption of Chronicles in Ezra 1, we stand once more before David (fashioned now in the form of Cyrus), as we are ordered to be up and building a new edifice. The vision of David stays in the text, too, as the people offer gifts and praise YHWH at the foundation of the new house, and as Ezra and Nehemiah themselves charge, exhort, and celebrate. As in Chronicles, the great moments are those of giving and thanksgiving in the service of YHWH by a community which finds its identity in its ordering in and around his house. Ultimately this is the only house that matters. At the dedication of the wall—the bulwark around the house and its servants (cf. Neh. 12: 44–7)—Ezra's company of praise processes with the musical instruments of David the 'man of God', above David's house (12: 31–7).

Yet the actuality of house-building competes with David's vision: there is no end to the business of establishment (Neh. 13: 30). Rather the story is one of struggle and contention and ever renewed invitation—by exhortation or paradigm (see e.g. Neh. 12: 47)—to give. Again and again we see commitment lapsed. The ending, set against the celebration in chapter 12, with Nehemiah again attempting to untangle the potential damage done by ever resurgent self-interest and human banality, is realistic, if a touch pathetic: the zealot berates, curses, contends, chases, and pulls out hair. Remember the forces of evil, he urges God; and 'remember me, O God, for good' (13: 23–31). His righteousness risks mocking itself. The sentiment is not unlike that of David's last words (2 Sam. 23: 1–7). It works to pull Chronicles and Samuel together again.

David's vision in Chronicles–Ezra–Nehemiah is a splendid one, a call to build a house in order to seek YHWH in the service of praise and thanksgiving—a call which reverberates particularly readily with today's reader in church or synagogue. When we read between the texts, this vision reasserts, alongside the liberating ironies of Samuel and Kings, the constructive power of order and institution.

Yet for us to end thus in security may be to betray both narratives. For insecurity is also the burden of these stories of houses. Better perhaps to break off with a question: Must the story always end this way, as it does with Nehemiah—not with praise and thanksgiving in the house of YHWH but with desperate judgement and claims to righteousness?

The end of this reading is full of judgements—not least our own value judgements. As we have made explicit in the Introduction, and implicit in our subsequent discussions, who we are, where we read from, and what we stand for constantly shape our reading and the meanings we try to secure from texts. To return to our opening metaphors, we single out the pattern, we choose the lure.

8

Nebuchadnezzar and the Three Jews: Daniel 3

While some narrators tell their stories rather matter-of-factly, avoiding repetition, ambiguity, and metaphor, others revel in the wonder of words, the play of patterns and images. In Daniel 3 we find such a playful story-teller.

Nebuchadnezzar the king made an image of gold. Its height was sixty cubits; its width six cubits. He erected it in the plain of Dura in the province of Babylon. Nebuchadnezzar the king summoned for assembly the satraps, the prefects and the governors, the counsellors, the treasurers, the judges, the officials and all the authorities of the province to come to the dedication of the image which Nebuchadnezzar the king had erected. Then the satraps, the prefects and the governors, the counsellors, the treasurers, the judges, the officials and all the authorities of the province assembled themselves for the dedication of the image which Nebuchadnezzar the king had erected. They stood before the image that Nebuchadnezzar had erected and the herald called loudly to them, saying, 'Peoples, nations, and languages! When you hear the sound of the horn, the pipe, the lyre, the trigon, the harps, the bagpipes, and every kind of music, you will fall down and pay homage to the gold image that Nebuchadnezzar the king has erected. Whoever does not fall down and pay homage will immediately be cast into the midst of a blazing fiery furnace.' Consequently, as soon as all the people heard the sound of the horn, the pipe, the lyre, the trigon, the harp, the bagpipes and every kind of music, all the peoples, nations, and languages fell down and paid homage to the gold image that Nebuchadnezzar the king had erected. (Dan. 3: 1–7)

The historical Babylonian King Nebuchadrezzar destroyed Jerusalem and took most of its citizens into captivity. As one can well imagine, this figure was not exactly a popular hero among the ancient Israelites. The characterization of Nebuchadnezzar in this story is, like that in Daniel 1, 2, and 4, a parody of this ruthless king. The narrator's repetitious style and love of tedious detail set a tone of ridicule and absurdity.

Nebuchadnezzar builds an image of ludicrous dimensions: ninety feet by nine feet—a top-heavy statue if ever there was one. The delicately balanced mass of gold alludes to the preceding story in Daniel 2 in which Nebuchadnezzar dreams of a similar statue with a head of gold. The sage Daniel had identified the golden head with Nebuchadnezzar himself, but, in the dream, the statue fell when a great stone crushed its feet of clay. The dream in Daniel 2 functions as a divine warning against hubris, but Nebuchadnezzar's sculpting feat in Daniel 3 indicates that the stupid king has totally missed the point. He builds the preposterous gold image and, though we are not explicitly told why he builds it, we might easily surmise that it is to represent the golden age of his reign. The structure is a visual symbol of the way in which he wants himself and his reign to be perceived, both now and in the years to come.

That the king is preoccupied with public perceptions is verified in his next action. He assembles a long list of officials to the dedication of his image. No sooner is the long-winded list uttered than it is repeated in the narrator's report of the officials' arrival. On the surface, this (almost) verbatim repetition of the list tells us precisely who is summoned and precisely who appears at the dedication of the image. It gives a guide to the nature of the gathering. All the people involved are identified by political status. This is not an occasion for the general populace; it is an administrative assembly. The list's extent suggests a rather sophisticated political network. The repetition of the list, however, also enacts the power structure of the story world. It shows the king's control of this network. Precisely what the king wills is precisely what takes place. The precise people whom he summons are the precise people who assemble. Thus, through repetition, the narrator pictures (and mocks) a setting in which conformity is normative, disobedience unthinkable.

The repetition slows the pace of narration and the list's content

broadens our range of vision. We began with a view limited to the
king and his top-heavy image; now our vision is broadened to
include the assembled multitude. As we look upon the crowd with
our wide-angle vision, we hear the herald make the royal announcement that all are to bow to the image or be thrown into a furnace.
This dedication, it seems, involves more than simply admiring the
king's handiwork. The people are required to swear allegiance to
(that is, to worship) this image. If they refuse, they are sentenced to
death by burning. By threatening death, Nebuchadnezzar attempts
to control the behaviour of the crowd. But why is such behaviour
so important? What is this image? Is it a god? We are not expressly
told so. In fact, the only description of the image (besides its odd
dimensions) is the insistence that Nebuchadnezzar the king erected
it. The recurrence of this qualifier (vv. 2, 3 (twice), 5, 7, 12, 14, 18)
suggests that the significance of the image lies in the identity of
its progenitor. Nebuchadnezzar the king has made it. It is his
accomplishment.

The herald's address may also be of help in deciphering the
import of the situation. When the herald addresses the congregation,
we might have expected: 'O satraps, prefects and governors, etc.' Instead, he makes a substitution: 'O peoples, nations, and languages!'
When reporting the congregation's obedience to the order, the
narrator also employs the herald's terminology: 'All the peoples,
nations, and languages fell down and paid homage . . .' While the
previous list of political offices identifies the people with the
Babylonian administration, thus signalling affinity, the variation
'peoples, nations, and languages' acknowledges a broad national
spectrum, thus signalling difference. The people gathered may be
part of the Babylonian political structure, but they also come from a
variety of national backgrounds. They represent nations who have
been conquered and subjugated by the fierce Nebuchadnezzar. To
worship the image is to swear allegiance to their conqueror. The
dedication is a manœuvre on Nebuchadnezzar's part to rally political
solidarity. Even the religious nuances of the dedication fit well into
the promotion of political unity. One need only recall the reforms
of Hezekiah and Josiah (2 Kings 18 and 23) to understand that
religious homogeneity and political autonomy go hand in hand.

The narrator's tone ridicules this attempt on Nebuchadnezzar's part to reassure himself of his power and control. The tedious repetitions (of which we have not heard the last) undermine the solemnity of the occasion and leave the reader wondering about the hierarchy of significance in the story world. Rather than explaining what the image represents, the narrator spends time repeatedly listing officials and musical instruments. The pomp of the event is given more emphasis that the meaning of the event. And, lest we should forget for even a second, the narrator constantly reminds us that the image is something that 'Nebuchadnezzar the king has erected', thus mocking the king's attempt to be regarded and remembered as a head of gold. Royal insecurity is exposed to all who have eyes to see.

When reporting the crowd's response to the command, the narrator includes the redundant catalogue of musical instruments as well as the herald's nomenclature, 'peoples, nations, and languages'. The narrator, however, adds the word *all*—'all the peoples, nations, and languages bowed down and worshipped the gold image . . .' The addition of 'all' emphasizes the wholesale compliance of the assembly and thus accentuates the point made by the earlier repeated list of officials: precisely what the king commands is precisely what happens. The wholesale compliance of the assembly can put the king's political worry to rest.

Or can it? Does the word 'all' represent the narrator's point of view or does it merely represent Nebuchadnezzar's? By using the absurd repetition, might the narrator be mocking the king's perspective that he has now attained the unanimous allegiance of his subjects?

The word 'all' unsettles a reader who has already read Daniel 1 and 2. The reader's interest would be focused on Daniel and his friends who, when we last heard of them, had been appointed as officials over the province of Babylon. Presumably they too are at this dedication. In an earlier episode (Daniel 1) the Jewish friends would not eat food from the king's table for fear of compromising authority. How are they now to respond to the command to worship an image as a gesture of political allegiance?

Suddenly the scene shifts and the scope of our vision narrows. We are made to focus on 'certain Chaldaeans' who approach the king accusing 'certain Jews' of disobeying the royal order.

They said to Nebuchadnezzar the king, 'O King, live forever! You, O King, have given a command that everyone who hears the sound of the horn, the pipe, the lyre, the trigon, the harp, the bagpipes, and every kind of music must fall down and pay homage to the gold image and whoever does not fall down and pay homage will be cast into the midst of a blazing fiery furnace. There are certain Jews whom you have appointed over the administration of the province of Babylon: Shadrach, Meshach, and Abednego. These men, O King, show no deference to you. They do not serve your gods and they do not pay homage to the gold image that you have erected.'   (Dan. 3: 9–12)

Since the behaviour of 'certain Jews' is on our minds, we are not terribly surprised by this turn in the plot. As the Chaldaeans speak, we realize that, if their testimony is reliable, our vantage point in the first scene has been so distant that we have obviously missed something. We could see the crowd, but not the individuals. If the Chaldaeans are telling the truth, the little word 'all' has merely told us what we and the king *think* we have seen, not what has actually taken place.

The narrator could have handled in several different ways the scene in which Nebuchadnezzar learns of the disobedience. The story could have been told in the passive voice: 'And it was told to King Nebuchadnezzar that the Jews had refused to worship the image.' Or the king, while officiating at the dedication, could simply have witnessed the disobedience himself. Instead, the narrator, who never seems to miss a chance of a verbose repetition, introduces another party to give the report to the king.

However, though they mimic with absurd accuracy the herald and the narrator before them, they expand and, to a certain extent, reorganize the material in order to move the king to take action against the three Jews. As they reiterate the king's order, they carefully include the condition for failure to comply. Since their purpose is to inform on Shadrach, Meshach, and Abednego, the pointed reminder of the fiery furnace serves as a subtle challenge to the king to act upon his word.

The most striking addition that the informants make in their speech is, of course, the information about the three Jews. The Chaldaeans do not simply say 'these men did not pay homage to the gold image'. Rather, they first mention the political position that these three hold: they are the king's personal appointees over the administration of the province of Babylon. As the Chaldaeans continue, they craftily voice the affront as a personal one. Notice that they do not say 'These men show no deference to the royal decree' or 'to Babylonian law'. They do not refer to the divine as 'Babylonian gods' or 'our gods'. Instead, they pointedly make the king the target of the affront by employing the second person singular: 'they show no deference to *you*'; 'they do not serve *your* gods'; 'they do not worship the image *you* have erected'.

The rhetoric of their speech accomplishes several things. The use of the second person singular turns political betrayal into personal betrayal. In other words, the king himself appointed them to office and now they are stabbing him in the back. The reference to not serving the king's gods plays upon the king's attitude implicit in this whole affair, namely, that religious affinity is political affinity and, conversely, religious difference is political difference. Difference, emphasize the Chaldaeans, is suspect. The speech also plants the idea that this particular disobedience is the manifestation of their *complete* untrustworthiness—they show *no deference* to the king. Moreover, through their rhetoric, the Chaldaeans implicitly contrast themselves to the three Jews. Unlike the Jews, their speech suggests, they are obedient to the king, of the same religious persuasion as the king, and politically loyal to the king. They present themselves as dutiful subjects who have only the king's interests in mind.

However questionable the Chaldaeans' motives, the reader may suspect with good reason that they are in fact telling the truth about the incident itself. After all, Shadrach, Meshach, and Abednego had followed Daniel's lead in chapter 1 and refused to eat the indenturing royal food. It seems most likely that they have also refused to worship the image. What they might do when publicly challenged on this issue is another matter, however. Daniel is not around to take charge and, as every dissenter knows, discreet disobedience is remarkably easier than overt defiance.

To the king's credit, he does not accept the Chaldaean's report unquestioningly. He summons the three before him for interrogation.

'Is it true, Shadrach, Meshach, and Abednego, that you do not serve my gods nor do you pay homage to the god image I have erected? Now, if you are ready, when you hear the sound of the horn, the pipe, the lyre, the trigon, the harp, the bagpipes and every kind of music, you will fall down and pay homage to the image that I have made. If you do not pay homage, you will promptly be cast into the midst of a blazing fiery furnace—and who is the god who will deliver you from my hands?'

(Dan. 3: 14–15)

Each repetition of the original royal order has brought us a step closer to the central confrontation of the story. With this fourth and final repetition there are no mediators—no herald speaking on the king's behalf, no narrator reporting obedience, no Chaldaeans reporting disobedience. The king and the three Jews are face to face.

Despite the verbose repetition, Nebuchadnezzar also offers his own creative version. Rather than giving the order straight away, he first echoes, in a question to the three, the last statements of the Chaldaeans. But rather than waiting for an answer, he hurries on with the order. By proceeding this way, he seems to be communicating that the important thing is their performance of the act of homage. What they did earlier is irrelevant; what they do now is critical. That is to say, he is less concerned with their belief than he is with their conduct. They may not believe in his gods; they may set no store by the image itself; but they should at least bow down out of respect for and fear of the king who has made it. He deserves their homage because he has the power to put them to death.

In Nebuchadnezzar's major variation on the repetition, he correctly perceives that the three men are motivated by religious devotion: 'Who is the god who will deliver you from my hands?' The object of such loyalty, suggests the king, should be powerful. He himself is ultimately powerful because he can have them killed; their god cannot possibly compete with this control over life and death. His rhetorical question challenges, what is in his view, their misplaced loyalty and plays upon their fear.

Shadrach, Meshach, and Abednego are no longer three faceless people in the obscurity of a multitude. They stand alone, front and centre. Whatever they do now determines what becomes of them. Suspense builds as we wait through the king's listing of musical instruments, his command, his threat for disobedience, and his gibe at the folly of their religious commitment.

The speech of Shadrach, Meshach, and Abednego marks the first and the major climactic point in the story.

'O Nebuchadnezzar, we have no need to respond to you concerning this matter. If our god whom we serve is able to deliver us from a blazing fiery furnace and from your hands, O King, then he will deliver. But if not, be it known to you, O King, that we do not serve your gods nor will we pay homage to the gold image that you have erected.'

(Dan. 3: 16–18)

Their speech breaks the verbal rules of the story. Their speech stands apart from all the others heard thus far in that they refuse to answer with the extensive repetition that has come to be expected. Not only do they fail to use the full-scale repetition themselves, they speak without waiting for the musical signal and thus deprive the narrator of the final chance to relist the instruments.

The response of the three friends does, however, echo smaller segments of the earlier material. None the less, they do not attempt to buy time with verbosity. They offer no self-defence. Although Nebuchadnezzar had intended his closing question to be rhetorical, Shadrach, Meshach, and Abednego refuse to interpret it as such. They answer affirming loyalty, not to Nebuchadnezzar, but to their god.

Their words overpower the words of the king. By refusing to acknowledge his rhetoric, they render his speech impotent. By not flinching at his ordained punishment, they emasculate his threat.

Furthermore, their response separates all the issues that have been fused together by the king and the Chaldaeans. Deliverance and divine ability are distinguished from the decision between loyalty and idolatry. Whether or not their god is able to deliver, they will not succumb to idolatry or tyranny. Their action is independent of divine action. Their loyalty is not contingent upon divine power.

The words of Shadrach, Meshach, and Abednego put the king in his place—his human place—and are a judgement upon his hubris. Though the three Jews may be uncertain about their god's *ability* to deliver them, they are confident that their god is *willing* to deliver them. Their confidence communicates something about the nature of their god: whether or not their god is omnipotent, their god still has a sense of fidelity, justice, righteousness. These are qualities that the king does not obviously possess. Here is a confession of faith that if their god is able to right this evil, unjust situation, then indeed their god will do so.

The narrator turns our attention to the king and observes that, at this point, the 'image', that is, the expression, of Nebuchadnezzar's face changes toward the three men (3: 19). By employing the same word that has been used to refer to the image of gold, the narrator playfully connects the image of gold with the image of Nebuchadnezzar's face. The word-play satirizes the king's audacity through allusion. In Genesis 1 God creates humankind in the divine image; in Daniel 3 Nebuchadnezzar creates, in his own (very human) image, an object (a god? see v. 28) to be worshipped.

The changing of Nebuchadnezzar's 'image' marks a turning-point in the story. The king proceeds to order that the three be thrown into the furnace (3: 19). When reading this story for the first time, readers are likely to anticipate an execution because the story has promised it: the king has threatened it, the Chaldaeans have forced it, the Jews have accepted it. At this point, the reader might recall the theme 'The king's fury is a messenger of death' (Prov. 16: 14), not only from personal experience of the world, but also from stories like 2 Samuel 12 and Daniel 2 that mimic common human experiences of power structures. The reader might also be aware that, in the larger story of Genesis–2 Kings, people have been known to die by fire for any number of reasons (for example, Numbers 16; Joshua 7; Judges 11; cf. Jer. 29: 22).

Although prepared for an execution, readers may also recognize certain literary allusions in the story that allow for other possibilities. The king's manipulative question, 'Who is the god who will deliver you from my hands?', not only echoes Deuteronomy 32: 39, in which YHWH himself says, 'there is no one who can deliver from my hand', but it also brings to mind the story of Sennacherib's attempt to take Jerusalem in 2 Kgs. 18: 13–19: 37. Through the voice of his messenger, Sennacherib sends a similar taunt to the people of the city: 'Has any of the gods of the nations ever delivered his land out of the hand of the king of Assyria? . . . Who among all the gods of the lands have delivered their land from my hand, that YHWH should deliver Jerusalem from my hand?' (2 Kgs. 18: 33, 35). Both allusions prompt a reader to see the king's audacity and to realize that, though the king does not view himself so, the narrator is portraying him to be blasphemous. The 2 Kings passage, because it, too, is narrative, is particularly suggestive concerning the plot of Daniel 3. Sennacherib threatens to take Jerusalem, but a miracle occurs that keeps him from doing so. The allusion suggests an analogy, and thereby foreshadows what is to come in Daniel 3. A miraculous deliverance is a possible plot alternative. We are being led to expect a miracle that prevents the threatened punishment from taking place.

This expectation is supported by another possible allusion. As the story continues, the three men are bound in preparation for the burning. The binding and the fire are reminiscent of another binding for another fire—the binding of Isaac for a holocaust on Mount Moriah in Genesis 22. In that story, too, divine intervention prevents the destruction.

The Isaac story also invites us to see the sacrificial nature of the execution. The three Jews are bound to be burned as a kind of sacrifice, a turn of events foreshadowed in Daniel 1 by the levitical description that the young men are 'without blemish'.

Standing in tension with the narrative elements that point to certain death, the allusions to miraculous deliverance may alert an imaginative reader to the possibilities and therefore hope, if not expectation, that something will happen to prevent the three from being thrown into the furnace. We look for something to happen to the king to cause him to change his mind, a divine voice, perhaps, or we hope for an angel to appear and extinguish the flames.

As first-time readers we are pulled between that which we fear and that for which we hope. The narrator holds us in suspense, teetering between the two possibilities. On subsequent readings we are likely to savour the suspense less, the texture of the narrative more. The preparations for the execution proceed with a meticulous cadence similar to that in the Genesis 22 story. The furnace is heated beyond customary proportion. Strong men are selected from the army to conduct the execution. The three men are bound. Their state of dress is described to the last detail. And then, in the moment most likely for divine intervention to take place, the three are cast into the furnace (3: 20–1). Suddenly the matter is closed, the men are gone, and with a stroke of finality, the narrator informs us that the men who threw them in are killed by the intensity of the flame

(3: 22-3). If those outside the furnace are slain by its heat, those cast inside stand no chance.

At this second climactic juncture, a sensitive reader might well pause in cadence with the text to ponder this monstrous event. Although we have been prepared for this possibility, we feel no sense of resolution. We may well feel unsettled by the lack of justice.

As we return to the narrative, our thoughts are on the three men in the fire, but the narrator forces our attention to Nebuchadnezzar (3: 24). Although something is happening in the furnace, we are only allowed to watch his response to it. We hear his dismay, we witness his alarm, but we are blinded to the source of his astonishment. We wait with wonder as he questions his counsellors and they give answer:

'Did we not cast three bound men into the midst of the fire?'
'It is true, O King.'
'Lo, I see four men, unbound, walking around in the midst of the fire and no harm has come to them! And the appearance of the fourth is like that of a son of the gods.'   (Dan. 3: 24-5)

The king's announcement comes as a surprise. What we thought had been settled has not been settled at all. Execution is not the last word. If we had hoped for deliverance *from* the fire, we had probably not expected deliverance *within* the fire. But, if so, perhaps we should have considered that possibility since fire often accompanies theophany in biblical literature (e.g., Exod. 3; 13: 21-2; Num. 16: 35). We should have recognized earlier the irony involved in the choice of fire as a means of execution. The often repeated phrase 'blazing fiery furnace' has been foreshadowing this outcome all along. Not only does a divine representative appear in the flames, but, like the burning bush, the men are not consumed.

Nebuchadnezzar summons the three men from the furnace, and calls them 'servants of the highest god' (3: 26). They step forth from the fire, but immediately lose the narrator's focus. That moves to the perceptions of those gathered around. The assembled officials—'the satraps, the prefects and the governors and the king's counsellors' —witness that the men are completely untouched by the flames: 'the fire had no power over the bodies of these men. The hair of their heads was not singed; their mantles were not changed; and the smell of fire had not passed onto them' (3: 27).

Although not every group of officials is mentioned by name, enough of the list is here to indicate that the same people who were called to worship the image are the very ones who witness the miraculous survival of the three Jews. Hence an irony: the assembly is gathered for one purpose, namely to acknowledge the ultimate sovereignty of Nebuchadnezzar; however, the crowd bears witness to the work of a sovereign more powerful than a human king could ever be. Nebuchadnezzar's intention for the dedication, like his intention to kill the three Jews, is thwarted. The gold image is forgotten.

Shadrach, Meshach, and Abednego say nothing else throughout the remainder of the story. We know nothing of their perceptions. They give us no account of their experience in the fire; they tell us nothing about the one 'like a son of the gods'. Their character is one that does not change through the course of the story. The narrator has structured the ordeal like a rite of passage, a mythical hero's journey from old life to (symbolic) death to new life. Yet even this ordeal designed to bring about change brings about none for those who participate in it. Their faith is no stronger. They acquire no new powers. Their unchanged appearance, so deliberately stressed by the narrator, is symbolic of their unchanged character.

Besides being static, the character of Shadrach, Meshach, and Abednego is, like all the other characters in the story with the exception of Nebuchadnezzar, collective. The three Jews, the administrators who attend the dedication, the 'certain Chaldaeans', the 'certain strong men' from the royal army, and the king's counsellors all are completely uniform. They speak and act as one. No individual personalities emerge. Shadrach, Meshach, and Abednego, though they appear as heroic figures, are likewise never portrayed as individuals.

Consequently, we may decide that the story is not their story. It is not a story of their heroism. The story is about the effect of their heroism on the world around them, in particular, on the king who has tried to transform them and, failing that, has tried to kill them.

The consistent collective and static characterization of Shadrach, Meshach, and Abednego, as well as of the others, highlights the single individual in the story, King Nebuchadnezzar. The narrator has focused our attention on the king more than on any other character. For the remainder of the story, he continues to fill our range of vision. As the only one to have seen inside the furnace (not even the narrator admits to having witnessed what has transpired there), Nebuchadnezzar is now the one who offers testimony. Ironically, it is he, rather than Shadrach, Meshach, and Abednego, who is changed by the fiery ordeal. He acquires a new knowledge, and it is this acquisition of knowledge around which the story turns.

As Nebuchadnezzar shares his new knowledge of God, we realize how dependent we are on the characters for *our* knowledge of this god. The deity who answers the king's challenge is never presented as an actual character in the story. We know the power of this god because we see the three men unharmed by the fire. We know the presence of this god because we hear Nebuchadnezzar report seeing a divine representative. God's power has an effect on the story world, but God's character cannot be seen. Our vision of God in the story, like our vision of God in real life, is severely limited and often comes only in our encounters with other people.

Nebuchadnezzar responds to what he has witnessed with

'Blessed be the god of Shadrach, Meshach, and Abednego. [He] . . . has delivered his servants who set their trust upon him . . . and gave their bodies because they would not serve nor would they pay homage to any god except their god.' (3: 28)

One might have expected him to use the often-heard repetition in this concession: 'they would not serve my gods nor would they pay homage to the gold image I have erected.' However, 'my gods' and 'the gold image I have erected' has been pre-empted by 'any god except their god'. He is reticent about his own involvement in the preceding ordeal. By making the issue strictly a religious one, by omitting the political elements, by exempting himself from culpability, he saves face (preserves his image!).

The limits of Nebuchadnezzar's new knowledge become apparent as he continues his speech. Though he recognizes the power of the Hebrew god, he does not even ask the name or nature of this god. Instead, he defines and identifies the divine in terms of the human: he refers to the deity as 'the god of Shadrach, Meshach, and Abednego'. He never admits that his own power should be subject to this divine power. In fact, he immediately makes the deity politically useful:

'I make a decree that any people, nation, or language that says anything against the god of Shadrach, Meshach, and Abednego will be dismembered and his house will be laid in ruins because there is no other god who is able to deliver like this'. (3: 29)

The structural balance of the story lends an ironic force to the climactic confession of Nebuchadnezzar. This decree concerning the god of Shadrach, Meshach, and Abednego mirrors the earlier decree concerning the gold image. Both order some type of religious subservience. Both threaten death for disobedience. Nebuchadnezzar is again in the business of controlling the religious attitudes of others by wielding his political power.

This story that speaks of unequalled tyranny, unsullied faith, unflinching heroism, and unquestionable divine presence is a story too good to be true. For us real life is not so simple, and we would do well to suspect that real life for Israelites in Babylonian exile wasn't so simple either. The prophetic writings of that period indicate a time of ambiguous politics, compromised faith, confused response, and an elusive god. If this story is a paradigm, as some commentators have suggested, of Israel in exile, then it must be recognized that this is an exceptionally clean story of clear choices made by model characters—a clean story that attempts to make sense of uncertainty, to see with clarity what is blurred in reality. The story as metaphor offers an answer, a meaning, a lens with and through which we can view suffering and exile.

The key image of this metaphorical reading is that of the fiery furnace. Both 'fire' and 'furnace' are metaphors of captivity. In Deut. 4: 20 the exodus from Egypt is described in terms of deliverance from an 'iron furnace'. In a speech of comfort to those in exile, Isaiah 43: 2 uses the image of fire to describe the exilic experience: 'When you pass through the waters I will be with you; and through the rivers, they shall not overwhelm you; when you walk through the fire you shall not be burned, and the flame shall not consume you.'

The fiery furnace of exile tests the fidelity of Israel and the fidelity of God. Both are found, despite the suspense, to endure. Israel survives, unwavering in its loyalty to YHWH, and the nature of God is revealed as one who does not prevent the suffering of Israel but who is with Israel in the midst of suffering.

The meaning of the ordeal, however, is more than a test for God and Israel. Like the narrator of Daniel 3, God is concerned, perhaps primarily, with the perspectives of those outside Israel, particularly those outside Israel with political power. It is not enough for Israel to recognize God—other 'peoples, nations, and languages' must acknowledge God's sovereignty as well. Through the faith of Israel, God's power is exposed to the world.

9

Readers and Responsibility

A Man and a Lion were discussing the relative strength of
men and lions in general. The Man contended that he and
his fellows were stronger than lions by reason of their
greater intelligence. 'Come now with me,' he cried, 'and I
will soon prove that I am right.' So he took him into the
public gardens and showed him a statue of Hercules
overcoming the Lion and tearing his mouth in two.

'That is all very well,' said the Lion, 'but proves nothing,
for it was a Man who made the statue.'

Aesop's *Fables* (The Lion and the Statue)

Literature and ideology

This book has been about producing meaning from biblical narrative
in ways that have long been familiar to literary critics of secular
literature. In some cases we have seen that conventions of composition in biblical narrative are not entirely familiar. For example,
Hebrew narrative is tolerant of, indeed enjoys, the repetition of key
words or even scenes in ways that defy modern conventions of
composition in English. And the mixture of genres—narrative, law,
poetry—in Genesis–2 Kings may disturb our sense of unity. So,
too, the way this story appears to be 'strung together' out of a seemingly heterogeneous collection of stories. Nevertheless, we have been
able to speak of character and plot and point of view, of ambiguity
and metaphor and allusion, in terms that connect our reading of this
ancient literature with readings of literature of the modern western,
especially English-speaking, world.

But our book has not just been about poetics, about understanding the 'mechanics' of biblical narrative. It has offered a way of reading that has serious, and probably obvious, implications for how a reader evaluates the narrative being read and how that reading relates to his or her own values. Our way of reading and our particular readings raise questions of values, personal and social. Both the shaping of a narrative poetics and the production of meaning from texts are ideological endeavours.

The term 'ideology' tends to have a rather pejorative sense in common usage. Ideology is what extremists have; sensible, moderate people like ourselves are fortunately unburdened with such obsessions. But social theorists tell otherwise. Ideology is a fundamental aspect of society. As one scholar puts it, ideology is the sort of picture of society that 'individuals in it carry around in their heads':

Ideology designates a rich 'system of representations', worked up in specific material practices, which helps form individuals into social subjects who 'freely' internalize an appropriate 'picture' of their social world and their place in it. Ideology offers the social subject not a set of narrowly 'political' ideas but a fundamental framework of assumptions that defines the parameters of the real and the self; it constitutes what Althusser calls the social subject's 'lived relation to the real' . . . [It] is a social process that works on and through every social subject . . . whether or not they 'know' or understand it. It has the function of producing an *obvious* 'reality' that social subjects can assume and accept, precisely as if it had not been socially produced and did not need to be 'known' at all.   (Kavanagh 1990: 310–11 ¶B)

That is to say, ideologies are like opinions—everybody has one. Some people are just more conscious of theirs. Ideology affects what we do and how we think. Even in our most scientific and apparently objective endeavours it colours and shapes our research and conclusions. Recent decades have seen a growing awareness that all inquiry is to some extent subjective and contextually based. Western scholarly tradition has been shaped by an exclusive set of cultural values. In particular, certain social constructions of gender, race, and class have determined, for example, what kind of scientific projects have been approved, what kind of histories have been written, what literature is deemed to be classic, and who gets to decide all these things. In short, academics in the western world have been until recently mostly white, male, and upper or middle class. Even those who do not fit this description have been trained to adopt as a norm the values of these people.

The western intellectual tradition has been preoccupied with the pursuit of truth, *the* truth, as though it were somehow definable, locatable, something all reasonable people may finally agree upon. The statue in the garden is such a truth for the man in the fable. The sculpture, depicting Hercules' defeat of the lion, supports the man's world-view and thus, for him, it represents some kind of transcendent reality. The prophetic voice of the lion, however, reveals the incongruity of this viewpoint. Meaning, says the lion, is a matter of perspective. Or, to use the term of the critical theorists, meaning is a matter of ideology.

Recent theorists have advocated that all criticism is political and that the experiences of neglected and/or oppressed members of society are also valid standards of critical investigation. In other words, the statue looks a lot different if you are a lion; and to examine it from the lion's perspective renders a whole new understanding of the nature of the statue. The construction of the statue and the decision to read as a man or as a lion carries social responsibility. The statue is in the public garden, open to view as a symbol of the community's ideology. It thus has the potential to construct social roles or relationships, those of man and lion. As the man interprets it in terms of his hierarchical dominance over the natural world he (re)constructs social reality for himself and those who listen to him. His reading therefore has political force. If he were to admit the lion to public debate on the meaning of the statue, that, in turn, would be an act of political significance. If the lion were able to articulate an alternative interpretation—say that here is a representation of 'Man' at his most typical, at odds with nature and exercising violence—that would have political significance. And if the lion were to discredit the statue as propaganda—to assert, in other words, 'This is not truth or reality but a Man's fantasy' —then that would also be a political countermove.

Today more readers are reading like lions. They recognize, like the lion, that texts are not objective representations of reality, but representations of particular value systems.

How we respond to such value systems is determined by our own values. Granted, sometimes we read like the man in the fable—the text seems so familiar, so congruent with our own views, that we do not even realize that these views are there. Like the man in the fable, we think that the text, so read, is a true representation of the way the world really is. When we meet a value system that is totally incongruent with what we think, our lion mentality comes into play. We usually deem the text unacceptable and we resist what it seems to be trying to say. Sometimes we may decide that to reject the text totally is the responsible thing to do. More often, the text has some worthwhile meaning to us or we would not be reading it in the first place. In such cases we sometimes meet a value system that is different from but not incompatible with our own.

Resistance is more likely to be satisfying and productive when it is partial, when we find ourselves in genuine disagreement with some parts of a work without entirely losing our respect for it. In these cases, we talk with the text and its author more as equals, acknowledging their power, but, for that very reason, required to think hard about the nature and meaning of their limits.   (Phelan 1989: 188 ¶A)

Read thus, the text then might cause us to re-examine our values, to reflect upon who we are and what the world is like and the ways in which we relate to it. In such instances, whether our reading modifies or confirms our views, we are challenged and, to some degree, changed. If the point of ideology is to 'constitute, adjust, and/or transform social subjects' (Kavanagh: 314) then the point of ideologically aware criticism is to determine *how* any given discourse is doing that and exactly *which* constitutive social conditions or values are at stake. In the process such criticism shares ideology's potential to shape both the critic (the reader) and the critic's reader.

The Bible and ideology

What happens when we enter the story world of the Hebrew Bible? We have been conditioned to relate to the heroes and to look to them for examples for living our own lives. But what if we find ourselves reading as a lion?

What if, when we encounter the ancient Israelite ancestors, we find ourselves relating, not to Abraham the chosen patriarch who has been promised land, prosperity, and progeny, but to the Canaanites who are told they must forfeit their native land because another people's god has chosen to give it to them? (Indeed this is where many people—native American 'Indians' or Australian Aboriginals or Palestinians—find themselves today; see, for example, Warrior 1989 and Ateek 1989 ¶D.) What if we relate more to the patriarch's wife whose sexuality is pawned to strangers because of her husband's cowardice? What if we find ourselves drawn to the Egyptian servant woman who, having fled slavery and oppression, is told by God to return to the chosen ones and submit to more affliction?

The Bible, like all other writings, is a product of culture. Whatever their view of the Bible's nature as scripture, most biblical scholars today recognize that the social world of ancient Israel, with its particular notions of politics, nationalism, and racial/ethnic, gender, and class difference, is an indelible presence in biblical literature. Israelite society, however, was not monolithic, so that when we talk of *the* social world we are really speaking of some elements of that world. As historical criticism has taught us, it is a world spanning many centuries and so encompassing much diversity over time. We should remember, too, that very probably literature was the product of an intellectual and economic elite. Even what may originally have been oral 'folk' tales and sayings have most likely come into written form through such a filter. Modern readers may find some of the social attitudes and practices encoded in the text strange. More than that, those attuned to the injustice of racism, classism, and sexism may not find the Bible's dominant ideologies—as they reconstruct them—at all agreeable. The result is interpretation that expresses a conflict, or at least conversation, between modern and ancient contexts and values.

Reconstructing the ideology of a text is a delicate process due to the complicated relationship between text and reader. As we have already observed, meaning lies in the interaction between the two. Consequently we may very reasonably be confident that ancient cultural notions are encoded in the text and yet find ourselves arguing over the identification of those notions. Part of the complication is that inevitably (whatever they may say about being 'neutral' or 'objective') readers not only bring their own ideologies to bear on the interpretations of texts, but they use texts to push their ideologies on to others.

Genesis 2–3: women, men, and God

The story found in Genesis 2–3, for example, has long been used to justify women's subordinate place in society. Phyllis Trible (1978 ¶H.1), however, argues that the history of interpretation has shown more misogynist tendencies than does the text itself. Rather than a justification of woman's inferiority, Trible discerns in the text a remarkable equality between the sexes in the original creation of humankind, arguing that it is only after the 'fall' that hierarchy is imposed upon human existence. Her interpretation of the first human being as a sexually undifferentiated creature has merit. The *'adam*, literally, the human, is created from the *'adamah*, the humus, the earth. Though a masculine pronoun is used for this 'earth crea-ture' (Hebrew has no neuter pronoun), it is not until the female is differentiated from this creature (literally, made from its side) that the original human being acquires a gender. This line of interpretation is actually not new. The famous tenth-century Jewish commentator Rashi suggested that the first human was male on one side and female on the other and that God simply divided the crea-ture in half. The interpretation may not be supported by the gram-mar of the text, but it appeals to our sense of binary logic. We know things by their opposites: we only know light because we know dark-ness, we know hot because we know cold, we know male because we know female.

Trible offers further arguments. She interprets the woman as the crown of creation rather than God's afterthought, she argues that the word 'helper' (*'ezer*) used to describe the woman is most often used in reference to God and therefore denotes a superior being rather than an inferior one, and she observes that the woman is assertive and decisive while the man is passive and compliant. These points all have a definite attraction to some of us, perhaps because we would like to think that this text indeed affirms women as much as Trible thinks it does. In other words, we want to believe that the lion in the statue is holding its own against Hercules.

More recent work on Genesis 2–3 has been less idealistic about the patriarchal nature of the text, but has none the less attempted to rehabilitate the character of the woman who later comes to be known as Eve. For Mieke Bal (1987 ¶H.1), Eve develops into a character of great power. Her decision to eat the fruit from the tree of the knowledge of good and evil is the first act of human independence and puts the human creatures on a more equal footing with God. For Bal, this is not a negative thing because now the human and the divine are in a real relationship of give and take rather than an artificial relationship of puppet and puppeteer. Eve did not 'sin'; she opted for reality. She chose real life, and her choice marks the emergence of human character. (Bal, unlike many of the other feminists under discussion, does not see the Bible as a book having religious authority for her. She does, however, recognize that the Bible has been a powerful authority for Western culture in general, and this is what motivates her to devote attention to it.)

Text-affirming or character-affirming readings reflect (consciously or unconsciously) a 'role model' hermeneutic. The search for heroes, or at least admirable characters, makes a rather strong statement about how literature works in general and, more specifically, about the nature of biblical authority. The underlying assumption here is that the Bible is in the business of offering us characters to emulate, people after whom we can pattern our lives.

This, of course, fails to take ambiguity into account. Can we really be sure that there are unambiguous characters in the Hebrew Bible, that there are clearly good and perfect heroes? Probably not. The figure of Eve is a case in point: where Trible and Bal see an independent, assertive, and intelligent character, others for thousands of years have seen a gullible and stupid one. While Eve may be a more obvious case of ambiguity, other characters who traditionally have been acclaimed as heroes (or villains) can be found, upon close examination, to be just as ambiguous: Abraham, Moses, Saul, or David, for example.

Role-modelling, it must be recognized, is a product of the reader's ideology. As hopelessly subjective readers, we often can see in biblical characters only our own values. In modern Western society, aggressiveness, decisiveness, and a clear sense of reality are considered to be admirable qualities. Hence, it is scarcely surprising that many feminist interpreters, when reading Genesis 2–3, see an aggressive, decisive, and realistic Eve.

Some critics have confronted this text-affirming approach, suspicious of the sexual politics of biblical composers, the men who made the statue. Who defines positive and negative female qualities? they ask. Are the womanly assets commended in the Bible merely those characteristics deemed valuable by the patriarchy? And what about less than admirable female characters? Are they being portrayed thus because of some political strategy at work to control women's self-understanding?

Gender is, after all, a social construction. Unlike biological sexual difference, gender identity is socially defined. People are born male and female, but they become men and women through adhering to cultural constructions of what men and women are supposed to be like. 'Femininity is a performance and not a natural mode of being' (Jehlen 1990: 269 ¶B). Or as one of Mark Twain's characters puts it in *Huckleberry Finn*: 'Hellfire Hotchkiss [the girl] is the only genuwyne male man in this town and [the boy] Thug Carpenter's the only genuwyne female girl, if you leave out sex and just consider the business facts' (see Jehlen: 272).

Genesis 2–3, as a story of origins, is, among other things, in the business of constructing gender roles and relating them to an accepted social hierarchy. If the portrayal of woman is as positive here as Trible thinks it is, then we could ask: Who, in ancient Israel, would have entertained such radical thinking and written such a feminist story? (So David Jobling (1986:42 ¶H.1) and most recently David Clines (1990: 29 ¶H.1).) Critics who have asked this question have usually found no likely candidates. Without endorsing the androcentricity they see in the text—on the contrary—these critics are convinced that the values endemic to the production of this text can hardly be other than male-centred, given the pervasive patriarchal ideology of ancient Israelite society generally. This answer, however, is not as conclusive as its advocates suppose. In male-dominated fifth-century Athens the comic playwright Aristophanes successfully staged plays, notably *The Thesmophoriazousai* and *Lysistrata*, which mocked conventional male values and behaviour, both personal and political. Among other evidence of counter-cultural thinking in classical Athens, Eva Keuls (1985 ¶B) has drawn attention to vase painting that satirizes men's glorification of war (and militant patriotism) at the expense of the women and children who are war's victims. That sounds very like the ending of the book of Judges. In other words, to discern in an ancient text a challenge to patriarchal values is not necessarily to propose an anachronism.

The argument here involves an appeal to the biblical author's intention as a guide to valid interpretation. Such an appeal is involved, too, when Susan Lanser (1988 ¶H.1) disputes Trible's reading of sexual equality by applying the principles of speech-act theory to the text. She argues that when a character is introduced into a story, that character is assumed to have a gender. *Ha'adam* would have been, and should be, understood to be a male human. There is nothing in the text to indicate otherwise, she maintains, though others might well disagree.

David Clines has argued at length that the word 'helper' does not, as Trible has suggested, designate a superior being. While a helper may have superior status, she or he is, nevertheless, secondary to the project of the one who is being helped. Eve is, in Clines's reading, unalterably subordinate to Adam. Finding support among the church fathers, Clines concludes that Eve is necessary to help Adam do the only task he cannot seem to accomplish by himself, namely, procreate.

If men built the statue, then Hercules will always dominate the lion. No feminist reformation of surface elements, suggests Pamela Milne (1988, 1989 ¶H.1), is going to disguise the fact that Genesis 2–3 is essentially male mythology and has been consistently perceived as such by male scholars who have analysed it. Readers who look to the Bible for spiritual direction and yet disagree with the values found there face a dilemma. In Milne's judgement, our alternatives are few:

We can either accept the patriarchal biblical text as sacred and content ourselves with exposing its patriarchy ... or we can expose its patriarchy and reject it as sacred and authoritative. But if we are looking for a sacred scripture that is not patriarchal, that does not construct woman as 'other' and that does not support patriarchal interpretations based on this otherness, we are not likely to find it or to recover it in texts such as Genesis 2–3. If we want an authoritative sacred scripture that does not make it possible to believe that women are secondary and inferior humans, it appears that we need to make new wine to fill our new wineskins.   (Milne 1989: 22)

Clines takes a wider tack. Authority, he suggests, is not the point:

The authority of a text has to do with its nature; we want to be saying things about the Bible that have to do with its *function*. We want to be saying, not so much that the Bible is right, not even that the Bible is wrong, but that it impacts for good upon people. Despite its handicaps, despite the fact that it has misled people and promoted patriarchy, it has an unquenchable capacity—when taken in conjunction with a commitment to personal integrity—to inspire people, bring out the best in them and suggest a vision they could never have dreamed of for themselves. Think of it as dogma and you will at times, as over the matter of men and women, either be wrong or get it wrong. Think of it rather as a resource for living which has no authority but which nevertheless manages to impose itself powerfully upon people.   (Clines 1990: 48)

Clines, like Milne, reads Genesis 2–3 as an irredeemably androcentric text. Yet whereas for her the androcentrism is fatal to the notion of the Bible as scripture, for him this 'simple and mindless androcentricity' (Clines: 41) is only a 'handicap'. The biblical text, in conjunction with the reader's personal integrity, can bring out the best in people. How this is possible given his reading of Genesis 2–3, however, he does not show us. (Nor is his notion of the text imposing itself powerfully upon people one that is likely to hold out much appeal to a reader resisting the patriarchal valuation of dominance.) Furthermore, it is not clear that appeal to personal integrity helps much. Church fathers such as Augustine and Aquinas no doubt read with integrity, yet between them and the text these men constructed *and propagated* the most debasingly (as we now see it) misogynist interpretation. Personal integrity is never without its own agenda.

Gender analysis in biblical studies, most often going by the title of feminist criticism, has had a tendency to focus on the roles and characterizations of women in the biblical text. While inevitable and crucial to the project, such study is not without its drawbacks. To some extent, the focus on women has, paradoxically, slipped into the patriarchal syndrome of defining women as 'other'. Women, because they differ from men, are the subject of investigation. Whether women emerge as positive figures, as in the analysis of Trible, or whether they are hopelessly minimalized, as Clines sees the text, the implication is the same. Men, and men's interests, somehow remain the standard. Even the recognition that writing itself is gendered, that is, it reflects gendered experience, has often occasioned little more than observation in biblical criticism.

Gender, of course, is not simply a matter of difference. It is (in patriarchy at least) a matter of power. Thus to say, for example, that a text is androcentric or racist, as if that were an ideological perspective equal to any other, and to leave it at that, may sound scholarly, but it is not neutral—it is according some value, if only by default, to certain oppressive relations of power between people. How critics write of gender, then, is a matter of grave responsibility. Categories like gender, race, and class hierarchically structure our lives and our texts, but not without troubling tensions and contradictions. To say that a text is androcentric, even when taking a clear stand on the question of value, and to leave it at that, may also be missing an opportunity to deal with inherent tensions and contradictions in androcentrism's disposition of power.

Scholars who are scrutinizing the power relations both within texts and in the writing of texts are producing readings in which tension and contradiction are part of the text's meaning. David Jobling (1986 ¶H.1), employing structuralist methodology clearly informed by Marxist and feminist ideology, finds several conflicts at work in Genesis 2–3. First there is a conflict between two narrative programmes (or plots, to use our terminology). On the one hand, the story explains the creation and fall of humankind—this is the programme traditionally recognized. On the other hand this plot agenda competes with a more basic agenda—explaining how there came to be a man to till the earth (which is the problem or lack set forth at the beginning of the story). Conflict also exists on the ideological level. The patriarchal tendency of the story is to subordinate the woman in the social order and to blame the woman for the misfortune that has fallen humankind. In tension with this agenda are the undeniable positive characteristics of the woman in the text.

There is, he insists, asymmetry in the creation of the man and the woman and in their subsequent offences. Yet, while the patriarchal culture that produced and received this text would have assumed the first human to be male, an assumption grounded in the grammar of the text, the logic, Jobling admits, is on Trible's side: 'male' is meaningless without 'female'. While the woman sins first and is implicated in the man's sin, the woman is (as Trible has also observed) active and intelligent while the man is passive and oblivious. How do such characterizations come to be in a patriarchal text?

They are inevitable expressions of the logic of the myth: woman and sexuality belong to the same semantic configuration as knowledge. Part of the price the male mindset pays is the admission that woman is more aware of the complexity of the world, more in touch with 'all living'. And finally, at the deepest level of the text, where the fall myth as a whole is in tension with 'a man to till the earth', the possibility is evoked that the human transformation in which the woman took powerful initiative was positive, rather than negative, that the complex human world is to be preferred over any male ideal.

But these 'positive' features are not the direct expression of a feminist consciousness . . . Rather, they are the effects of the patriarchal mindset tying itself in knots trying to account for woman and femaleness in a way which *both* makes sense *and* supports patriarchal assumptions.

(Jobling: 42–3)

Bal, writing after Jobling, recognizes the same phenomenon. The text reveals a problem with man's priority and domination.

The reason for this situation is obvious. The burden of domination is hard to bear. Dominators have, first, to establish their position, then to safeguard it. Subsequently, they must make both the dominated *and* themselves believe in it. Insecurity is not a prerogative exclusively of the dominated. The establishing of a justifying 'myth of origin', which has to be sufficiently credible and realistic to account for common experience, is not that simple a performance. Traces of the painful process of gaining control can therefore be perceived in those very myths. They serve to limit repression to acceptable, viable proportions.

(Bal 1987: 110 ¶H.1)

Consequently, the story may be designed to communicate male priority and superiority over females and to justify thereby the social dominance of men over women, but texts often say more than, and sometimes even quite the opposite of, what they intend.

The point here is that language attempts to build up positions of authority which language itself calls into question . . . the very expressions by which we claim . . . credibility betray how fragile and challengeable [that credibility] is. (Graff 1990: 170 ¶A).

We are dealing here, however, not simply with instability or indeterminacy within texts, but with a particular way of reading. 'Reading against the grain' is, in Graff's terms, 'a method which does not take the texts' apparent contexts and intentions at face value, but looks at the doubts they repress or leave unsaid and how this repressed or 'absent' element can undermine or undo what the text says' (Graff: 171). It is, in short, choosing to read as a lion, choosing to question the priorities and hierarchies that are conventionally seen or assumed in a text.

In the case of Genesis 2—3, the questioning of hierarchies might extend beyond the roles of man and woman. The divine, the human, and the animal realms also fall into a prioritized order. The divine character, YHWH Elohim, not surprisingly, has a large investment in authority. He is the 'author' of the garden and all that is in it. He created not only the man, but the woman and the serpent who are traditionally blamed for the 'fall'. And it was he who placed that momentous tree in the midst of the garden and circumscribed it with arbitrary prohibition.

Most commentators, for obvious theological reasons, want to 'protect' God, to remove the divine character from scrutiny, much as God pronounces the tree of the knowledge of good and evil to be off limits to the humans in the garden. Some readers, however, are willing to pluck the fruit, eager to learn what the knowledge of good and evil is all about. Tensions and contradictions within the text, and between text and reader, may challenge us to re-enter the garden with our eyes opened, even if that means eventually running up against the contradictory, unstable character of God.

David Jobling's structural analysis reveals that YHWH Elohim is both the initiator and the opponent of the action. God creates what the earth needs, a man to till it, but then acts as villain by retaining the man to keep his own private garden. Furthermore, YHWH counteracts his own villainy by creating the tree of knowledge, the serpent, and the woman, who converge to foil the divine conspiracy.

Francis Landy, in a more poetical reading, also sees the ambiguity inherent in the behaviour of God.

> The prohibition of the Tree of Knowledge . . . sets the tree apart . . . Not only is it biologically the purveyor of evil, but functionally, apparently arbitrarily, it stands for being naughty, it introduces the idea of rebellion and trespass into the world. God gives no reason for his command; he merely asserts his authority . . . In doing so, he raises the crucial question of power and obedience that will determine the coming course of the story . . . Regulation ensures infringement, in our world and in the fairy tale, where the arbitrary or incomprehensible command is infallibly broken . . . Man (*sic*) is not yet curious; in presenting him with a mystery . . . God very subtly rouses him . . . Suddenly it is revealed that man has no independence, no rights, and that his harmonious enterprise in the garden . . . is part of a rigorous divine order.
>
> (Landy 1983: 215 ¶H.1)

When this rigorous divine order is seen as an allegory of human politics, we begin to see how the text might work ideologically. 'The distinctive effect of ideology is not theoretical but pragmatic, to enable various social subjects to feel at home, and to act (or not act), within the limits of a given social project' (Kavanagh 1990: 314 ¶B). James Kennedy (1990 ¶H.1) has aligned YHWH Elohim with the political élite in the Israelite monarchy and Adam and Eve with the peasant class. The same sorts of hierarchies and privileges pertain. YHWH Elohim co-opts the labour of the man to take care of his private garden as a king would use peasant labour to work a private estate. The labourers receive their sustenance from and are answerable to the lord of the manor. Knowledge and education are the privilege of the élite; the intellectual confines of the peasantry are kept in strict control because education leads to dissatisfaction. Any rebellion on the part of the peasant, that is, the eating of the fruit of the tree of knowledge, is doomed to failure and will result in further hardship.

Read in terms of social class, the text's ideology keeps a peasant class in tow. Read in terms of gender, the text explains why women are and should be subordinate to men. Read in terms of theology, the text promotes the frailty of humanity over against the sovereignty of God. All of these dimensions assign people their places in a social or theological structure. On the surface, the text seeks to assure a status quo. When read 'against the grain', however, it can be heard to call for transformation.

In a more recent attempt to 'read against the grain', David Gunn (1990 ¶H.1) has suggested that certain characteristics of God, established in Genesis 1 and transferred to the humans who were created in the divine image, keep the text from completely succeeding in shifting the blame of the fall on to the woman and the serpent. God's desire for dominion (evident in such language as 'rule' [1: 16], 'subjugate' [1: 26], and 'subdue' [1: 28]), for dividing and naming, for creating self-likeness, and for discovery, colour both God and humans with a mixture of control and freedom. Domination, categorization, labelling, and ensuring sameness or conformity are all manifestations of the need to control. The capacity for discovery ('And God saw that it was good'), however, undermines control, valuing exploration and venture. Furthermore, as the divine pronouncements of 'good' reveal, God can differentiate between good and evil and, in the slippage between plural self-reference and singular verbs ('Elohim [plural] said [singular], "Let us make humankind in our image . . ."'), God admits differentiation within the divine self.

The contradictions in the creator are likewise manifested in the creature. We see the first human categorizing and naming the animals. We see the man labelling the woman, declaring her likeness and yet her difference. We see the woman's curiosity and love of discovery, her desire to be 'like' God, to know good and evil. And we see humankind divided among itself, aware of and attempting to conceal its differences. The man blames the 'other' one and eventually subjugates her.

The language of the text allows the blame to shift from man to woman to serpent, and there the buck-passing stops, because 'the serpent's mouth is stopped with dust'. But hard as the words try to blame humans in general, and women and their animal counterparts specifically, the silences, the tensions, the contradictions whisper that God is ultimately responsible for the 'fallen', or perhaps more to the point, the 'realistic' state of creation.

Reading against the grain is a call to responsibility. It is a call to see how texts and their interpretations oppress people—and sometimes even creation itself—physically, emotionally, economically, theologically. It is a call to expose domination in order to bring about change.

Conclusion

An awareness of ideology recognizes that the Bible is composed of many voices, and a few of those are even the voices of lions. Because of its multivocal nature, the Bible, despite its biases of gender, race/ethnicity, and class, makes provision for its own critique. It points to its own incongruity. Every characterization of a passive, weak, irresponsible male ridicules 'maleness' as an ultimate value. Every message of liberation passes judgement on celebrations of domination. The Bible shows us not merely patriarchy, élitism, and nationalism; it shows us the fragility of these ideologies through irony and counter-voices. Xenophobic Joshua and Ezra are undermined by the book of Ruth. David is countered by Hannah and Rizpah. The patriarchy of Persia is threatened by the single woman Vashti (Esther 1). Voices from the margins, voices from the fissures and cracks in the text, assure us that male sovereignty is contrived and precarious, that racial/ethnic chauvinism is ultimately insupportable, that social élitism is self-deluding, that religious rectitude is self-serving.

For people who believe in social equality and yet for whom the Bible is a source of religious authority, reading has become a complicated matter. Critical readers cannot naïvely accept the Bible as an unmediated word of liberation. Jewish or Christian readers trying to be faithful to their tradition cannot easily reject the Bible as an unredeemable word of subjugation. Yet there are some steps we can take, those of us who find ourselves in such a position. We can learn to recognize our own world in the text. We can try to relate to all the characters and not just the heroes. We can listen to more than one voice and particularly to those faint, niggling voices that whisper 'all is not right with the world'. We can open ourselves to the Bible's irony. Above all, we can recognize that texts *do* more than they *say*.

These texts may be *saying* that patriarchy is a mandatory way of life, that men are more important than women, that one group of people is superior, that one class is more deserving, in short, that men are more able than lions. What they may be *doing* is reinforcing these ideas in the contemporary world. All that may be 'obvious'. (The 'ideological struggle over whether a pleasurable/beautiful/ fascinating cultural text will be used to reaffirm or to challenge the prevailing sense of self and social order', observes Kavanagh, is 'always a struggle over what is 'obvious' ' [1990:318 ¶B]). But most of these texts may also be *doing* something very different, something no less 'obvious' when exposed by the ideological critic. They may be uncovering a world in need of redemption and healing and a world-view much in need of change. This is the kind of reading that can transform us. If we realize that the world of the Bible is a broken world, that its people are human and therefore limited, that its social system is flawed, then we might start to see more clearly our own broken world, our own human limitations, our own defective social systems. And who knows? Maybe we shall find ourselves called to be the agents of change.

BIBLIOGRAPHY

This bibliography contains the works cited in the text, listed by section number (¶A, ¶H.7, etc.). It also contains English language studies that have helped shape our own readings and this book. Beyond that, however, it lists materials which have had no direct bearing on our own work, but which point the reader to the depth and diversity of the larger matrix out of which our book has emerged. (We have not distinguished between works consulted by us or not.) While by no means a complete bibliography of current literary criticism (in English) of Hebrew Bible narrative, it is sufficiently comprehensive to enable readers both to see the larger picture, including the development of the discipline, and to find help with particular topics and texts. We have more than one kind of reader in mind. For students beginning to explore, we have asterisked some more accessible starting-points. For more advanced readers, for example those using this book for teaching, the additional listings provide leads in similar or (often) variant directions to those we have taken.

Commentaries are not listed, with a few exceptions. As yet few commentaries in literary-critical vein have been written, a situation which will clearly change. Notable, however, are several volumes in the Interpretation series (Westminster/John Knox) with literary-critical sympathies: Walter Brueggemann on Genesis and 1 and 2 Samuel, Terence Fretheim on Exodus, Richard Nelson on 1 and 2 Kings, Gerald Janzen on Job, and Sibley Towner on Daniel. New commentary series planned are Readings (Sheffield Academic Press) and Studies in Hebrew Narrative (Michael Glazier Books/Liturgical Press).

From the inception of this literary-critical movement in biblical · studies in the early seventies articles and essays have been, with some notable exceptions, the mainstay of the published discussion. But extended book-length treatments of method and texts have been appearing with growing frequency since the early eighties. With graduate (Ph.D.) programmes in the USA conceding the legitimacy of literary criticism in biblical studies, an increasing number of doctoral dissertations are now prefiguring significant books. Important sources of books, both monographs and essay collections, are the JSOT Supplement

Series (JSOT/Sheffield Academic, 1976–; David Clines, David Gunn [–1984], Philip Davies, eds.), the Bible and Literature Series (Almond, 1981–; David Gunn, ed.), Semeia Studies (Scholars, 1982–; Dan Via [–1987], Edward Greenstein, eds.), Indiana Studies in Biblical Literature (Indiana UP, 1985–; Herbert Marks, Robert Polzin, eds.), and Literary Currents in Biblical Interpretation (Westminster/John Knox, 1990–; Danna Nolan Fewell, David Gunn, eds.). Overtures to Biblical Theology (Fortress, 1977–; Walter Brueggemann, John Donahue, eds.) has also furnished significant studies.

The major journals in the field have all been founded within the past two decades: *Semeia* (Scholars, 1974–; Robert Funk [–1980], Robert Culley, eds.), *Journal for the Study of the Old Testament* (Sheffield Academic, 1976–; David Clines, David Gunn, Philip Davies, eds.), and *Prooftexts* (Johns Hopkins UP, 1981–; Alan Mintz, David G. Roskies, eds.). Germane articles can often be found in *Journal of Feminist Studies in Religion* (Scholars), *Journal of Literature and Theology* (Oxford UP), and *Christianity and Literature* (Seattle Pacific University). *Biblical Interpretation*, a new journal of 'contemporary approaches', is due to appear in 1993 from Brill in the Netherlands (Cheryl Exum, Mark Brett, eds.).

This bibliography begins with some introduction to critical theory (¶A–B) and biblical hermeneutics (¶C–D) before listing work on biblical narrative in general (¶E). A section on collected essays of criticism (¶F) precedes the major part of the bibliography, a listing of work relating to particular biblical texts (¶G–V). The sequence of biblical books follows the traditional (Jewish) Masoretic text of the Hebrew Bible, according to the standard critical edition (Biblia Hebraica Stuttgartensia), with guides to the common alternatives of (Christian) English versions which follow an order found in ancient Greek translations (the Septuagint). Further bibliographic resources may be found in a valuable work which appeared after our own book was completed: Mark Alan Powell with Cecile G. Gray and Melissa C. Curtis, *The Bible and Modern Literary Criticism: A Critical Assessment and Annotated Bibliography*, New York: Greenwood (1992).

Abbreviations

B&L   Bible and Literature Series (Sheffield: Almond)
CBQ   *Catholic Bible Quarterly*

C&L   *Christianity and Literature*
ISBL   Indiana Studies in Biblical Literature (Bloomington: Indiana
        UP)
JAAR   *Journal of the American Academy of Religion*
JBL   *Journal of Biblical Literature*
JFSR   *Journal of Feminist Studies in Religion*
JLT   *Journal of Literature and Theology*
JSOT   *Journal for the Study of the Old Testament*
JSOTS   JSOT Supplement Series (Sheffield: JSOT/Sheffield Aca-
        demic)
LCBI   Literary Currents in Biblical Interpretation (Louisville, Ky.:
        Westminster/John Knox)
OBT   Overtures to Biblical Theology (Minneapolis: Fortress—
        previously published in Philadelphia)
SS   Semeia Studies (Atlanta: Scholars—previously published vari-
        ously in Missoula, Mont.; Chico, Calif.; and Decatur, Ga.)

¶A. Introducing Literary Theory

Alter, Robert (1990). *The Pleasures of Reading in an Ideological Age*,
    New York: Simon and Schuster.
Atkins, G. Douglas, and Morrow, Laura, eds. (1989). *Contemporary
    Literary Theory*, Amherst: Massachusetts UP.
Bal, Mieke (1985). *Narratology: Introduction to the Theory of Narrative*,
    Toronto: Toronto UP. (Rev. from Dutch 2nd edn. 1980.)
—— (1991). *On Story-Telling*, Sonoma, Calif.: Polebridge.
Booth, Wayne C. (1983). *The Rhetoric of Fiction*, 2nd edn.; Chicago UP.
    (1st edn. 1961.)
—— (1974). *A Rhetoric of Irony*, Chicago and London: Chicago UP.
Brooks, Peter (1985). *Reading for the Plot: Design and Intention in
    Narrative*, New York: Vintage Books. (And see Willett, below.)
*Chatman, Seymour (1978). *Story and Discourse: Narrative Structure in
    Fiction and Film*, Ithaca, NY: Cornell UP.
Eagleton, Terry (1983). *Literary Theory: An Introduction*, Oxford:
    Blackwell; Minneapolis: Minnesota UP.
Fish, Stanley (1980). 'Interpretive Authority in the Classroom and in
    Literary Criticism', in *Is There a Text in this Class? The Authority of
    Interpretive Communities*, Cambridge, Mass.: Harvard UP, 303–71.

* Fish, Stanley (1990). 'Rhetoric', in Lentricchia and McLaughlin, eds. (below), 203–22.

Forster, E. M. (1927). *Aspects of the Novel*, London and New York: Harcourt, Brace, and World.

Genette, Gérard (1980). *Narrative Discourse: An Essay in Method*, Ithaca, NY: Cornell UP. (From French edn. 1972.)

* Graff, Gerald (1990). 'Determinacy/Indeterminacy', in Lentricchia and McLaughlin, eds. (below), 163–76.

* Hartman, Geoffrey H. (1989). 'The State of the Art of Criticism', in Ralph Cohen, ed., *The Future of Literary Theory*. New York and London: Routledge, 86–101.

Hochman, Baruch (1985). *Character in Literature*, Ithaca, NY, and London: Cornell UP.

Lanser, Susan (1981). *The Narrative Act: Point of View in Prose Fiction*, Princeton UP.

* Leitch, Thomas (1986). *What Stories Are: Narrative Theory and Interpretation*, Univ. Park, Pa.: Pennsylvania State UP.

* Lentricchia, Frank, and McLaughlin, Thomas, eds. (1990). *Critical Terms for Literary Study*, Chicago UP.

* Miller, J. Hillis (1990). 'Narrative', in Lentricchia and McLaughlin, eds. (above), 66–79.

Mintz, Alan (1984). 'On the Tel Aviv School of Poetics', *Prooftexts* 4: 215–35.

Muecke, D. C. (1969). *The Compass of Irony*, London: Methuen.

* Norris, Christopher (1987). *Derrida*, London: Fontana; Cambridge, Mass.: Harvard UP.

—— (1990). *What's Wrong with Postmodernism: Critical Theory and the Ends of Philosophy*, Baltimore: Johns Hopkins UP.

—— (1991). *Deconstruction: Theory and Practice*, rev. edn., London and New York: Routledge. (1st edn., London: Methuen, 1982.)

Phelan, James (1989). *Reading People, Reading Plots: Character, Progression, and the Interpretation of Narrative*, Chicago and London: Chicago UP.

Prince, Gerald (1982). *Narratology: The Form and Functioning of Narrative*, New York: Mouton.

Propp, Vladimir (1968). *Morphology of the Folktale*, 2nd edn.; Austin: Texas UP. (1st Russian edn. 1928).

Ray, William (1984). *Literary Meaning: From Phenomenology to Deconstruction*, Oxford: Blackwell.

*Rimmon-Kenan, Shlomith (1983). *Narrative Fiction: Contemporary Poetics*, London: Methuen.

Sarap, Madan (1989). *An Introductory Guide to Post-Structuralism and Postmodernism*, Athens, Ga.: Univ. of Georgia; London: Harvester-Wheatsheaf. (See esp. on Lacan, Derrida, and Foucault.)

Siebers, Tobin (1988). *The Ethics of Criticism*, Ithaca, NY, and London: Cornell UP. (See esp. 1–43.)

Silverman, Kaja (1983). *The Subject of Semiotics*, New York: Oxford UP.

Spivak, Gayatri Chakravorty (1976). 'Translator's Preface', in Jacques Derrida, *Of Grammatology*, Baltimore: Johns Hopkins UP, ix–lxxxvii.

Suleiman, Susan R., and Crosman, Inge, eds. (1980). *The Reader in the Text: Essays on Audience and Interpretation*, Princeton UP.

White, Hayden (1989). ' "Figuring the nature of the times deceased": Literary Theory and Historical Writing', in Ralph Cohen, ed., *The Future of Literary Theory*, New York and London: Routledge, 19–43.

Willett, Susan (1990). 'Coming Unstrung: Women, Men, Narrative, and Principles of Pleasure', *PMLA* 105: 505–18. (On Brooks (above) and plot.)

¶B. Literature, Culture, Ideology

Ashley, Kathleen M., ed. (1990). *Victor Turner and the Construction of Cultural Criticism: Between Literature and Anthropology*. Bloomington: Indiana UP.

*Belsey, Catherine (1991). 'Constructing the Subject: Deconstructing the Text', in Robyn R. Warhol and Diane Price Herndl, eds., *Feminisms: An Anthology of Literary Theory and Criticism*. New Brunswick: Rutgers UP, 593–609. (Orig. 1985.)

Best, Steven, and Kellner, Douglas (1991). *Postmodern Theory: Critical Interrogations*, New York: Guilford.

*Bové, Paul A. (1990). 'Discourse', in Lentricchia and McLaughlin, eds. (¶A), 50–65. (On Foucault.)

*Culler, Jonathan (1982). 'Reading as a Woman', in *On Deconstruction: Theory and Criticism after Structuralism*. Ithaca, NY: Cornell UP, 43–64.

Dowling, William C. (1984). *Jameson, Althusser, Marx: An Introduction to the Political Unconscious*, Ithaca, NY: Cornell UP.

Erickson, Joyce Quiring (1983). 'What Difference? The Theory and Practice of Feminist Criticism.' *C&L* 33: 65–74.

Flax, Jane (1990). 'Postmodernism and Gender Relations in Feminist Theory', in Nicholson, ed. (below), 39–62.

Flynn, Elizabeth A., and Schweickart, Patrocinio P. (1986). *Gender and Reading: Essays on Readers, Texts, and Contexts*, Baltimore and London: Johns Hopkins UP.

Frow, John (1986). *Marxism and Literary Criticism*, Cambridge, Mass.: Harvard UP.

Gates, Henry Louis, Jr. (1984). 'Criticism in the jungle', in *Black Literature and Literary Theory*, New York and London: Methuen, 1–24.

Geertz, Clifford (1973). *The Interpretation of Cultures*, New York: Basic Books.

hooks, bell (1984). *Feminist Theory: From Margin to Center*, Boston: South End.

*Humm, Maggie (1990). *The Dictionary of Feminist Theory*, Columbus: Ohio State UP.

Jacobus, Mary (1986). 'Reading Woman (Reading)', in *Reading Woman: Essays in Feminist Criticism*, New York: Columbia UP, 3–26.

Jameson, Fredric (1981). *The Political Unconscious: Narrative as a Socially Symbolic Act*, Ithaca, NY: Cornell UP.

Jardine, Alice, and Smith, Paul, eds. (1987). *Men in Feminism*, New York and London: Methuen.

*Jehlen, Myra (1990). 'Gender', in Lentricchia and McLaughlin, eds. (¶A), 263–73.

*Kavanagh, James H. (1990). 'Ideology', in Lentricchia and McLaughlin, eds. (¶A), 306–20.

Keuls, Eva C. (1985). *The Reign of the Phallus: Sexual Politics in Ancient Athens*, New York: Harper and Row. (See esp. ch. 16, 'Love, Not War.')

Kolodny, Annette (1985). 'Dancing Through the Minefield: Some Observations on the Theory, Practice, and Politics of Feminist Literary Criticism', in Showalter, ed. (below), 144–67. (Orig. 1980.)

*Lanser, Susan S. (1991). 'Toward a Feminist Narratology', in Warhol and Herndl, eds. (see Belsey, above), 610–29.

Leigh, David J. (1983). 'Michel Foucault and The Study of Literature and Theology.' *C&L* 33: 75–85.

Moi, Toril (1985). *Sexual/Textual Politics: Feminist Literary Theory*, London: Methuen.

Nicholson, Linda J., ed. (1990). *Feminism/Postmodernism*, New York and London: Routledge.

Rabinowitz, Peter J. (1987). *Before Reading: Narrative Conventions and the Politics of Interpretation*, Ithaca, NY: Cornell UP.

*Ryan, Michael (1989). 'Political Criticism', in Atkins and Morrow, eds. (¶A), 200–13.

Showalter, Elaine, ed. (1985). *The New Feminist Criticism: Essays on Women, Literature and Theory*. New York: Pantheon.

*—— (1989). 'Introduction: The Rise of Gender', in *Speaking of Gender*, New York and London: Routledge, 1–13.

Siebers, Tobin (1988). 'The Ethics of Sexual Difference', in *The Ethics of Criticism*, Ithaca, NY, and London: Cornell UP, 186–219.

Todd, Janet (1988). 'Men in Feminist Criticism', in *Feminist Literary History*, New York: Routledge, 118–34.

Tong, Rosemarie (1989). *Feminist Thought: A Comprehensive Introduction*, Boulder, Colo., and San Francisco: Westview.

Torsney, Cheryl B. (1989). 'The Critical Quilt: Alternative Authority in Feminist Criticism', in Atkins and Morrow, eds. (¶A), 180–93.

*Weedon, Chris (1987). *Feminist Practice and Poststructuralist Theory*, Oxford: Blackwell.

¶C. Biblical Interpretation

Barr, James (1989). 'The Literal, the Allegorical, and Modern Biblical Scholarship', *JSOT* 44: 3–17.

*Barton, John (1984). *Reading the Old Testament: Method in Biblical Study*, London: Darton, Longman and Todd.

Berlin, Adele (1982). 'On the Bible as Literature', *Prooftexts* 2: 323–7. (With response by James Kugel.)

Boyarin, Daniel (1990). *Intertextuality and the Reading of Midrash*, ISBL.

Brueggemann, Walter (1991). *Abiding Astonishment: Psalms, Modernity, and the Making of History*, LCBI.

Burnett, Fred W. (1990). 'Postmodern Biblical Exegesis: The Eve of Historical Criticism', in Phillips, ed. (below), 51–80.

Childs, B. S. (1990). 'Critical Reflections on James Barr's Understanding of the Literal and the Allegorical', *JSOT* 46: 3–9.

Clines, David J. A. (1980). 'Story and Poem: The Old Testament as Literature and as Scripture', *Interpretation* 34: 115–27.

*Coggins, Richard (1990). *Introducing the Old Testament*. Oxford Bible Series; Oxford and New York: Oxford UP.

*Cormie, Lee (1991). 'Revolutions in Reading the Bible', in Jobling *et al.*, eds. (¶D), 173–93.

Croatto, J. Severino (1987). *Biblical Hermeneutics: Toward a Theory of Reading as the Production of Meaning*. Maryknoll, NY: Orbis.

Crossan, John Dominic, ed. (1975). *Paul Ricoeur on Biblical Hermeneutics*, Semeia 4.

Detweiler, Robert, ed. (1982). *Derrida and Biblical Studies*. Semeia 23.

—— ed. (1985). *Reader Response Approaches to Biblical and Secular Texts*, Semeia 31.

*Edgerton, W. Dow (1992). *The Passion of Interpretation*, LCBI.

Fishbane, Michael (1989). *The Garments of Torah: Essays in Biblical Hermeneutics*, ISBL.

Flanagan, James W. (1991). 'New Constructs in Social World Studies', in Jobling *et al.*, eds. (¶D), 209–23.

Frei, Hans W. (1974). *The Eclipse of Biblical Narrative: A Study in Eighteenth and Nineteenth Century Hermeneutics*, New Haven, Conn., and London: Yale UP.

Gerhart, Mary. (1989). 'The Restoration of Biblical Narrative', in Amihai *et al.*, eds. (¶F). 13–29.

Greenstein, Edward L. (1989*a*). 'Deconstruction and Biblical Narrative.' *Prooftexts* 9: 43–71.

—— (1989*b*). *Essays on Biblical Method and Translation*, Atlanta: Scholars.

Greidanus, Sidney (1988). *The Modern Preacher and the Ancient Text: Interpreting and Preaching Biblical Literature*, Grand Rapids, Mich.: Eerdmans.

*Haynes, Stephen, and McKenzie, Steven L. (1993). *To Each Its Own Meaning: An Introduction to Biblical Interpretations and Their Applications*, Louisville, Ky.: Westminster/John Knox.

Jasper, David (1989). 'Hermeneutics, Literary Theory and the Bible', in *The Study of Literature and Religion: An Introduction*, Minneapolis: Fortress, 83–96.

Jobling, David, and Moore, Stephen D. (1992). *Poststructuralism as Exegesis*, Semeia 54.

Josipovici, Gabriel (1990). 'The Bible in Focus', *JSOT* 48: 101–22.

* Keegan, Terence J. (1985). *Interpreting the Bible: A Popular Introduction to Biblical Hermeneutics*, New York: Paulist.

Kugel, James L. (1990). *In Potiphar's House: The Interpretive Life of Biblical Texts*, San Francisco: HarperSanFrancisco.

—— and Greer, Rowan A. (1986). *Early Biblical Interpretation*, Philadelphia: Westminster.

* Longman III, Tremper (1987). *Literary Approaches to Biblical Interpretation*, Grand Rapids, Mich.: Academie Books (Zondervan).

McKnight, Edgar V. (1985). *The Bible and the Reader: An Introduction to Literary Criticism*, Philadelphia: Fortress.

—— (1988). *Post-Modern Use of the Bible: The Emergence of Reader-Oriented Criticism*, Nashville: Abingdon.

* Miscall, Peter D. (1986). 'Introduction', in *1 Samuel* (¶N), vii–xxv.

Moore, Stephen D. (1989). *Literary Criticism and the Gospels: The Theoretical Challenge*, New Haven, Conn., and London: Yale UP.

* Morgan, Robert, with John Barton (1988). *Biblical Interpretation*, Oxford Bible Series; Oxford and New York: Oxford UP.

Mosala, Itumeleng J. (1989). *Biblical Hermeneutics and Black Theology in South Africa*, Grand Rapids, Mich.: Eerdmans.

Muilenburg, James (1969). 'Form Criticism and Beyond', *JBL* 88: 1–18.

Parker, T. H. L. (1986). 'The Exposition of History', in *Calvin's Old Testament Commentaries*, Edinburgh: Clark, 83–121.

Patrick, Dale, and Scult, Allen (1990). *Rhetoric and Biblical Interpretation*, B&L 26.

Phillips, Gary A., ed. (1990). *Poststructural Criticism and the Bible: Text/History/Discourse*, Semeia 51. (Esp. 7–49, 'Exegesis as Critical Praxis'.)

* Polzin, Robert (1980a). 'Criticism and Crisis within Biblical Studies', in *Moses and the Deuteronomist* (¶K), 1–24.

—— (1980b). 'Literary and Historical Criticism of the Bible: A Crisis in Scholarship', in Richard A. Spencer, ed., *Orientation by*

Disorientation: Studies in Literary Criticism and Biblical Literary Criticism, Pittsburgh: Pickwick, 99–127.

Polzin, Robert, and Rothman, Eugene (1982). *The Biblical Mosaic: Changing Perspectives*, SS.

Radzinowicz, Mary Ann (1989). 'How and Why the Literary Establishment Caught Up with the Bible: Instancing the Book of Job', *C&L* 39: 77–90.

Rashkow, Ilona (1993). *The Phallacy of Genesis: A Psychoanalytic Approach to the Hebrew Bible*, LCBI.

Ricoeur, Paul (1978). 'The Narrative Function', *Semeia* 13: 177–202.

Robertson, David (1977). *The Old Testament and the Literary Critic*, Philadelphia: Fortress.

Ryken, Leland (1990). 'The Bible as Literature', *Bibliotheca Sacra* 147: 3–15, 131–42, 259–69, 387–98.

Tate, W. Randolph (1991). *Biblical Interpretation: An Integrated Approach*, Peabody, Mass.: Hendrikson.

Thiselton, Anthony C. (1990). 'On Models and Methods: A Conversation with Robert Morgan', in Clines *et al.*, eds. (¶F), 337–56.

Thoma, Clemens, and Wyschogrod, Michael, eds., *Understanding Scripture: Exploration of Jewish and Christian Traditions of Interpretation*, New York and Mahwah, NJ: Paulist.

White, Hugh C., ed. (1988). *Speech Act Theory and Biblical Criticism*, Semeia 41.

Wink, Walter (1973). *The Bible In Human Transformation: Towards a New Paradigm for Biblical Study*, Philadelphia: Fortress.

¶D. Bible, Culture, Ideology

Ateek, Naim Stifan (1989). 'The Bible and Liberation: A Palestinian Perspective', in *Justice, and Only Justice: A Palestinian Theology of Liberation*, Maryknoll, NY: Orbis, 74–114.

Bach, Alice, ed. (1990). *The Pleasure of Her Text: Feminist Readings of Biblical and Historical Texts* (¶E).

Bailey, Randall C. (1991). 'Beyond Identification: The Use of Africans in Old Testament Poetry and Narrative', in Felder, ed., (below), 165–84.

Bailey, Randall C. (1992). 'Doing the Wrong Thing: Male-Female Relationships in the Hebrew Canon', in Sarah Cunningham, ed., *We Belong Together*, New York: Friendship, 18–29.

Bal, Mieke (1987). *Lethal Love: Feminist Literary Readings of Biblical Love Stories*, ISBL.

—— (1988a). *Murder and Difference: Gender, Genre, and Scholarship on Sisera's Death*, trans. Matthew Gumpert. ISBL. (And see the response by Robert Detweiler, 'Parerga: Homely Details, Secret Intentions, Veiled Threats', *JLT* 5 (1991), 1–10.)

—— (1988b). 'The Coherence of Politics and the Politics of Coherence', in *Death and Dissymmetry* (¶M), 9–39.

*Beal, Timothy K. (1992). 'Ideology and Intertextuality in Biblical Studies: Surplus of Meaning and Controlling the Means of Production', in Fewell, ed. (¶E), 27–39.

* —— and Gunn, David M. (1993). 'The Book of Judges', in John H. Hayes, ed., *A Dictionary of Biblical Interpretation*, Nashville: Abingdon.

Cannon, Katie Geneva and Fiorenza, Elisabeth Schüssler, eds. (1989). *Interpretation for Liberation*, Semeia 47.

Collins, Adela Yarbro, ed. (1985). *Feminist Perspectives on Biblical Scholarship*, Chico, Calif.: Scholars.

*Craig, Kerry M., and Kristjansson, Margret A. (1990). 'Women Reading as Men/Women Reading as Women: A Structural Analysis for the Historical Project', in Phillips, ed. (¶C), 119–36.

*Darr, Katheryn Pfisterer (1991). *Far More Precious than Jewels: Perspectives on Biblical Women*, Louisville, Ky.: Westminster/John Knox.

Day, Peggy L., ed. (1989). *Gender and Difference in Ancient Israel*, Minneapolis: Fortress.

Exum, J. Cheryl, and Bos, Johanna W. H., eds. (1988). *Reasoning with the Foxes: Female Wit in a World of Male Power*, Semeia 42.

Felder, Cain Hope (1989). *Troubling Biblical Waters: Race, Class, and Family*, Maryknoll, NY: Orbis.

—— ed. (1991). *Stony the Road We Trod: African American Biblical Interpretation*, Minneapolis: Fortress.

*Fewell, Danna Nolan (1987). 'Feminist Criticism of the Hebrew Bible: Affirmation, Resistance, and Transformation', *JSOT* 39: 65–75.

* Fewell, Danna Nolan (1993). 'Feminist Criticism', in Haynes and McKenzie, eds. (¶C).

* —— and Gunn, David M. (1993). *Gender, Power, and Promise: The Subject of the Bible's First Story*, Nashville: Abingdon.

Fuchs, Esther (1985). 'Who Is Hiding the Truth? Deceptive Women and Biblical Androcentrism', in Collins, ed. (above), 137–44.

—— (1989). 'The Literary Characterization of Mothers and Sexual Politics in the Hebrew Bible', in Amihai *et al.*, eds. (¶F), 151–68.

* Fulkerson, Mary McClintock (1991). 'Contesting Feminist Canons: Discourse and the Problem of Sexist Texts', *JFSR* 7: 53–73.

Gottwald, Norman K., ed. (1983). *The Bible and Liberation: Political and Social Hermeneutics*, Maryknoll, NY: Orbis.

Jobling, David (1990). 'Writing the Wrongs of the World: The Deconstruction of the Biblical Text In the Context of Liberation Theologies', in Phillips, ed. (¶C), 81–118.

* —— (1991). 'Feminism and 'Mode of Production' in Ancient Israel: Search for a Method', in Jobling *et al.*, eds. (below), 239–51.

—— Day, Peggy L., and Sheppard, Gerald T., eds. (1992). *The Bible and the Politics of Exegesis: Essays in Honor of Norman K. Gottwald* . . . , Cleveland: Pilgrim.

* Kwok Pui Lan (1989). 'Discovering the Bible in the Non-Biblical World', *Semeia* 47: 25–42.

LaCocque, André (1990). *The Feminine Unconventional: Four Subversive Figures in Israel's Tradition*, OBT. (On Susanna, Judith, Esther, and Ruth.)

Laffey, Alice L. (1988). *An Introduction to the Old Testament: A Feminist Perspective*, Philadelphia: Fortress.

Mosala, Itumeleng J. (1991). 'Bible and Liberation in South Africa in the 1980s: Toward an Antipopulist Reading of the Bible', in Jobling *et al.*, eds. (above), 267–74. (And see Mosala 1989 ¶C.)

Newsom, Carol (1989). 'Woman and the Discourse of Patriarchal Wisdom: A Study of Proverbs 1–9', in Day, ed. (above), 142–60.

* —— and Ringe, Sharon, eds. (1992). *The Women's Bible Commentary*, Louisville, Ky.: Westminster/John Knox.

Penchansky, David (1990). *The Betrayal of God: Ideological Conflict in Job*, LCBI.

Rashkow, Ilona (1990). *Upon the Dark Places: Anti-Semitism and Sexism in English Renaissance Biblical Translation*, B&L 28.

Rashkow, Ilona (1993). *The Phallacy of Genesis* (¶C).

*Ringe, Sharon H. (1992). 'When Women Interpret the Bible', in Newsom and Ringe, eds. (above), 1–9.

*Russell, Letty, ed. (1985). *Feminist Interpretation of the Bible*, Philadelphia: Westminster.

Sprague, Minka Shura (1991). 'Exegetical Storytelling: Liberation of the Tradition from the Text', in Jobling *et al.*, eds. (above), 83–93.

*Tolbert, Mary Ann, ed. (1983). *The Bible and Feminist Hermeneutics*, Semeia 28.

*Trible, Phyllis (1978). *God and the Rhetoric of Sexuality*, OBT.

*—— (1984). *Texts of Terror: Literary-Feminist Readings of Biblical Narratives*, OBT.

*—— ed. (1982). 'The Effects of Women's Studies on Biblical Studies: An Introduction', *JSOT* 22: 3–71.

*Warrior, Robert Allen (1989). 'Canaanites, cowboys, and Indians: Deliverance, conquest, and liberation theology today', *Christianity and Crisis* (11 Sept.), 261–5.

*Weems, Renita (1991). 'Reading *Her Way* Through the Struggle: African American Women and the Bible', in Felder, ed. (above), 3: 57–77.

Williams, James G. (1991). *The Bible, Violence, and the Sacred: Liberation from the Myth of Sanctioned Violence*, San Francisco: HarperSanFrancisco.

Wimbush, Vincent L. (1989). 'Historical/Cultural Criticism as Liberation. A Proposal for an African American Biblical Hermeneutic', in Cannon and Fiorenza, eds. (above), 43–55.

—— (1991). 'The Bible and African Americans: An Outline of an Interpretive History', in Felder, ed. (above), 81–97.

¶E. Literary Criticism in the Hebrew Bible: Collections

Alter, Robert and Kermode, Frank, eds. (1987). *The Literary Guide to the Bible*, Cambridge, Mass.: Harvard UP; London: Collins.

Bach, Alice, ed. (1990). *The Pleasure of Her Text: Feminist Readings of Biblical and Historical Texts*, Philadelphia: Trinity Press International.

Bal, Mieke, ed. (1989). *Anti-Covenant: Counter-Reading Women's Lives in the Hebrew Bible*, B&L 22.

Clines, David J. A. (1990). *What Does Eve Do to Help? and Other Readerly Questions to the Old Testament*, JSOTS 94.

—— Gunn, David M., and Hauser, Alan J., eds. (1982). *Art and Meaning: Rhetoric in Biblical Literature*, JSOTS 19.

—— Fowl, Stephen E., and Porter, Stanley E., eds. (1990). *The Bible in Three Dimensions*, JSOTS 87.

Culley, Robert C., ed. (1975). *Classical Hebrew Narrative*, Semeia 3.

—— ed. (1979). *Perspectives on Old Testament Narrative*, Semeia 15.

Exum, J. Cheryl and Johanna W. H. Bos, eds. (1988). *Reasoning with the Foxes* (¶D).

—— ed. (1989). *Signs and Wonders: Biblical Texts in Literary Focus*, SS.

Fewell, Danna Nolan, ed. (1992). *Reading Between Texts: Intertextuality and the Hebrew Bible*, LCBI.

Gros Louis, Kenneth R. R., with Ackerman, James S., and Warshaw, Thayer S., eds. (1974). *Literary Interpretations of Biblical Narratives*, i, Nashville: Abingdon.

—— with Ackerman, James S., eds. (1982). *Literary Interpretations of Biblical Narratives*, ii, Nashville: Abingdon.

Long, Burke O., ed. (1981). *Images of Man and God: Old Testament Short Stories in Literary Focus*, B&L 1.

Niditch, Susan, ed. (1990). *Text and Tradition: The Hebrew Bible and Folklore*, SS.

Preminger, Alex, and Greenstein, Edward L., eds. (1986). *The Hebrew Bible in Literary Criticism*, New York: Ungar.

Rosenblatt, Jason P., and Sitterson, Joseph C., Jr., eds. (1991). *'Not in Heaven': Coherence and Complexity in Biblical Narrative*, ISBL.

Schwartz, Regina, ed. (1990). *The Book and the Text: The Bible and Literary Theory*, Oxford: Blackwell.

¶F. Narrative in the Hebrew Bible: In General

* Alter, Robert (1981). *The Art of Biblical Narrative*, New York: Basic Books. (And see extended reviews by David Jobling in *JSOT* 27 (1983), 87–99, David Gunn in *JSOT* 29 (1984), 109–16, Susan Einbinder in *Prooftexts* 4 (1984), 301–8, and Robert Cohn in *Biblical Research* 31 (1986), 13–18.; also Long 1991 (below).)

Amihai, Miri, Coats, George W., and Solomon, Ann M., eds. (1989). *Narrative Research on the Hebrew Bible*, Semeia 46. (A variety of social, historical, and literary criticism; see the response by James G. Williams, 169–79.)

Amit, Yairah (1989). 'The Multi-Purpose "Leading Word" and the Problems of its Usage', *Prooftexts* 9: 99–114.

Auerbach, Erich (1953). 'Odysseus' Scar', in *Mimesis: The Representation of Reality in Western Literature*, Princeton UP, ch. 1. (German orig. 1946.)

Bal, Mieke (1987). *Lethal Love: Feminist Literary Readings of Biblical Love Stories* (¶D).

* Bar-Efrat, Shimon (1989). *Narrative Art in the Bible*, B&L 17. (Hebrew orig. 1979, 1984.)

* Berlin, Adele (1983). *Poetics and Interpretation of Biblical Narrative*, B&L 9. (And see the review by Joel Rosenberg in *Prooftexts* 5 (1985), 287–95).

* Coats, George W., ed. (1985). *Saga, Legend, Tale, Novella, Fable: Narrative Forms in Old Testament Literature*, JSOTS 35.

Culley, Robert C. (1992). *Themes and Variations: A Study of Action in Biblical Narrative*, SS.

Damrosch, David (1987). *The Narrative Covenant: Transformations of Genre in the Growth of Biblical Literature*, San Francisco: Harper and Row. (And see the review by Edward L. Greenstein ('On the Genesis of Biblical Prose Narrative') in *Prooftexts* 8 (1988), 347–54.)

Eslinger, Lyle M. (1989). 'Narratorial Situations in the Bible', in *Into the Hands of the Living God* (¶K), 1–24.

* Exum, J. Cheryl (1992). *Tragedy and Biblical Narrative: Arrows of the Almighty*, Cambridge UP.

—— ed. (1984). *Tragedy and Comedy in the Bible*, Semeia 32.

Fewell, Danna Nolan, and Gunn, David M. 1991. 'Tipping the Balance: Sternberg's Reader and the Rape of Dinah', *JBL* 110: 193–211.

* —— (1993). *Gender, Power, and Promise: The Subject of the Bible's First Story* (¶D).

Funk, Robert W. (1988). *The Poetics of Biblical Narrative*, Sonoma, Calif.: Polebridge. (Mostly about NT.)

Frye, Northrop (1982). *The Great Code: The Bible and Literature*, Toronto: Academic. (And see the review by Susan Einbinder ('Alter vs. Frye: Which Bible?') in *Prooftexts* 4 (1984), 301–8; also Lynn Poland's review in *Journal of Religion* 64 (1984), 513–19.)

Good, Edwin M. (1981). *Irony in the Old Testament*, 2nd edn., B&L 3, 56–80. (1st edn., Philadelphia: Westminster, 1965.)

Greenstein, Edward L. (1981). 'Biblical Narratology', *Prooftexts* 1: 201–8.

* —— (1989). 'Deconstruction and Biblical Narrative', *Prooftexts* 9: 43–71.

Gunn, David M. (1984). 'The Anatomy of Divine Comedy: On Reading the Bible as Comedy and Tragedy', in Exum, ed. (above), 115–29.

* —— (1987). 'New Directions in the Study of Biblical Hebrew Narrative', *JSOT* 39: 65–75.

—— (1990). 'Reading Right: Reliable and Omniscient Narrator, Omniscient God, and Foolproof Composition in the Hebrew Bible', in Clines *et al.*, eds., *The Bible in Three Dimensions* (¶E), 53–64. (On Sternberg's poetics.)

Holbert, John C. (1991). *Preaching Old Testament: Proclamation and Narrative in the Hebrew Bible*, Nashville: Abingdon.

* Humphreys, W. Lee. (1985). *The Tragic Vision and the Hebrew Tradition*, OBT.

Jobling, David (1978/1986). *The Sense of Biblical Narrative: Structural Analyses in the Hebrew Bible*, i (1978, 2nd edn. 1986) and ii (1986), JSOTS 7, 39.

—— (1992). ' "Forced Labor": Solomon's Golden Age and the Question of Literary Representation, in Jobling and Moore, eds. (¶C), 57–76.

Josipovici, Gabriel (1988). *The Book of God: A Response to the Bible*, New Haven, Conn., and London: Yale UP.

Kort, Wesley A. (1988). *Story, Text, and Scripture: Literary Interests in Biblical Narrative*, University Park, Pa., and London: Pennsylvania State UP.

Lasine, Stuart (1986). 'Indeterminacy and the Bible: A Review of Literary and Anthropological Theories and their Application to Biblical Texts', *Hebrew Studies* 27: 48–80.

Leach, Edmund (1969). *Genesis as Myth and Other Essays*, London: Jonathan Cape.

* Licht, Jacob (1978). *Storytelling in the Bible*, Jerusalem: Magnes.

Long, Burke O. (1988). 'A Figure at the Gate: Readers, Reading, and Biblical Theologians', in Gene M. Tucker, David L. Petersen and Robert R. Wilson, eds., *Canon, Theology, and Old Testament Interpretation*, Philadelphia: Fortress, 166–86.

* —— (1991). 'The "New" Biblical Poetics of Alter and Sternberg', *JSOT* 51: 71–84.

* McCarthy, Carmel, and Riley, William (1986). *The Old Testament Short Story: Explorations into Narrative Spirituality*, Wilmington: Michael Glazier. (On Ruth, Esther, Jonah, Tobit, and Judith.)

McConnell, Frank, ed. (1986). *The Bible and the Narrative Tradition*, New York: Oxford UP.

Milne, Pamela J. (1988). *Vladimir Propp and the Study of Structure in Hebrew Biblical Narrative*, B&L 13.

Miscall, Peter D. (1979). 'Literary Unity in Old Testament Narrative', *Semeia* 15: 27–44.

—— (1983). *The Workings of Old Testament Narrative*, SS.

Niditch, Susan (1987). *Underdogs and Tricksters: A Prelude to Biblical Folklore*, New Voices in Biblical Studies; San Francisco: Harper and Row.

Patrick, Dale (1981). *The Rendering of God in the Old Testament*, OBT. (On the characterization of God.)

Radday, Yehuda T., and Brenner, Athalya (1990). *On Humour and the Comic in the Hebrew Bible*, B&L 23.

Rosenberg, Joel (1986). *King and Kin: Political Allegory in the Hebrew Bible*, ISBL.

Savran, George (1985). 'The Character as Narrator in Biblical Narrative', *Prooftexts* 5: 1–17.

—— (1988). *Telling and Retelling: Quotation in Biblical Narrative*, ISBL. (And see the review by Alice Bach in *Prooftexts* 9 (1989) 264–7.)

Schwartz, Regina (1990). 'Introduction: On Biblical Criticism', in *The Book and the Text* (¶E), 1–15; also 40–59 (includes discussion of Frye and typological interpretation).

Simon, Uriel (1990). 'Minor Characters in Biblical Narrative', *JSOT* 46: 11–19.

Sternberg, Meir (1985). *The Poetics of Biblical Narrative: Ideological Literature and the Drama of Reading*, ISBL. (And see the reviews by Adele Berlin in *Prooftexts* 6 (1986), 273–84, Walter Reed in *JLT* 1 (1987), 154–66, and Lynn Poland in *Journal of Religion* 68 (1988), 426–34. Also see Gunn 1990, Fewell and Gunn 1991, and Long 1991 (above); and Mintz 1984 (¶A).

—— (1990). 'Time and Space in Biblical (Hi)story Telling: The Grand Chronology', in Schwartz, ed. (¶E), 81–145.

* Trible, Phyllis (1978). *God and the Rhetoric of Sexuality* (¶D).

Weiss, Meir, ed. (1984). *The Bible from Within*, Jerusalem: Magnes.

White, Hugh C. (1991). '*A Functional Theory of Narrative*', in *Narration and Discourse* (¶H), 1–91.

Wilder, Amos N. (1991). 'Story and Story-World', in *The Bible and the Literary Critic*, Minneapolis: Fortress, 132–48. (Orig. 1983.)

Williams, James G. (1982). *Women Recounted: Narrative Thinking and the God of Israel*, B&L 6.

¶G–W. Narrative in the Hebrew Bible: In Particular

¶G. *Genesis–Deuteronomy–2 Kings*

Clines, David J. A. (1978). *The Theme of the Pentateuch*, JSOTS 10.

* —— (1990). 'The Old Testament Histories: A Reader's Guide', in *What Does Eve Do to Help?* (¶E), 85–105. (Rev. of 'Introduction to the Biblical Story: Genesis–Esther,' in James L. Mays, ed., *Harper's Bible Commentary*, San Francisco: Harper and Row (1988), 74–84.)

* Fewell, Danna Nolan, and Gunn, David M. (1993), *Gender, Power, and Promise* (¶D).

* Mann, Thomas W. (1988). *The Book of the Torah: The Narrative Integrity of the Pentateuch*, Atlanta: John Knox.

Rendtorff, Rolff (1990). *The Problem of the Process of Transmission in the Pentateuch*, JSOTS 89. (German orig. 1977.) (Historical-critical study.)

Whybray, R. N. (1987). *The Making of the Pentateuch: A Methodological Study*, JSOTS 53. (Historical-critical study.)

¶H. *Genesis*

Bloom, Harold (1990). 'The Representation of Yahweh' and 'The Psychology of Yahweh', in David Rosenberg and Harold Bloom, *The Book of J*, New York: Grove Weidenfeld, 279–306.

Brisman, Leslie (1990). *The Voice of Jacob: On the Composition of Genesis*, ISBL.

* Clines, David J. A. (1990). 'What Happens in Genesis', in *What Does Eve Do to Help?* (¶E), 48–66.

Cohn, Robert L. (1983). 'Narrative Structure and Canonical Perspective in Genesis', *JSOT* 25: 3–16.

Dahlberg, Bruce (1982). 'The Unity of Genesis', in Gros Louis *et al.*, eds. (¶E), 126–34.

Fokkelman, J. P. (1975). *Narrative Art in Genesis: Specimens of Stylistic and Structural Analysis*, Assen/Amsterdam: Van Gorcum.

—— (1987). 'Genesis', in Alter and Kermode, eds. (¶E), 36–55.

Fox, Everett (1989). 'Can Genesis Be Read as a Book?', in Amihai *et al.*, eds. (¶F), 31–40.

* Jeansonne, Sharon Pace (1990). *The Women of Genesis*, Minneapolis: Fortress.

* Mann, Thomas W. (1988). 'The Primeval Cycle', in *The Book of the Torah* (¶G), 10–29.

Moye, Richard H. (1990). 'In the Beginning: Myth and History in Genesis and Exodus', *JBL* 109: 577–98.

* Niditch, Susan (1992). 'Genesis', in Newsom and Ringe, eds. (¶D), 10–25.

Rashkow, Ilona (1993). *The Phallacy of Genesis* (¶C).

Robinson, Robert B. (1986). 'Literary Functions of the Genealogies of Genesis', *CBQ* 48:595–608.

Steinberg, Naomi (1989). 'The Genealogical Framework of the Family Stories in Genesis', in Amihai *et al.*, eds. (¶F), 41–50. (Uses the formalist Tsvetan Todorov.)

—— (1991). 'Alliance or Descent? The Function of Marriage in Genesis', *JSOT* 51: 45–55.

Steinmetz, Devora (1991). *From Father to Son: Kinship, Conflict, and Continuity in Genesis*, LCBI.

Turner, Laurence A. (1990). *Announcements of Plot in Genesis*, JSOTS 96.

White, Hugh C. (1991). *Narration and Discourse in the Book of Genesis*, Cambridge UP.

¶H.1 Genesis 1–3: Adam and Eve

* Alter, Robert (1981). *The Art of Biblical Narrative* (¶F), 140–47. (On composite artistry.)

Bal, Mieke (1987). 'Sexuality, Sin, and Sorrow: The Emergence of the Female Character', in *Lethal Love* (¶D), 104–32.

Clines, David J. A. (1990). 'What Does Eve Do to Help? and Other Irredeemably Androcentric Orientations in Genesis 1–3', in *What Does Eve Do to Help?* (¶E), 25–48.

Dragga, Sam (1992). 'Genesis 2–3: A Story of Liberation', *JSOT* 55: 3–13.

Gunn, David M. (1990). 'Shifting the Blame: God and Patriarchy in the Garden (Genesis 1–3)'. Paper presented to Society of Biblical Literature, Central States. See now Fewell and Gunn, *Gender, Power, and Promise* (¶D), ch. 1.

Hauser, Alan Jon (1982). 'Genesis 2–3: The Theme of Intimacy and Alienation', in Clines *et al.*, eds., *Art and Meaning* (¶E), 20–36.

Jobling, David (1986). 'Myth and its Limits in Genesis 2.4b–3.24', in *The Sense of Biblical Narrative* (¶F), ii. 17–43.

Josipovici, Gabriel (1988). 'The Rhythm Established', in *The Book of God* (¶F), 53–74.

Kennedy, James M. (1990). 'Peasants in Revolt: Political Allegory in Genesis 2–3', *JSOT* 47: 3–14.

Landy, Francis (1983). 'Two Versions of Paradise', in *Paradoxes of Paradise: Identity and Difference in the Song of Songs*, B&L 7, 183–265.

Lanser, Susan (1988). '(Feminist) Criticism in the Garden: Inferring Genesis 2–3', *Semeia* 41: 67–84.

* Milne, Pamela J. (1988). 'Eve and Adam—Is a Feminist Reading Possible?', *Bible Review* 4: 12–21, 39.

—— (1989). 'The Patriarchal Stamp of Scripture: The Implications of Structural Analyses for Feminist Hermeneutics', *JFSR* 5: 17–34.

Patrick, Dale, and Scult, Allen (1990). 'Genesis and Power: An Analysis of the Biblical Story of Creation', in *Rhetoric and Biblical Interpretation* (¶C), 103–25.

* Trible, Phyllis (1978). 'A Love Story Gone Awry', in *God and the Rhetoric of Sexuality* (¶D), 72–143.

Van Wolde, E. J. (1989). *A Semiotic Analysis of Genesis 2–3*, Assen: Van Gorcum.

White, Hugh (1991). ' "Who told you that you were naked?" Genesis 2, 3', in *Narration and Discourse* (¶H), 115–45.

¶ H.2 *Genesis 4–11: Cain and Abel, Noah, and Babel*

Boesak, Alan (1984). *Black and Reformed: Apartheid, Liberation and the Calvinist Tradition*, Maryknoll, NY: Orbis.

Bowker, John (1969). *The Targums and Rabbinic Literature: An Introduction to Jewish Interpretations of Scripture*, Cambridge UP. (For Targum Pseudo-Jonathan on Genesis 4, see pp. 132–41.)

Calvin, John (1554). English transl. by John King 1847, *Commentaries on the First Book of Moses Called Genesis*, Edinburgh: Calvin Translation Soc., 187–224.

*Derrida, Jacques (1992). 'Des Tours de Babel', in Jobling and Moore, eds. (¶C), 3–34. (In English.)

Luther, Martin. (*c*.1536). English transl. by George V. Schick, ed. Jaroslav Pelikan, *Luther's Works, i. Lectures on Genesis Chapters 1–5*, Saint Louis: Concordia, 237–331.

Mosala, Itumeleng J. (1989). 'The Use of the Bible in Black Theology', in *Biblical Hermeneutics and Black Theology in South Africa* (**C**), 13–42. (And see Mosala, 1991 (¶D).)

Philo. English transl. by F. H. Colson and G. H. Whitaker (1929). 'On the Birth of Abel and the Sacrifices Offered by Him and by His Brother Cain [Gen. 4:2–4]', 88–195, and 'That the Worse is Wont to Attack the Better [Gen. 4:8–16]' 198–319, *Philo*, ii. Loeb Classical Library; London: Heinemann; New York: Putnam's Sons. See also *Philo. Supplement I: Questions and Answers on Genesis*. Transl. by Ralph Marcus, Cambridge, Mass.: Harvard UP; London: Heinemann (1953), 'Genesis, Book I' [including questions on Genesis 4], 36–49.

Speiser, E. A. (1964). *Genesis*, Anchor Bible; Garden City: Doubleday.

Sprague, Minka Shura (1991). 'Exegetical Storytelling' (¶D). (On Noah.)

Targum Pseudo-Jonathan. See Bowker (above).

Voltaire (764). English trans., *Philosophical Dictionary*. (French orig.)

West, Gerald O. (1989). 'Reading "the Text" and Reading "Behind the Text": The Cain and Abel Story in a Context of Liberation', in Clines *et al.*, eds., *The Bible in Three Dimensions* (¶E), 299–320.

Westermann, Claus (1984). *Genesis 1–11: A Commentary*, Minneapolis: Augsburg. (German orig. 1974.)

White, Hugh (1991). ' "Where is your brother?" Genesis 4', in *Narration and Discourse* (¶H), 146–68.

*Wiesel, Eli (1976). 'Cain and Abel: The First Genocide', in *Messengers of God: Biblical Portraits and Legends*, New York: Random House, 37–64.

Williams, Arnold (1948). *The Common Expositor: An Account of the Commentaries on Genesis, 1527–1633*, Chapel Hill: Univ. of North Carolina.

Williams, James G. (1991). 'Enemy Brothers', in *The Bible, Violence, and the Sacred* (¶D), 33–70.

¶*H.3 Genesis 12–26: Abraham, Sarah, Isaac*

Brisman, Leslie (1990). 'The Calls to Abraham', in *The Voice of Jacob* (¶H) 27–47.

Clines, David J. A. 'The Ancestor in Danger: But Not the Same Danger', in *What Does Eve Do to Help?* (¶E), 67–84.

* Darr, Katheryn Pfisterer (1991). 'More than the Stars of the Heavens: Critical, Rabbinical, and Feminist Perspectives on Sarah', in *Far More Precious than Jewels* (¶D), 85–131.

Delaney, Carol (1989). 'The Legacy of Abraham', in Bal, ed. (¶E), 27–41.

* Exum, J. Cheryl, and Whedbee, J. William (1985). 'Isaac, Samson, and Saul: Reflections on the Comic and Tragic Visions', in Exum, ed. (¶F), 5–40.

* Fewell, Danna Nolan (1989). 'Divine Calls, Human Responses: Another Look at Abraham and Sarah', *The Perkins School of Theology Journal*, 13–16.

* Gros Louis, Kenneth R. R. (1982). 'Abraham: I and II', in Gros Louis *et al.*, eds. (¶E), ii. 53–84.

* Mann, Thomas W. (1988). 'The Abraham Cycle', in *The Book of the Torah* (¶G), 29–50.

Marmesh, Ann (1989). 'Anti-Covenant', in Bal, ed. (¶E), 43–60.

Miscall, Peter (1983). 'Genesis 12 and Related Texts', in *The Workings of Old Testament Narrative* (¶F), 11–46.

Niditch, Susan (1987). 'The Three Wife-Sister Tales of Genesis', in *Underdogs and Tricksters* (¶F), 23–69.

Polzin, Robert (1975). '"The Ancestress of Israel in Danger" in Danger', in Culley, ed. (¶E), 81–98. (See also Miscall 1979 (¶F), followed by Polzin's response, 45–50.)

Rashkow, Ilona N. (1992). 'Intertextuality, Transference, and the Reader in/of Genesis 12 and 20', in Fewell, ed. (¶E), 57–73.

White, Hugh (1991). 'Why did you say, "She is my sister"? Genesis 12: 10–20', in *Narration and Discourse* (¶H), 174–86.

Williams, James G. (1980). 'The Beautiful and the Barren: Conventions in Bible Type-Scenes', *JSOT* 17: 107–19.

¶H.4 Genesis 16–21: Hagar, Ishmael, Lot and his Daughters

Alter, Robert (1990). 'Sodom as Nexus: The Web of Design in Biblical Narrative', in Schwartz, ed. (¶E), 146–60.

*Darr, Katheryn Pfisterer (1991). 'More than a Possession: Critical, Rabinical, and Feminist Perspectives on Hagar', in *Far More Precious than Jewels* (¶D), 132–63.

*Gunn, David M. (1993). 'Narrative Criticism', in Haynes and McKenzie (¶C). (Includes a reading of the story of Lot and his wife at Sodom.)

*Hawk, L. Daniel (1992). 'Strange Houseguests', in Fewell, ed. (¶E), 89–97. (On Genesis 19 and Judges 2, 6.)

Helyer, Larry R. (1983). 'The Separation of Abraham and Lot: Its Significance in the Patriarchal Narratives', *JSOT* 26: 77–88.

*Jeansonne, Sharon Pace (1988). 'The Characterization of Lot in Genesis', *Biblical Theology Bulletin* 18: 123–9.

Penchansky, David (1992). 'Staying the Night: Intertextuality in Genesis and Judges', in Fewell, ed. (¶E), 77–88. (On Genesis 19, 24 and Judges 19.)

Tapp, Anne Michele (1989). 'An Ideology of Expendability: Virgin Daughter Sacrifice in Genesis 19.1–11, Judges 11.30–39 and 19.22–26', in Bal, ed. (¶E), 157–74.

*Trible, Phyllis (1984). 'Hagar: The Desolation of Rejection', in *Texts of Terror* (¶D), 9–35.

Turner, Laurence A. (1990). 'Lot as Jekyll and Hyde: A Reading of Genesis 18–19', in Clines *et al.*, eds., *The Bible in Three Dimensions* (¶E), 85–101.

*Weems, Renita J. (1988). 'A Mistress, a Maid, and No Mercy', in *Just a Sister Away: A Womanist Vision of Women's Relationships in the Bible*, San Diego: LuraMedia, 1–21. (On Hagar.)

¶H.5 Genesis 22: Abraham and Isaac

Auerbach, Erich (1953). 'Odysseus' Scar', in *Mimesis*. (¶F) (On Genesis 22, Abraham and Isaac.)

Brisman, Leslie (1990). 'The Disappearances of Isaac', in *The Voice of Jacob* (¶H), 48–65.

* Crenshaw, James L. (1984). 'A Monstrous Test: Genesis 22', in *A Whirlpool of Torment: Israelite Traditions of God as an Oppressive Presence*, OBT, 9–29.

* Edgerton, W. Dow (1992). 'The Exegesis of Echoes', in *The Passion of Interpretation* (¶C), 66–93.

Landy, Francis (1989). 'Narrative Techniques and Symbolic Transactions in the Akedah', in Exum, ed. (¶E), 1–40. (And see the response by Jan P. Fokkelman: 41–57.)

Mazor, Yair (1986). 'Genesis 22: The Ideological Rhetoric and the Psychological Component', *Biblica* 67: 81–8.

Saldarini, Anthony J. (1982). 'Interpretation of the *Akedah* in Rabbinic Literature', in Polzin and Rothman, eds. (¶C), 149–65.

* Swindell, Anthony C. (1975). 'Abraham and Isaac: An Essay in Biblical Appropriation', *Expository Times* 87: 50–3. (A brief history of interpretation.)

White, Hugh (1991). ' "Where is the lamb for the burnt offering?" Genesis 22', in *Narration and Discourse*. (¶H), 187–203.

* Wiesel, Elie (1976). 'The Sacrifice of Isaac: A Survivor's Story', in *Messengers of God: Biblical Portraits and Legends*, New York: Random House, 69–97.

¶H.6 Genesis 24: Rebekah

* Alter, Robert (1981). *The Art of Biblical Narrative* (¶F), 51–4. (On Genesis 24, Rebekah.)

* Fewell, Danna Nolan and Gunn, David M. (1993). *Gender, Power, and Promise* (¶D), ch. 2.

Fuchs, Esther (1987). 'Structure and Patriarchal Functions in the Biblical Betrothal Type-Scene', *JFSR* 3: 7–13.

Penchansky, David (1992). 'Staying the Night' (¶H.4).

Sternberg, Meir (1990). 'The Wooing of Rebekah', in *The Poetics of Biblical Narrative* (¶F), 131–52.

* Turner, Mary Donovan (1985). 'Rebekah: Ancestor of Faith', *Lexington Theological Quarterly* 20: 42–50.

* Williams, James G. (1982). 'The Arche-Mother: The Mother of Israel's Beginnings', in *Women Recounted* (¶F), 42–66.

⁴ *H.7 Genesis 25–36: Jacob, Esau, Laban, Leah and Rachel*

* Alter, Robert (1981). *The Art of Biblical Narrative* (⁴ F), 42–5 (on Jacob) and 185–8 (on Rachel).

Barthes, Roland (1974). 'The Struggle with the Angel: Textual Analysis of Genesis 32: 23–33', in Barthes *et al.*, eds., *Structural Analysis and Biblical Exegesis: Interpretational Essays*, Pittsburgh: Pickwick, 21–33.

Berger, David (1987). 'On the Morality of the Patriarchs in Jewish Polemic and Exegesis', in Thoma and Wyschogrod, eds. (⁴ C), 49–62.

* Evans, Carl (1986). 'The Patriarch Jacob—An "Innocent Man"', *Bible Review* 2: 32–7.

* Fishbane, Michael (1979). 'Genesis 25:19–35:22/The Jacob Cycle', in *Text and Texture: Close Readings of Selected Biblical Texts*, New York: Schocken, 40–52.

Fokkelman, J. P. (1975). *Narrative Art in Genesis: Specimens of Stylistic and Structural Analysis*, Assen/Amsterdam: Van Gorcum, Part II (chs. III–V), 86–236.

Fuchs, Esther (1988). ' "For I Have the Way of Women": Deception, Gender, and Ideology in Biblical Narrative', *Semeia* 42: 68–83.

Furman, Nelly (1989). 'His Story Versus Her Story: Male Genealogy and Female Strategy in the Jacob Cycle', in Amihai *et al.*, eds. (⁴ F), 141–9.

* Mann, Thomas W. (1988). 'The Jacob Cycle', in *The Book of the Torah* (⁴ G), 51–66.

Miscall, Peter D. (1978). 'The Jacob and Joseph Stories as Analogies', *JSOT* 6: 28–40.

Niditch, Susan (1987). *Underdogs and Tricksters* (⁴ F), 70–125. (On Jacob and Joseph.)

White, Hugh (1991). ' "Who then is he who was hunting game . . . before you came?" Genesis 25:19–34; 26:34–5; and 27:1–28:9', in *Narration and Discourse* (⁴ H), 204–31.

Williams, James G. (1991). 'Enemy Brothers', in *The Bible, Violence, and the Sacred* (⁴ D), 33–70.

⁴ *H.8 Genesis 34: Dinah*

Caspi, Mishael Maswari (1985). 'The Story of the Rape of Dinah: The Narrator and the Reader', *Hebrew Studies* 26: 25–45.

* Fewell, Danna Nolan, and Gunn, David M. (1991). 'Tipping the Balance: Sternberg's Reader and the Rape of Dinah', *JBL* 110: 193–211.

Geller, Stephen A. (1990). 'The Sack of Shechem: The Use of Typology in Biblical Covenant Religion', *Prooftexts* 10: 1–15.

* Jeansonne, Sharon Pace (1990). 'Dinah: The Fracturing of a Tenuous Peace in a Troubled Land', in The *Women of Genesis* (¶H), 87–97.

Rashkow, Ilona (1990). 'The Rape of Dinah', in *Upon the Dark Places* (¶D), 97–117.

Sternberg, Meir (1990). 'Delicate Balance in the Rape of Dinah', in *The Poetics of Biblical Narrative* (¶F), 445–75.

¶H.9 Genesis 37–50: Joseph

Ackerman, James S. (1982). 'Joseph, Judah, and Jacob', in Gros Louis *et al.*, eds. (¶E), ii. 85–113.

Alter, Robert (1981). *The Art of Biblical Narrative* (¶F), 107–13 (on Potiphar's wife) and 155–77 (on Joseph).

* Berlin, Adele (1983). *Poetics and Interpretation of Biblical Narrative* (¶F), 48–51, 113–21. (On Genesis 37.)

Coats, George W. (1976). *From Canaan to Egypt: Structural and Theological Context for the Joseph Story*, Washington: Catholic Biblical Assoc.

* Greenstein, Edward L. (1982). 'An Equivocal Reading of the Sale of Joseph', in Gros Louis *et al.*, eds. (¶E), ii. 114–25.

* Humphreys, W. Lee (1988). *Joseph and His Family: A Literary Study*, Columbia, SC: Univ. of South Carolina. (See esp. Part I, 'The Poetics of the Joseph Novella'.)

Josipovici, Gabriel (1988). 'Joseph and Revelation', in *The Book of God* (¶F), 75–89.

* Mann, Thomas W. (1988). 'The Joseph Cycle', in *The Book of the Torah* (¶G), 66–77.

Miscall, Peter D. (1978). 'The Jacob and Joseph Stories as Analogies', *JSOT* 6: 28–40.

Savage, M. (1980). 'Literary Criticism and Biblical Studies: A Rhetorical Analysis of the Joseph Narrative', in Carl D. Evans *et al.*, eds., *Scripture in Context*, Pittsburgh: Pickwick, 79–100.

Schwartz, Regina (1990). 'Joseph's Bones and the Resurrection of the Text: Remembering in the Bible', in *The Book and the Text* (¶E), 40–59.

Sternberg, Meir (1990). 'Joseph and His Brothers: Making Sense of the Past' and 'Repetition and Communication: Pharaoh's Dream', in *The Poetics of Biblical Narrative* (¶F), 285–308 and 394–402. (Also 423–27, on Potiphar's wife.)

White, Hugh C. (1985). 'Reuben and Judah: Duplicates or Complements?', in James T. Butler *et al.*, eds., *Understanding the Word: Essays in Honor of Bernhard W. Anderson*, JSOTS 37, 73–97.

—— (1991). ' "Where do you come from?" Genesis 37, 39–45, 50', in *Narration and Discourse* (¶H), 232–75.

Williams, James G. (1991). 'Enemy Brothers', in *The Bible, Violence, and the Sacred* (¶D), 33–70.

¶*H.10 Genesis 38: Tamar and Judah*

* Alter, Robert (1981). *The Art of Biblical Narrative* (¶F), 5–12.

Bird, Phyllis A. (1989). 'The Harlot as Heroine: Narrative Art and Social Presupposition in Three Old Testament Texts', in Amihai *et al.*, eds. (¶F), 119–39. (On Genesis 38, Joshua 2, 1 Kings 3.)

* Fewell, Danna Nolan, and Gunn, David Miller (1990). 'A Lapful of Grain: Reading Ruth in a Biblical Collage', in *Compromising Redemption* (¶R), Part I.

Goldin, Judah (1977). 'The Youngest Son or Where Does Genesis 38 Belong?', *JBL* 96: 27–44.

* Jeansonne, Sharon Pace (1990). 'Tamar: The Woman Who Demanded Justice', in *The Women of Genesis* (¶H), 98–106.

Niditch, Susan (1979). 'The Wronged Woman Righted: An Analysis of Genesis 38', *Harvard Theological Review* 72: 143–9.

van Dijk-Hemmes, Fokkelien (1989). 'Tamar and the Limits of Patriarchy: Between Rape and Seduction (2 Samuel 13 and Genesis 38)', in Bal, ed. (¶E), 135–56.

¶*I. Exodus*

* Ackerman, James S. (1974). 'The Literary Context of the Moses Birth Story (Exodus 1–2)', in Gros Louis *et al.*, eds. (¶E), i. 74–119.

Chirichigno, C. G. (1987). 'The Narrative Structure of Exodus 19–24', *Biblica* 68: 457–79.

Daube, David (1963). *The Exodus Pattern in the Bible*, London: Faber and Faber.

*Exum, J. Cheryl (1983). ' "You Shall Let Every Daughter Live": A Study of Exodus 1:8–2:10', *Semeia* 28: 63–82.

Fokkelman, J. P. (1987). 'Exodus', in Alter and Kermode, eds. (¶E), 56–65.

*Gunn, David M. (1982). 'The "Hardening of Pharaoh's Heart": Plot, Character and Theology in Exodus 1–14', in Clines *et al.*, eds., *Art and Meaning* (¶E), 72–96.

Holbert, John (1990). 'A New Literary Reading of Exodus 32, The Story of the Golden Calf', *Quarterly Review* 10/3: 46–8.

Isbell, Charles (1982). 'Exodus 1–2 in the Context of Exodus 1–14: Story Lines and Key Words', in Clines *et al.*, eds., *Art and Meaning* (¶E), 37–61.

*Mann, Thomas W. (1988). 'Exodus', in *The Book of the Torah* (¶G). 78–112.

Moberly, R. W. L. (1983). *At the Mountain of God: Story and Theology in Exodus 32–34*, JSOTS 22.

Nohrnberg, James (1981). 'Moses', in Long, ed. (¶E), 35–57.

Setel, Drorah (1992). 'Exodus', in Newsom and Ringe, eds. (¶D), 26–35.

Trible, Phyllis (1989). 'Bringing Miriam out of the Shadows', *Bible Review* 5: 14–25, 34.

Waldavsky, Aaron (1984). *The Nursing Father: Moses as a Political Leader*, University, Ala.: Univ. of Alabama.

Walzer, Michael (1985). *Exodus and Revolution*, New York: Basic Books.

Williams, James G. (1991). 'Moses and the Exodus', in *The Bible, Violence, and the Sacred* (¶D), 71–103.

¶ J. Leviticus and Numbers

*Ackerman, James S. (1987). 'Numbers', in Alter and Kermode, eds. (¶E), 78–91.

*Alter, Robert (1981). *The Art of Biblical Narrative* (¶F), 131–7 (on Numbers 16) and 104–7 (on Numbers 22–4).

Clark, Ira (1982). 'Balaam's Ass: Suture or Structure?', in Gros Louis *et al.*, eds. (¶E), 137–44.

Culley, Robert C. (1990). 'Five Tales of Punishment in the Book of Numbers', in Niditch, ed. (¶E), 25–34. (And see the comments by Dan Ben-Amos, 35–45.)

Damrosch, David (1987). 'Law and Narrative in the Priestly Work', in *The Narrative Covenant* (¶F), 261–97.

Greenstein, Edward L. (1989). 'Deconstruction and Biblical Narrative', *Prooftexts* 9: 43–71. (On the deaths of Aaron's sons, Nadab and Abihu; Leviticus 10.)

Hickcox, Alice McCracken (1994). *Between Redemption and Promise: Exodus and Exile in Numbers*, LCBI.

Jobling, David (1978). 'A Structural Analysis of Numbers 11–12', in *The Sense of Biblical Narrative* (¶F), i. 26–62.

—— (1986). ' "The Jordan a Boundary": Transjordan in Israel's Ideological Geography', in *The Sense of Biblical Narrative* (¶F), ii. 88–134.

* Mann, Thomas W. (1988). 'Leviticus' and 'Numbers', in *The Book of the Torah* (¶G), 113–42.

Newing, Edward G. (1987). 'The Rhetoric of Altercation in Numbers 14', in Edward W. Conrad and Edward G. Newing, eds., *Perspectives on Text and Language*, Winona Lake, Ind.: Eisenbrauns, 211–29.

Safran, Jonathan D. (1988). 'Balaam and Abraham', *Vetus Testamentum* 38: 105–13.

Sakenfeld, Katharine Doob (1988). 'In the Wilderness, Awaiting the Land: The Daughters of Zelophehad and Feminist Interpretation', *Princeton Seminary Bulletin* 9: 179–96.

—— (1992). 'Numbers', in Newsom and Ringe, eds. (¶D), 45–51.

Wegner, Judith Romney (1992). 'Leviticus', in Newsom and Ringe, eds. (¶D).

¶K. Deuteronomy–Kings

Eslinger, Lyle M. (1989). *Into the Hands of the Living God*, B&L 24.

* Fewell, Danna Nolan, and Gunn, David M. (1993). *Gender, Power, and Promise* (¶D).

Frymer-Kensky, Tikva (1992). 'Deuteronomy', in Newsom and Ringe, eds. (¶D), 52–62.

* Freedman, David Noel (1976). 'The Deuteronomic History', in K. Crim, ed., *The Interpreter's Dictionary of the Bible*, Nashville: Abingdon, 226–28.

* Mann, Thomas W. (1988). 'Deuteronomy', in *The Book of the Torah* (¶G), 143–56.

Polzin, Robert (1980). *Moses and the Deuteronomist: A Literary Study of the Deuteronomic History. Part One: Deuteronomy, Joshua, Judges*, New York: Seabury.

—— (1987). 'Deuteronomy', in Alter and Kermode, eds. (¶E), 92–101.

¶L. Joshua

Bird, Phyllis A. (1989). 'The Harlot as Heroine, (¶H.10). (On Joshua 2.)

Culley, Robert C. (1984). 'Stories of the Conquest: Joshua 2, 6, 7, and 8', *Hebrew Annual Review* 8: 25–44.

Eslinger, Lyle M. (1989). 'Those Nations that Remain', in *Into the Hands of the Living God* (¶K), 25–54.

* Fewell, Danna Nolan (1992). 'Joshua', in Newsom and Ringe, eds. (¶D), 63–6.

* Gunn, David M. (1987). 'Joshua and Judges', in Alter and Kermode, eds. (¶E), 102–21.

* Hawk, L. Daniel (1991). *Every Promise Fulfilled: Contesting Plots in Joshua*, LCBI.

* —— (1992). 'Strange Houseguests: Rahab, Lot, and the Dynamics of Deliverance', in Fewell, ed. (¶E), 89–97.

Jobling, David (1986). 'The Jordan a Boundary' (¶J).

Koopmans, William T. (1990). *Joshua 24 as Poetic Narrative*, JSOTS 93.

Polzin, Robert (1980). 'The Book of Joshua', in *Moses and the Deuteronomist* (¶K), 73–145.

* Rowlett, Lori (1992). 'Inclusion, Exclusion and Marginality in the Book of Joshua', *JSOT* 55: 15–23.

* Warrior, Robert Allen (1989). 'Canaanites, cowboys, and Indians: Deliverance, conquest, and liberation theology today', *Christianity and Crisis* (11 Sept.), 261–5.

¶M. Judges

Bal, Mieke (1988). *Death and Dissymmetry: The Politics of Coherence in the Book of Judges*, Chicago UP.

* Beal, Timothy K., and Gunn, David M. (1993). 'The Book of Judges' (¶D). (History of interpretation.)

Brettler, Marc (1989). 'The Book of Judges: Literature as Politics', *JBL* 108: 395–418.

* Exum, J. Cheryl (1990). 'The Centre Cannot Hold: Thematic and Textual Instabilities in Judges', *CBQ* 52: 410–31.

* Fewell, Danna Nolan (1992). 'Judges', in Newsom and Ringe, eds. (¶D), 67–77.

* Gunn, David M. (1987). 'Joshua and Judges', in Alter and Kermode, eds. (¶E), 102–21.

* Hamlin, E. John (1990). *Judges: At Risk in the Promised Land*, Grand Rapids, Mich.: Eerdmans; Edinburgh: Handsel.

Jobling, David (1986). 'Deuteronomic Political Theory in Judges and 1 Samuel 1–12', in *The Sense of Biblical Narrative* (¶F), ii. 44–87.

Josipovici, Gabriel (1988). 'The Rhythm Falters: The Book of Judges', in *The Book of God* (¶F), 108–31.

Klein, Lillian R. (1988). *The Triumph of Irony in the Book of Judges*, B&L 14.

* Polzin, Robert (1980). 'The Book of Judges', in *Moses and the Deuteronomist* (¶K), 146–204.

Webb, Barry G. (1987). *The Book of the Judges: An Integrated Reading*, JSOTS 46.

¶*M.1 Judges 1–3*

* Alter, Robert (1981). *The Art of Biblical Narrative* (¶F), 37–41. (On Ehud, Judges 3.)

* Amit, Yairah (1989). 'The Story of Ehud (Judges 3:12–30): The Form and the Message', in Exum, ed. (¶E), 97–123. (And see the response by David Jobling: 125–31.)

Eslinger, Lyle M. (1989). 'A New Generation in Israel', in *Into the Hands of the Living God* (¶K), 55–80. (On Judges 1–2.)

Webb, Barry G. (1987). *The Book of the Judges* (¶M), 81–122.

¶*M.2 Judges 4 and 5: Deborah, Barak and Jael*

* Amit, Yairah (1987). 'Judges 4: Its Contents and Form', *JSOT* 39: 89–111.

Bal, Mieke (1988). *Murder and Difference* (¶D).

Brenner, Athalya (1990). 'A Triangle and a Rhombus in Narrative Structure: A Proposed Integrative Reading of Judges iv and v', *Vetus Testamentum* 40: 129–38.

*Exum, J. Cheryl (1985). '"Mother in Israel": A Familiar Figure Reconsidered', in Russell, ed. (¶D), 73–85.

Fewell, Danna Nolan, and Gunn, David M. (1990). 'Controlling Perspectives: Women, Men, and the Authority of Violence in Judges 4 and 5', *JAAR* 56: 389–411.

Murray, D. F. (1979). 'Narrative Structure and Techniques in the Deborah-Barak Story (Judges iv 4–22)', *Vetus Testamentum Supplements* 30: 155–89.

Niditch, Susan (1989). 'Eroticism and Death in the Tale of Jael', in Day, ed. (¶D), 43–57.

Sternberg, Meir (1990). 'Darkness in Light, or: Zigzagging toward Sisera's End', in *The Poetics of Biblical Narrative* (¶F), 270–83.

¶*M.3 Judges 6–9: Gideon and Abimelech*

Boogaart, T. A. (1985). 'Stone for Stone: Retribution in the Story of Abimelech and Shechem', *JSOT* 32: 45–56.

Janzen, J. Gerald (1987). 'A Certain Woman in the Rhetoric of Judges 9', *JSOT* 38: 33–7.

Klein, Lillian R. (1988). *The Triumph of Irony in the Book of Judges* (¶M), 49–80.

¶*M.4 Judges 10–12: Jephthah and Jephthah's Daughter*

Bal, Mieke (1989). 'Between Altar and Wandering Rock: Toward a Feminist Philology', in *Anti-Covenant* (¶E), 211–31.

—— (1990). 'Dealing/With/Women: Daughters in the Book of Judges', in Schwartz, ed. (¶E), 16–39.

Exum, J. Cheryl (1989). 'The Tragic Vision and Biblical Narrative: The Case of Jephthah', in Exum, ed. (¶E), 59–83. (And see the response by W. Lee Humphreys: 85–96.)

* —— (1990). 'Murder They Wrote: Ideology and the Manipulation of Female Presence in Biblical Narrative', in Bach, ed. (¶E), 45–67.

Fuchs, Esther (1989). 'Marginalization, Ambiguity, Silencing: The Story of Jephthah's Daughter', *JFSR* 5: 35–45.

* Trible, Phyllis (1984). 'The Daughter of Jephthah: An Inhuman Sacrifice', in *Texts of Terror* (¶D), 93–116.

  Webb, Barry G. (1987). *The Book of the Judges* (¶M), 41–78.

¶M.5 Judges 13–16: Samson

* Alter, Robert (1983). 'How Convention Helps Us Read: The Annunciation Type-Scene in the Bible', *Prooftexts* 3: 115–30.

—— (1990). 'Samson Without Folklore', in Niditch, ed. (¶E), 47–56.

  Bal, Mieke (1987). 'Delilah Decomposed: Samson's Talking Cure and the Rhetoric of Subjectivity', in *Lethal Love* (¶D), 37–67.

* Camp, Claudia V., and Fontaine, Carole R. (1991). 'The Words of the Wise and Their Riddles', in Niditch, ed. (¶E), 127–52.

* Crenshaw, James L. (1978). *Samson: A Secret Betrayed, a Vow Ignored*, Atlanta: John Knox.

  Exum, J. Cheryl (1980). 'Promise and Fulfillment: Narrative Art in Judges 13', *JBL* 99: 39–59.

—— (1981). 'Aspects of Symmetry and Balance in the Samson Saga', *JSOT* 19: 2–29.

—— (1983). 'The Theological Dimension of the Samson Saga', *Vetus Testamentum* 33: 30–45.

  Fuchs, Esther (1985). 'The Literary Characterization of Mothers and Sexual Politics in the Hebrew Bible', in Collins, ed. (¶D), 117–36. (Reprinted in Amihai *et al.*, eds. (¶F), 151–66.)

  Greenstein, Edward L. (1981). 'The Riddle of Samson', *Prooftexts* 1: 237–60.

* Gunn, David M. (1992). 'Samson of Sorrows: An Isaianic Gloss on Judges 13–16', in Fewell, ed. (¶E), 225–53.

* Niditch, Susan (1990). 'Samson As Culture Hero, Trickster, and Bandit: The Empowerment of the Weak', *CBQ* 52: 608–24.

  Reinhartz, Adele (1992). 'Samson's Mother: An Unnamed Protagonist', *JSOT* 55: 25–37.

* Vickery, John B. (1981). 'In Strange Ways: The Story of Samson', in Long, ed. (¶E), 58–73.

¶M.6 Judges 17–21: Micah and the Danites, and the Levite's Woman

  Bal, Mieke (1990). 'Dealing/With/Women: Daughters in the Book of Judges', in Schwartz, ed. (¶E), 16–39.

Klein, Lillian R. (1988). *The Triumph of Irony in the Book of Judges* (¶M), 141–92.

Lasine, Stuart (1984). 'Guest and Host in Judges 19: Lot's Hospitality in an Inverted World', *JSOT* 29: 37–59.

Niditch, Susan (1982). 'The "Sodomite" Theme in Judges 19–20: Family, Community, and Social Disintegration', *CBQ* 44: 365–78.

Penchansky, David (1992). 'Staying the Night' (¶H.4). (On Judges 19.)

* Trible, Phyllis (1984). 'An Unnamed Woman: The Extravagance of Violence', in *Texts of Terror* (¶D), 65–91.

Webb, Barry G. (1987). *The Book of the Judges* (¶D), 181–203.

[For the Book of Ruth, see below, ¶R]

¶N. *1 and 2 Samuel*

* Brueggemann, Walter (1985). *David's Truth in Israel's Imagination and Memory*, Philadelphia: Fortress.

* Exum, J. Cheryl (1992). *Tragedy and Biblical Narrative* (¶F).

Flanagan, James W. (1988). 'Domain of Notions: Literary Images of the David Figure', in *David's Social Drama: A Hologram of Israel's Early Iron Age*, Sheffield: Almond, 193–272.

Fokkelman, J. P. (1981). *Narrative Art and Poetry in the Books of Samuel, i. King David (II Sam. 9–20 and I Kg. 1–2)*, Amsterdam: Van Gorcum.

—— (1986). *Narrative Art and Poetry in the Books of Samuel, ii. The Crossing Fates (I Sam. 13–31 and II Sam. 1)*, Assen: Van Gorcum.

—— (1990). *Narrative Art and Poetry in the Books of Samuel, iii. Throne and City (II Sam. 2–8 & 21–24)*, Assen: Van Gorcum.

Garsiel, Moshe (1985). *The First Book of Samuel: A Literary Study of Comparative Structures*, Analogies and Parallels, Ramat-Gan: Revivim.

Gunn, David M. (1978). *The Story of King David: Genre and Interpretation*, JSOTS 6.

* —— (1980). *The Fate of King Saul: An Interpretation of a Biblical Story*, JSOTS 14.

—— (1989). 'In Security: The David of Biblical Narrative', in Exum, ed. (¶E), 133–51. (And the response by Peter D. Miscall: 153–63.)

Miscall, Peter D. (1986). 1 *Samuel: A Literary Reading*, ISBL.

Polzin, Robert (1989). *Samuel and the Deuteronomist: A Literary Study of the Deuteronomic History. Part Two: 1 Samuel*, San Francisco: Harper and Row.

Rosenberg, Joel (1986). *King and Kin (¶F)*.

* —— (1987). '1 and 2 Samuel', in Alter and Kermode, eds. (¶E), 122–45.

¶N.1   1 *Samuel: Samuel and Saul*

* Ackerman, James S. (1991). 'Who Can Stand before YHWH, This Holy God? A Reading of 1 Samuel 1–15', *Prooftexts* 11: 1–24.

* Alter, Robert (1981). The Art of Biblical Narrative (¶F), 81–7. (On the birth of Samuel.)

Eslinger, Lyle M. (1983). 'Viewpoints and Point of View in 1 Samuel 8–12', *JSOT* 26: 61–76.

—— (1985). *Kingship of God in Crisis: A Close Reading of 1 Samuel 1–12*, B&L 10.

—— (1989). 'A King in Whom There is No Profit', in *Into the Hands of the Living God* (¶K), 81–121.

Fokkelman, Jan P. (1989). 'Saul and David: Crossed Fates', *Bible Review* 5: 20–32.

* Good, Edwin M. (1981). 'Saul: The Tragedy of Greatness', in *Irony in the Old Testament* (¶F), 56–80.

* Gunn, David M. (1980). *The Fate of King Saul* (¶N).

* —— (1981). 'A Man Given Over to Trouble: The Story of King Saul', in Long, ed. (¶E), 89–112.

Humphreys, W. Lee (1978). 'The Tragedy of King Saul: A Study of the Structure of 1 Samuel 9–31', *JSOT* 6: 18–27.

* —— (1985). 'The Tragedy of King Saul', in *The Tragic Vision and the Hebrew Tradition* (¶F), 23–42.

Janzen, J. Gerald (1983). '"Samuel Opened the Doors of the House of Yahweh" (1 Samuel 3:15)', *JSOT* 26: 89–96.

Jobling, David. (1978). 'Jonathan: A Structural Study in 1 Samuel', in *The Sense of Biblical Narrative* (¶F), i. 4–25.

Long, V. Philips (1989). *The Reign and Rejection of King Saul: A Case for Literary and Theological Coherence*, Atlanta: Scholars.

Sternberg, Meir (1990). 'Ideology, Rhetoric, Poetics', in *The Poetics of Biblical Narrative* (¶F), 482–515. (On Saul.)

* Wiesel, Elie (1981). 'Saul', in *Five Biblical Portraits*, Notre Dame and London: Notre Dame UP, 69–95.

Williams, James G. (1991). *The Bible, Violence, and the Sacred* (¶D), 129–48. (On Saul.)

¶*N.2 1 Samuel 16–30: David, Saul, Michal, Abigail and Nabal*

* Alter, Robert (1981). *The Art of Biblical Narrative* (¶F), 114–30 (on Michal and David) and 147–53 (on 1 Samuel 16–17).

* Bach, Alice (1990). 'The Pleasure of Her Text', in Bach, ed. (¶E), 25–44. (On Abigail.)

* Berlin, Adele (1982). 'Characterization in Biblical Narrative: David's Wives', *JSOT* 23: 69–85. (Also in Poetics and Interpretation (¶F), 23–33.)

Beuken, W. A. M. (1878). '1 Samuel 28: The Prophet as 'Hammer of Witches', *JSOT* 6: 3–17.

Brueggemann, Walter (1989). 'Narrative Intentionality in 1 Samuel 29', *JSOT* 43: 21–35.

Clines, David J. A., and Eskenazi, Tamara C., eds. (1991). *Telling Queen Michal's Story: An Experiment in Comparative Interpretation*, JSOTS 119. (Includes recent essays by Richard Bowman, Cheryl Exum, Peter Miscall, Robert Polzin, and the editors.)

Eslinger, Lyle M. (1988). ' "A Change of Heart": 1 Samuel 16', in Lyle Eslinger and Glen Taylor, eds., *Ascribe to the Lord: Biblical and other studies in memory of Peter C. Craigie*, JSOTS 67, 341–61.

* Exum, J. Cheryl (1990). 'Murder They Wrote: Ideology and the Manipulation of Female Presence in Biblical Narrative', in Bach, ed. (¶E), 45–67. (On Michal.)

Lawton, Robert B. (1989). '1 Samuel 18: David, Merob, and Michal', *CBQ* 51: 423–25.

Levenson, Jon D. (1982). '1 Samuel 25 as Literature and History', in Gros Louis *et al.*, eds. (¶E), 220–42. (On Abigail.)

* Miscall, Peter D. (1983). *The Workings of Old Testament Narrative* (¶F), Part II. (On 1 Samuel 16–22.)

Rosenberg, Joel (1986). 'Nabal and Abigail', in *King and Kin* (¶F), 149–55.

Simon, Uriel (1988). 'A Balanced Story: The Stern Prophet and the Kind Witch', *Prooftexts* 8: 159–71. (On 1 Samuel 28.)

Sternberg, Meir (1990). 'Good Looks in Samuel', in *The Poetics of Biblical Narrative* (¶F), 354–64.

¶N.3 2 Samuel: King David

* Ackerman, James S. (1990). 'Knowing Good and Evil: A Literary Analysis of the Court History in 2 Samuel 9–20 and 1 Kings 1–2', *JBL* 109: 41–60.

Brueggemann, Walter (1971). 'Life and Death in Tenth Century Israel', *JAAR* 40: 96–109.

—— (1974). 'On Coping with Curse: A Study of 2 Sam. 16:5–14', *CBQ* 36: 175–92.

* —— (1985). *David's Truth in Israel's Imagination and Memory*, Philadelphia: Fortress.

—— (1988). '2 Samuel 21–24: An Appendix of Deconstruction?', *CBQ* 50: 383–97.

Conroy, Charles (1978). *Absalom Absalom! Narrative and Language in 2 Sam. 13–20*, Rome: Pontifical Biblical Institute.

Flanagan, James W. (1983). 'Social Transformation and Ritual in 2 Samuel 6', in C. Meyers and M. O'Connor, eds., *The Word of the Lord Shall Go Forth*, Winona Lake, Ind.: Eisenbrauns, 361–72.

—— (1988). 'Domain of Notions: Literary Images of the David Figure', in *David's Social Drama: A Hologram of Israel's Early Iron Age*, Sheffield: Almond, 193–272.

Fokkelman, J. P. (1981). *Narrative Art and Poetry*, (¶N), i.

* Gros Louis, Kenneth R. R. (1977). 'The Difficulty of Ruling Well: King David of Israel', *Semeia* 8: 15–33.

Gunn, David M. (1975). 'David and the Gift of the Kingdom (2 Sam 2–4, 9–20, 1 Kgs 1–2)', *Semeia* 3: 14–45.

* —— (1978). *The Story of King David* (¶N), ch. 3.

* —— (1988). '2 Samuel', in James L. Mays, gen. ed., *Harper's Bible Commentary*, San Francisco: Harper and Row, 287–304.

—— (1989). 'In Security: The David of Biblical Narrative' (¶N).

Hagan, Harry (1979). 'Deception as Motif and Theme in 2 Sam. 9–20; 1 Kings 1–2', *Biblica* 60: 301–26.

Jackson, Jared J. (1965). ' "David's Throne": Patterns in the Succession Story', *Canadian Journal of Theology* 11: 183–95.

Jensen, Hans J. L. (1992). 'Desire, Rivalry and Collective Violence in the "Succession Narrative" ', *JSOT* 55: 39–59.

Josipovici, Gabriel (1988). 'David and Tears', in *The Book of God* (¶F), 191–209.

Lasine, Stuart (1989). 'Judicial Narratives and the Ethics of Reading: The Reader as Judge of the Dispute between Mephibosheth and Ziba', *Hebrew Studies* 30: 49–69.

*Linafelt, Tod (1992). 'Taking Women: Readers/Responses/Responsibility in Samuel', in Fewell, ed. (¶E), 99–113.

*Marcus, David (1986). 'David the Deceiver and David the Dupe', *Prooftexts* 6: 163–71.

*Perdue, Leo G. (1984). ' "Is There Anyone Left of the House of Saul . . . ?" Ambiguity and the Characterization of David in the Succession Narrative', *JSOT* 30: 67–84.

Rosenberg, Joel (1986). 'From House to House', in *King and Kin* (¶F), 113–23.

Schwartz, Regina M. (1992). 'Adultery in the House of David: The Metanarrative of Biblical Scholarship and the Narratives of the Bible', in Jobling and Moore, eds. (¶C), 35–55.

Vorster, Willem S. (1986). 'Readings, Readers, and the Succession Narrative: An Essay on Reception', *ZAW* 98: 351–62.

¶*N.4 2 Samuel 11–12: David, Bathsheba and Uriah*

Bal, Mieke (1987). 'The Emergence of the Lethal Woman, or the Use of Hermeneutical Models', in *Lethal Love* (¶D), 10–36.

Bailey, Randall C. (1990). *David in Love and War: The Pursuit of Power in 2 Samuel 10–12*, JSOTS 75, esp. 83–90.

Lasine, Stuart (1984). 'Melodrama as Parable: The Story of the Poor Man's Ewe-Lamb and the Unmasking of David's Topsy-Turvy Emotions', *Harvard Annual Review* 8: 101–24.

*Nichol, George G. (1988). 'Bathsheba, A Clever Woman?' *Expository Times* 99: 360–3.

*Rosenberg, Joel (1989). 'The Institutional Matrix of Treachery in 2 Samuel 11', in Amihai *et al.*, eds. (¶F), 103–16.

Roth, Wolfgang (1977). 'You are the Man! Structural Interaction in 2 Samuel 10–12', *Semeia* 8: 1–13.

Sternberg, Meir (1990). 'Gaps, Ambiguity, and the Reading Process', in *The Poetics of Biblical Narrative* (¶F), 188–229.

—— and Perry, Menakhem (1986). 'The King through Ironic Eyes: Biblical Narrative and the Literary Reading Process', *Poetics Today* 7: 275–322. (Hebrew original, 1968.)

Vorster, Willem S. (1985). 'Reader-Response, Redescription, and Reference: "You Are the Man" (2 Sam. 12:7)', in Bernard C. Lategan and Willem S. Vorster, eds., *Text and Reality: Aspects of Reference in Biblical Texts*, SS, 95–112.

* Yee, Gale A. (1988). ' "Fraught With Background": Literary Ambiguity in II Samuel 11', *Interpretation* 42: 240–53.

¶*N.5   2 Samuel 13–14: Tamar, Amnon, and Absalom*

* Bar-Efrat, Shimon (1989). 'The Narrative of Amnon and Tamar', in *Narrative Art in the Bible* (¶F), 239–82.

* Long, Burke O. (1981). 'Wounded Beginnings: David and Two Sons', in Long, ed. (¶E), 26–34.

Ridout, George (1974). 'The Rape of Tamar', in Jared J. Jackson and Martin Kessler, eds., *Rhetorical Criticism: Essays in Honor of James Muilenburg*, Pittsburgh: Pickwick, 75–84.

* Rosenberg, Joel (1986). 'Amnon and Tamar', in *King and Kin* (¶F), 140–8.

* Trible, Phyllis (1984). 'Tamar: The Royal Rape of Wisdom', in *Texts of Terror* (¶D), 37–63.

van Dijk-Hemmes, Fokkelien (1989). 'Tamar and the Limits of Patriarchy: Between Rape and Seduction (2 Samuel 13 and Genesis 38)', in Bal, ed. (¶E), 135–56.

* Willey, Patricia K. (1992). 'The Importunate Woman of Tekoa and How She Got Her Way', in Fewell, ed. (¶E), 115–31.

¶*O.   1 and 2 Kings*

* Camp, Claudia V. (1992). '1–2 Kings', in Newsom and Ringe, eds. (¶D), 96–109.

Culley, Robert C. (1980). 'Punishment Stories in the Legends of the Prophets', in Richard A. Shemer, ed., *Orientation by Disorientation*, Pittsburgh: Pickwick, 167–82.

Long, Burke O. (1987). 'Framing Repetitions in Biblical Historiography', *JBL* 106: 385–99.

* McConville, J. G. (1989). 'Narrative and Meaning in the Books of Kings', *Biblica* 70: 31–49.

* Nelson, Richard D. (1988). 'The Anatomy of the Book of Kings', *JSOT* 40: 39–48.

Robertson, David (1982). 'Micaiah ben Imlah: A Literary View', in Polzin and Rothman, eds. (¶C), 139–46.

Savran, George (1987). '1 and 2 Kings', in Alter and Kermode, eds. (¶E), 146–64.

¶O.1 1 Kings

Bird, Phyllis A. (1989). 'The Harlot as Heroine' (¶H.10). (On 1 Kings 3.)

Brettler, Marc (1991). 'The Structure of 1 Kings 1–11', *JSOT* 49: 87–97.

Cohn, Robert L. (1982). 'The Literary Logic of 1 Kings 17–19', *JBL* 101: 333–50. (And see the further comments of Denise Dick Herr, 'Variations of a Pattern: 1 Kings 19', *JBL* 104 (1985), 292–4.)

——(1985). 'Literary Technique in the Jeroboam Narrative', *ZAW* 97: 23–35.

Eslinger, Lyle M. (1989). 'King Solomon's Prayers', in *Into the Hands of the Living God* (¶K), 123–81. (On 1 Kings 1–11.)

Frisch, Amos (1991). 'Structure and its Significance: The Narrative of Solomon's Reign (1 Kings 1–12.24)', *JSOT* 51: 3–14. (And see the response by Kim Ian Parker and rejoinder by Frisch: 15–24.)

* Gregory, Russell (1990). 'Irony and the Unmasking of Elijah', in Hauser and Gregory, *From Carmel to Horeb* (see Hauser, below), 91–175.

* Hauser, Alan J. (1990). 'Yahweh Versus Death—The Real Struggle in 1 Kings 17–19', in Alan J. Hauser and Russell Gregory, *From Carmel to Horeb: Elijah in Crisis*, B&L 19, 9–89.

Jobling, David (1978). 'Ahab's Quest for Rain: Text and Context in 1 Kings 17–18', in *The Sense of Biblical Narrative* (¶F), i. 63–88.

Jobling, David (1992). '"Forced Labor": Solomon's Golden Age and the Question of Literary Representation', in Jobling and Moore, eds. (¶C), 57–76.

Lasine, Stuart (1992). 'Reading Jeroboam's Intentions: Intertextuality, Rhetoric, and History in 1 Kings 12', in Fewell, ed. (¶E), 133–52.

*Long, Burke O. (1981). 'A Darkness Between Brothers: Solomon and Adonijah', *JSOT* 19: 79–94.

—— (1985). 'Historical Narrative and the Fictionalizing Imagination', *Vetus Testamentum* 35: 405–16. (On 1 Kings 20.)

Miscall, Peter D. (1989). 'Elijah, Ahab and Jehu: A Prophecy Fulfilled', *Prooftexts* 9: 73–83.

Parker, Kim Ian. (1988). 'Repetition as a Structuring Device in 1 Kings 1–11', *JSOT* 42: 19–27.

Prickett, Stephen (1986). 'Ways of Reading the Bible: The Problem of the Transparent Text', in *Words and* The Word: *Language, poetics and biblical interpretation*, Cambridge UP, 4–36. (On 1 Kgs. 8–12.)

Zakovitch, Yair (1984). 'The Tale of Naboth's Vineyard: 1 Kings 21', in Weiss, ed. (¶F), 379–405.

¶O.2 2 Kings

*Alter, Robert (1983). 'How Convention Helps Us Read: The Annunciation Type-Scene in the Bible', *Prooftexts* 3: 115–30. (On Elijah and the Shunammite woman, 2 Kings 4; also Genesis 18, 25; Judges 13; 1 Samuel 1.)

Cohn, Robert L. (1983). 'Form and Perspective in 2 Kings 5', *Vetus Testamentum* 33: 171–84.

Eslinger, Lyle M. (1989). 'Through the Fire', in *Into the Hands of the Living God* (¶K), 183–219. (On 2 Kings 17 and the Deuteronomistic History.)

*Fewell, Danna Nolan (1986). 'Sennacherib's Defeat: Words at War in 2 Kings 18.13–19.37', *JSOT* 34: 79–90.

Garcia-Treto, Francisco O. (1990). 'The Fall of the House: A Carnivalesque Reading of 2 Kings 9 and 10', *JSOT* 46: 47–65. (Also in Fewell, ed. (¶E), 153–71.)

*Granowski, Jan Jaynes (1992). 'Jehoiachin at the King's Table: A Reading of the Ending of the Second Book of Kings', in Fewell, ed. (¶E), 173–87.

Lasine, Stuart (1991). 'Jehoram and the Cannibal Mothers (2 Kings 6.24–33): Solomon's Judgement in an Inverted World', *JSOT* 50: 27–53.

Moore, Rick Dale (1990). *God Saves: Lessons from the Elisha Stories*, JSOTS 95, esp. 69–104. (On 2 Kings 5–7.)

*Shields, Mary E. (1993). 'Subverting a Man of God, Elevating a Woman: Role and Power Reversals in 2 Kings 4', *JSOT* forthcoming.

[See below: 1 and 2 Chronicles (¶V), Ezra and Nehemiah (¶U), Esther (¶S), Job (¶Q), and Daniel (¶T)]

¶P. Jonah

* Ackerman, James S. (1981). 'Satire and Symbolism in the Song of Jonah', in Baruch Halpern and Jon D. Levenson, eds., *Traditions in Transformation*, Winona Lake, Ind.: Eisenbrauns, 213–46.

*—— (1987). 'Jonah', in Alter and Kermode, eds. (¶E), 234–43.

Band, Arnold J. (1990). 'Swallowing Jonah: The Eclipse of Parody', *Prooftexts* 10: 177–95.

* Craig, Kenneth M., Jr. (1990). 'Jonah and the Reading Process', *JSOT* 47: 103–14.

Dozeman, Thomas (1989). 'Inner-Biblical Interpretation of Yahweh's Gracious and Compassionate Character', *JBL* 108: 207–23.

Eagleton, Terry (1990). 'J. L. Austin and the Book of Jonah', in Schwartz, ed. (¶E), 231–6.

Elata-Alster, Gerda and Salmon, Rachel (1989). 'The Deconstruction of Genre in the Book of Jonah: Towards a Theological Discourse', *JLT* 3: 40–60.

* Good, Edwin M. (1981). 'Jonah: The Absurdity of God', in *Irony in the Old Testament* (¶F), 39–55.

Goodhart, Sandor (1985). 'Prophecy, Sacrifice and Repentance in the Story of Jonah', *Semeia* 33: 43–63.

* Hauser, Alan Jon (1985). 'Jonah: In Pursuit of the Dove', *JBL* 104: 21–37.

* Holbert, John C. (1981). ' "Deliverance Belongs to Yahweh!" Satire in the Book of Jonah', *JSOT* 21: 59–81.

Landes, George M. (1967). 'The Kerygma of the Book of Jonah. The Contextual Interpretation of the Jonah Psalm', *Interpretation* 21: 3–31.

Magonet, Jonathan (1983). *Form and Meaning: Studies in Literary Techniques in the Book of Jonah*, 2nd edn.; B&L 8 (1st edn. Berne and Frankfurt am Main: Lang, 1976.)

Miles, John A. (1974–5). 'Laughing at the Bible: Jonah as Parody', *Jewish Quarterly Review* 65: 168–81.

Pelli, Moshe (1979–80). 'The Literary Art of Jonah', *Hebrew Studies* 20/21: 18–28.

West, Mona (1984). 'Irony in the Book of Jonah: Audience Identification with the Hero', *Perspectives in Religious Studies* 11: 233–42.

¶Q. Job

Brenner, Athalya (1989). 'Job the Pious? The Characterization of Job in the Narrative Framework of the Book', *JSOT* 43: 37–52.

Clines, David J. A. (1982). 'The Arguments of Job's Three Friends', in Clines, Gunn, and Hauser, eds. (¶E), 199–214.

—— (1987). 'False Naivety in the Prologue to Job', *Hebrew Annual Review* 9: 127–36.

* —— (1990). 'Deconstructing the Book of Job', in *What Does Eve Do to Help?* (¶E), 106–23.

Cooper, Alan (1990). 'Reading and Misreading the Prologue to Job', *JSOT* 46: 67–79.

Davis, Ellen F. (1992). 'Job and Jacob: the Integrity of Faith', in Fewell, ed. (¶E).

Fontaine, Carole R. (1987). 'Folktale Structure in the Book of Job', in Elaine R. Follis, ed., *Directions in Biblical Hebrew Poetry*, JSOTS 40, 205–32.

Good, Edwin M. (1990). *In Turns of Tempest: A Reading of Job*, Stanford UP.

Greenberg, Moshe (1987). 'Job', in Alter and Kermode, eds. (¶E), 283–304.

Habel, Norman C. (1983). 'The Narrative Art of Job: Applying the Principles of Robert Alter', *JSOT* 27: 101–11.

Miller, Ward S. (1989). 'The Structure and Meaning of Job', *Concordia Journal* 15: 103–20.

* Newsom, Carol A. (1992). 'Job', in Newsom and Ringe, eds. (¶D), 130–6.

Penchansky, David (1990). *The Betrayal of God* (¶D).

* Perdue, Leo G., and Gilpin, W. Clark, eds. (1991). *Voice From the Whirlwind: Interpreting the Book of Job*, Nashville: Abingdon.

Polzin, Robert, and Robertson, David (1977). *Studies in the Book of Job*, Semeia 7. (Includes Luis Alonso Schökel ('Toward a Dramatic Reading'), John J. Miles ('Gagging on Job'), and J. William Whedbee ('The Comedy of Job').)

Radzinowicz, Mary Ann (1989). 'How and Why the Literary Establishment Caught Up with the Bible: Instancing the Book of Job' (¶C).

And see further the recent commentaries of David J. A. Clines (Word; Waco, Tex.: Word Books, 1989), Norman Habel (Old Testament Library; Philadelphia: Westminster, 1985), and Gerald Janzen (Interpretation; Atlanta: John Knox, 1985).

¶R. Ruth

* Berlin, Adele (1983). 'Poetics in the Book of Ruth', in *Poetics and Interpretation of Biblical Narrative* (¶F), 83–110.

Bernstein, Moshe J. (1991). 'Two Multivalent Readings in the Ruth Narrative', *JSOT* 50: 15–26.

Black, James (1991). 'Ruth in the Dark: Folktale, Law and Creative Ambiguity in the Old Testament', *JLT* 5: 20–36.

* Campbell, Edward F. (1974). 'The Hebrew Short Story: A Study of Ruth', in Howard N. Bream *et al.*, eds. *A Light Unto My Path*, Philadelphia: Temple UP, 83–101. (Also in the 'Introduction' to *Ruth*, Anchor Bible; Garden City, NY: Doubleday, 1975, 1–41.

* Darr, Katheryn Pfisterer (1991). '"More than Seven Sons": Critical, Rabbinical, and Feminist Perspectives on Ruth', in *Far More Precious than Jewels* (¶D), 55–84.

Fewell, Danna Nolan, and Gunn, David M. (1988). '"A Son is Born to Naomi!": Literary Allusions and Interpretation in the Book of Ruth', *JSOT* 40: 99–108. (And see the response by Peter Coxon and rejoinder by Fewell and Gunn in *JSOT* 45 (1989), 25–37 and 39–43, respectively.)

Fewell, Danna Nolan, and Gunn, David M. (1989). 'Boaz, Pillar of Society: Measures of Worth in the Book of Ruth', *JSOT* 45: 45–59.

* —— (1990). *Compromising Redemption: Relating Characters in the Book of Ruth*, LCBI.

Feeley-Harnik, Gillian (1990). 'Naomi and Ruth: Building Up the House of David', in Niditch, ed. (¶E), 163–84. (And see the response by Edward L. Greenstein, 185–91.)

* Green, Barbara (1982). 'The Plot of the Biblical Story of Ruth', *JSOT* 23: 55–68.

Rashkow, Ilona N. (1990). 'The Book of Ruth', in *Upon the Dark Places* (¶D), 119–51.

* Rauber, D. F. (1970). 'Literary Values in the Bible: The Book of Ruth', *JBL* 89: 27–37. (Reprinted in Gros Louis *et al.*, eds. (¶E), i. 163–76.

Sasson, Jack M. (1979). *Ruth: A New Translation with a Philological Commentary and a Formalist-Folklorist Interpretation*, Baltimore: Johns Hopkins UP. (2nd edn., Sheffield: JSOT, 1989.)

* —— (1987). 'Ruth', in Alter and Kermode, eds. (¶E), 320–8.

* Trible, Phyllis (1978). 'A Human Comedy', in *God and the Rhetoric of Sexuality* (¶D), 166–99.

¶S. Esther

Bal, Mieke (1992). 'Lots of Writing', in Jobling and Moore eds. (¶C), 77–102.

Berg, Sandra Beth (1979). *The Book of Esther*, Missoula: Scholars.

* Clines, David J. A. (1984). 'The Story of Esther in Its Masoretic Form' and 'The Literary Art of the Esther Scroll', in *The Esther Scroll: The Story of the Story*, JSOTS 30, 9–38.

* —— (1990). 'Reading Esther from Left to Right: Contemporary Strategies for Reading a Biblical Text', in Clines *et al.*, eds., *The Bible in Three Dimensions* (¶E), 31–52.

* Fewell, Danna Nolan (1992). 'Introduction: Writing, Reading, and Relating', in Fewell, ed. (¶E), 11–20, esp. 11–17. (On Esther and Daniel.)

* Fox, Michael (1991). *Character and Ideology in the Book of Esther*, Columbia, SC: Univ. of South Carolina.

* Goldman, Stan (1990). 'Narrative and Ethical Ironies in Esther', *JSOT* 47: 15–31.
* Humphreys, W. Lee (1985). 'The Story of Esther and Mordecai: An Early Jewish Novella', in Coats, ed. (¶F), 97–113.
  Mosala, Itumeleng J. (1988). 'The Implications of the Text of Esther for African Women's Struggle for Liberation in South Africa', *Journal of Black Theology in South Africa* (Nov.): 3–9. Forthcoming in *Semeia*.
* Niditch, Susan (1987). 'Esther: Folklore, Wisdom, Feminism, and Authority', in *Underdogs and Tricksters* (¶F), 126–45.
* White, Sidnie Ann (1989). 'Esther: A Feminine Model for Jewish Diaspora', in Day, ed. (¶D), 161–77.

¶T. Daniel

* Brown, Robert McAfee (1984). 'Furnaces and Faith: But if not . . .', *Unexpected News: Reading the Bible With Third World Eyes*, Philadelphia: Westminster, 142–56.
* Craven, Toni (1992). 'Daniel and its Additions', in Newsom and Ringe, eds. (¶D), 191–4.
* Fewell, Danna Nolan (1991). *Circle of Sovereignty: Plotting Politics in the Book of Daniel*, Nashville: Abingdon. (Rev. and extended edn. of *Circle of Sovereignty: A Story of Stories in Daniel 1–6*, B&L 20, 1988.)
  —— (1992). 'Introduction' (¶S).
  Good, Edwin M. (1984). 'Apocalyptic as Comedy: The Book of Daniel', *Semeia* 32: 41–70.
  Kuhl, Curt (1930). *Die drei Männer im Feuer*, Giessen: Alfred Töpelmann.
  Milne, Pamela J. (1988). *Vladimir Propp and the Study of Structure in Hebrew Biblical Narrative* (¶F), 177–262.
* Niditch, Susan, and Doran, Robert (1977). 'The Success Story of the Wise Courtier: A Formal Approach', *JBL* 96: 179–93.
  Shea, William (1985). 'Further Literary Structures in Daniel 2–7: An Analysis of Daniel 4' and 'An Analysis of Daniel 5, and the Broader Relationships within Chapters 2–7', *Andrews University Seminary Studies* 23: 193–202 and 277–95.
* Wharton, James (1985). 'Daniel 3:16–18', *Interpretation* 39: 170–6.

¶*U. Ezra–Nehemiah*

* Clines, David J. A. (1990). 'The Nehemiah Memoir: The Perils of Autobiography', in *What Does Eve Do to Help?* (¶E), 124–64.

Eskenazi, Tamara Cohn (1988*a*). *In An Age of Prose: A Literary Approach to Ezra-Nehemiah*, SBL Monograph Series, 36; Atlanta: Scholars.

—— (1988*b*). 'The Structure of Ezra-Nehemiah and the Integrity of the Book', *JBL* 107: 641–56.

—— (1989). 'Ezra-Nehemiah: From Text to Actuality', in Exum, ed. (¶E), 165–97. (And see the response by David J. A. Clines: 199–215.)

* —— (1992). 'Ezra-Nehemiah', in Newsom and Ringe, eds. (¶D), 116–23.

¶*V. 1 and 2 Chronicles*

Ackroyd, Peter R. (1977). 'The Chronicler as Exegete', *JSOT* 2: 2–32.

—— (1988). 'Chronicles-Ezra-Nehemiah: The Concept of Unity', *ZAW* 100: 189–201. (Reprinted in *The Chronicler in His Age*, JSOTS 101, 1991, 344–59.)

Dillard, Raymond B. (1984). 'The Literary Structure of the Chronicler's Solomon Narrative', *JSOT* 30: 85–93.

Duke, Rodney K. (1990). *The Persuasive Appeal of the Chronicler: A Rhetorical Analysis*, B&L 25.

Fishbane, Michael (1985). 'Aggadic Exegesis in the Historiographical Literature', in *Biblical Interpretation in Ancient Israel*, Oxford UP, 380–407.

Gunn, David M. (1989). 'In Security: The David of Biblical Narrative', in Exum, ed. (¶E), 133–51. (And the response by Peter D. Miscall: 153–63.)

Knoppers, Gary N. (1990). 'Rehoboam in Chronicles: Villain or Victim?' *JBL* 109: 423–40.

Solomon, Ann M. (1989). 'The Structure of the Chronicler's History: A Key to the Organization of the Pentateuch', in Amihai *et al.*, eds. (¶F), 51–64.

INDEX OF PASSAGES CITED

INDEX OF BIBLICAL NAMES

GENERAL INDEX